T0314338

Animate to Harmony

Animate to Harmony

The Independent Animator's Guide to Toon Boom

Adam Phillips

Routledge
Taylor & Francis Group

New York London

First published 2015 by Focal Press

711 Third Avenue, New York, NY 10017, USA
2 Park Square, Milton Park, Abingdon, Oxon OX14 4RN

Routledge is an imprint of the Taylor & Francis Group, an informa business

First issued in hardback 2017

Library of Congress Cataloging in Publication Data
Phillips, Adam.
Animate to harmony : the independent animator's guide to Toon boom / Adam Phillips.
    pages cm
ISBN 978-0-415-70537-0 (paperback)
1. Toon boom. 2. Computer animation. I. Title.
    TR897.72.T66P45 2014
    777'.7–dc23
    2014012005

ISBN: 978-0-415-70537-0 (pbk)
ISBN: 978-1-138-42834-8 (hbk)

Typeset by Alex Lazarou

Contents

Introduction

In this book I'll teach you how to use Toon Boom software to create your own 2D animation. The three Toon Boom programs we cover are Animate, Animate Pro and Harmony.

Which one is right for you? There are significant differences between Animate at the low end, Animate Pro in the middle and Harmony at the top, but across all three, the interface is almost identical. This means that if you're familiar with one of them, you pretty much know your way around them all.

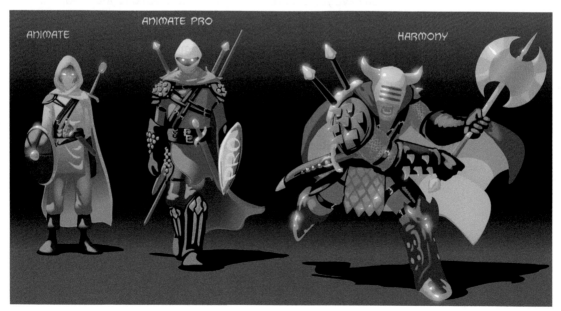

0.1

As of this writing, the current versions are Animate 3, Animate Pro 3 and Harmony 10.3. Throughout this book then, we'll start with the tools and techniques at the Animate level, most of which serves as a foundation for the other two. From time to time you'll see specific mention of 'Pro only features' or 'Harmony only features', indicated by the icons in Figure 0.2. These paragraphs, pages or chapters refer to advanced features available only in those programs.

0.2

When weighing up which program you need, the decision usually comes down to the list of tools you expect to use most in your work. If you're a complete beginner and just want to get a feel for the software, you don't necessarily need the high-end programs. However, with software it certainly doesn't hurt for the apprentice to have access to the master's cabinet. There will be tools that currently look like alien technology but they'll wait quietly until you're ready to use them.

If you have yet to make a decision about which one you need, you can download a free PLE (Personal Learning Edition) – a non-expiring, fully featured trial from Toon Boom's website, www.toonboom.com. The table opposite is not an exhaustive comparison; merely a short list of categorised features that you're likely to use most in your day-to-day work.

The red check marks ✓ indicate advanced features that were previously exclusive to Animate Pro or Harmony, but are now available in Animate 3 and Animate Pro 3. If you're using Animate 2, or Animate Pro 2, you won't have access to these red checked features.

Table 0.1

	ANIMATE	ANIMATE PRO	HARMONY
DRAWING			
Drawing Tools	✓	✓	✓
Textured Brush	✓	✓	✓
Variable-width Pencil Lines	✓	✓	✓
Textured Pencil Lines	✓	✓	✓
Rotate Workspace	✓	✓	✓
Sub Layers	2	4	4
ANIMATION			
Morphing	✓	✓	✓
Advanced Morping		✓	✓
Basic Rigging	✓	✓	✓
Advanced Rigging		✓	✓
Shift & Trace	✓	✓	✓
Bone Deformation		✓	✓
Curve Deformation			✓
Inverse Kinematics	✓	✓	✓
Advanced Inverse Kinematics		✓	✓
Timeline Display Modes	1	3	3
X-sheet Annotation Columns	✓	✓	✓
3D			
Multiplane	✓	✓	✓
Animated Camera	✓	✓	✓
Animated Camera in 3D space		✓	✓
Stereoscopic Ability		✓	✓
Rotate drawings in 3D		✓	✓
Import & Animate 3D objects			✓
EFFECTS			
Layer-based effects	15		
Node-based effects		50+	100+
Particles			✓

WHO THIS BOOK IS FOR

Whether this book is for you depends on your animation and software experience, as well as your future animation plans. In writing, I've targeted a broad range of 2D animators. If you can identify with any of the following, this book was written especially for you.

THE INDEPENDENT ANIMATOR

0.3

Animation isn't your career, but you create animation whenever you get the chance. You regularly complete short projects and have a few larger ones in the works. You have more ideas under construction than you can ever complete but ultimately wish you could do this full-time. You've animated a few pieces for payment but mostly your animation doesn't pay the bills. Lately you've been hearing about Toon Boom as an alternative to your current software choice and you decide it's time to take your work to the next level.

THE INDEPENDENT ANIMATION PROFESSIONAL

0.4

You earn a living by animating, probably from home. Contracts vary wildly, from simple web adverts, to games, to fully animated web cartoons. You rarely get a holiday and your own projects have sadly taken a backseat but in the eyes of many, you're living the dream. Your work has outgrown your usual software of choice and you're intrigued by what others are doing with Toon Boom. It's time to get serious.

THE PROFESSIONAL

0.5

You work for – or are applying for a job at – an animation studio. You have plenty of digital animation experience using other software but the studio is now hiring experienced Toon Boom animators and you need someone to show you the ropes, fast-like!

THE HOBBYIST

Because of your artistic talent, friends and family have always come to you for designs or illustrations. You're comfortable using digital animation software and have a few simple animated projects under your belt. Perhaps you've even submitted your work to YouTube or Newgrounds and received feedback, praise or insulting comments (it happens to us all!). Today, you believe you have a future in animation and want the best possible start.

0.6

THE DINOSAUR

Some may find it insulting to be referred to as a dinosaur but in anima-tion it's a badge of honour. It means you're a battle-scarred veteran of traditional 'pencil and paper' animation. You've spent decades honing your skills and taking great pride in your craft. Now with all this new-fangled digitrad or tradiggity or whatever the kids are calling it these days, you've decided it's time to drag your skills into the twenty-first century to show them how it's done. This book is your manual.

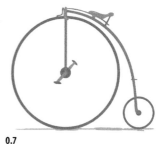

0.7

WHY SHOULD I USE TOON BOOM?

Toon Boom software is 100 per cent animation software. Everything you see in the program is designed for one thing – to create 2D anima-tion. This means that whatever power the program is drawing from your computer's resources, it's going entirely into helping you create animation.

Toon Boom is also *vector-based*. What that technically means, you'll find outlined in Appendix B, starting on page 436, but in practical terms it means that all art *created within the software* can be scaled up or down to any size. We can finish an entire movie at smartphone size, then in mere seconds, scale it up to cinema-screen size with no loss of quality. This flexibility isn't afforded to users of raster-based software such as TVPaint or Photoshop.

ADOBE FLASH AND THE SAGA OF FILE SIZE

A discussion of vector-based animation software wouldn't be complete without a mention of Adobe Flash.

From its very beginnings, Flash's biggest draw card as an animation tool has been its shallow learning curve and the low file size of the .swf (Shockwave Flash) movie format. Slick – and too many not-so-slick – animated banners lit up the web with sliding text, sound and colour transitions all for just a few kilobytes to download. Early on, an animated Flash intro was the must-have for every website and it wasn't long before entire websites were being built in Flash. Newgrounds.com still thrives as a Flash portal, with new animators seizing the opportunity to make their own games and movies.

As internet speeds increase and low file sizes become less important, HD video has become the new king of engaging web content. With the rise of YouTube have come filmmakers and animators showcasing their skills, experiments and telling their own stories. And while there are still many animators devoted to the super slim .swf format, there is nonetheless a now-dominant video presence as animators turn to more reliable and powerful software. Studios that once used Flash to develop entire seasons of primetime cartoons are now turning to Toon Boom for everything from web shorts and online games, to television series and feature films.

Speaking from personal experience, I believe the reason animators initially fall in love with Flash is generally the same reason they later become frustrated and outgrow it: Flash is great for *simple* animation. Those just starting out in digital animation take to it very quickly.

As your confidence, skills and animation ambitions grow, you may find that Flash starts to struggle. Your files grow larger and more complex, and you start to notice performance and stability issues. As much as you swear and scream, you can't really blame Flash because animation is only a thin wedge of what it's designed for.

I should add here that some animators' styles are so well-suited to Flash that they don't find a reason to move on. If you've never had any issues with Flash, congratulations!

ANIMATING GAMES WITHOUT USING FLASH

One major reason animators might stick with Flash is for its scripting language, ActionScript, and the ability to create interactivity for game development. You may think that to animate Flash games you have to use Flash. Actually it's possible – and perfectly acceptable – to create animation in another program, then bring it into Flash for coding. Toon Boom is no exception here. In fact, I created the animation in Toon Boom Animate Pro for my own game *Dashkin* then imported it all into Flash for programming.

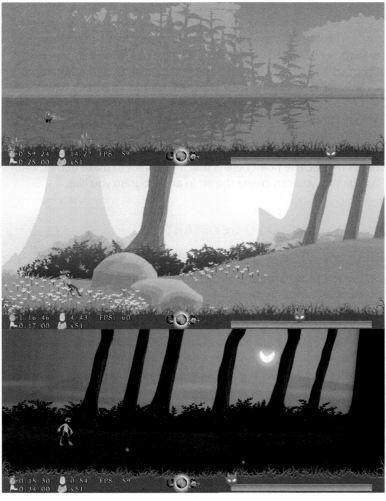

0.8
Dashkin art and animation were created entirely in Toon Boom Animate Pro, then imported into Flash for programming.

In March 2014, Toon Boom announced a new 'Gaming Pipeline' work-flow. Using this, game designers and animators can create art assets in Toon Boom Harmony and export them as sprite sheets and transform data, ready for use by almost any game engine.

MOBILE GAMES

Mobile game development is a squillion-dollar industry and because Flash has art, programming and mobile app export capability, it's running near the front of the pack.

There is, however, a number of other game development programs streaking ahead of Flash. Three examples are Unity3D, UDK (Unreal Development Kit) and GameMaker Studio. They're all inexpensive and easy to learn, ideal for web, mobile and console game development. However, when it comes to 2D, these three programs don't have their own inbuilt drawing tools, relying instead on 2D plugins, or imported assets, such as sprite sheets, backgrounds and animation sequences.

Whether you create these assets in Flash, Toon Boom or Photoshop, it doesn't matter. The point here is that if you want to make games, even Flash games, you can create the art in any program you like.

WHAT YOU NEED TO GET STARTED

Beside the fact that we're learning computer software and I therefore assume you know your way around a computer, I'll need to make a couple of other assumptions.

First, you have a basic grasp of how animation works – how the rapid, sequential display of images gives an illusion of movement. Ideally, you're familiar with the concept of frames on a timeline, or perhaps even cels on an X-sheet (for those coming from a traditional 2D background).

Second, you have some ability to draw, or at the very least a willing-ness to try. If you want to learn 2D animation software without ever making a single brush stroke, you might be in for a rough time. Sure, you can animate pre-drawn 2D assets, such as cut-out characters (more on those later in the book) but almost all of the exercises in this book will require you to draw something, or many somethings.

Finally, passion! Enthusiasm! When you're passionate about something, it never feels like work and you'll naturally improve with experience. Whether you're a mechanic, stuntman, wine-taster or an animator, without passion it gets tedious quicker.

0.9

HARDWARE

The number one essential piece of hardware for digital artists is a graphics tablet, or tablet monitor. The range of size, features and price varies across brands, but if you don't have any peripheral graphics hardware, you'll likely be stuck drawing with your mouse. For anyone who is comfortable drawing or painting with a real pencil or brush, the graphics tablet makes the most sense for translating your real-world pencil skills to digital art.

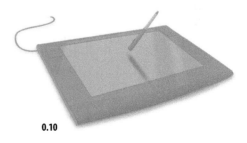

0.10

Apart from the usual freehand drawing and painting tools, most art software has an additional set of drawing tools for architectural precision with straight lines and perfect curves. The way these tools work makes them ideal for users who don't have a graphics tablet, or aren't comfortable drawing freehand. Especially if you're using a mouse, these helpful tools provide a little more control. One downside is that they're not ideal for organic shapes like faces, bodies and other natural objects. They can be very useful though, so we'll look closely at them in Chapter 2.

SOFTWARE

Generally speaking, Toon Boom exports video formats, so more often than not, when you finish a scene or project, you'll render it as a video file or image sequence. Video editing software is therefore required to stitch your scenes together.

0.11

Within Toon Boom we can preview animation with simple playback controls, as well as use Toon Boom Play: a kind of movie player that is built into Animate, Animate Pro and Harmony. We'll look closer at Play later in the book.

My personal solution for previewing and sequencing video outside of Toon Boom is QuickTime Pro. There are several other low-cost solutions available for quickly pasting together a few scenes so if you don't already have one, you can hunt around for an inexpensive or free solution.

For a final export though, you might want a more fully featured video editing program, like Adobe Premiere, After Effects or Final Cut. At the low-cost end, I've found that Adobe Premiere Elements has everything I need for simple video audio editing and export.

NOTE

In Toon Boom it is possible to create entire movies in a single file, but be warned, things can quickly get extremely large and messy unless you split the project into manageable parts. You're less likely to experience stability issues or slow computer response if your project is organised as individual scene files. Creating a new file for each scene is like writing with spaces between words; it's the best practise and makes the most sense.

DRIVERS

Installing the latest drivers for your graphics tablet will ensure you can use Toon Boom's drawing tools with pressure sensitivity enabled. This allows you to make pencil and brush strokes with variable thickness, depending on how hard you press the pen to the tablet.

TERMINOLOGY

There are one or two conflicts between 2D animation terminology and live action film terminology. For the information of readers who may be familiar with live action terminology, there are a couple of minor differences. In this book I'll be using the animation terms, so what is known as a 'shot' in live action is known as a 'scene' in animation. What is known as a 'scene' in live action is known as a 'sequence' in animation.

Animation and live action share the terms 'frames' and 'feet' (i.e., footage), which is the industry standard measurement for film. Scenes (or shots) are therefore measured by how many frames they have. For example, Scene 7 could be 60 frames long.

ANIMATION		LIVE ACTION
frame (single cel)		frame (single cel)
scene (multiple frames)		shot (multiple frames)
sequence (multiple scenes)		scene (multiple shots)
finished film (multiple sequences)		finished film (multiple scenes)

TIP
There was a time when 'animation' was a mass noun with no plural. Despite the word 'animations' becoming more and more common, most traditional 2D animators still wince whenever someone says 'Do you make animations?' or 'I did an animation!' Just like the words 'music' or 'poetry'. You never hear anyone say 'Do you make musics?' or 'I did a poetry!'

Therefore, if you ask a traditional 2D animator, we make animation. We don't make animations. I created seven animated shorts, seven pieces of animation, seven scenes, seven cartoons or seven cycles. But I did not make seven animations.

APPENDICES

What we can cover in this book is limited by the page count, so in order to get you up and running with the essentials, it has been necessary to skip over some technical explanations as well as some advanced features.

Appendices A and B at the end of the book will cover a range of these subjects in brief, explaining some of the more technical aspects of the software, as well as giving you a taste of some advanced tools.

Additionally, help is at hand with Toon Boom documentation for all their programs available at docs.toonboom.com.

SOFTWARE VERSIONS

This book covers Animate, Animate Pro and Harmony. While I was writing this book throughout 2013, Toon Boom released new versions of all three programs. At the time of publication, current versions are Animate 3, Animate Pro 3 and Harmony 11.

If you're using Harmony 11, you will find that some parts of the program differ from the screenshots. Be sure to visit this book's companion website at www.focalpress.com/cw/Phillips for a 'What's New in Harmony 11' video, as well as forthcoming updates of screenshots, errata and downloadable files.

HOW TO USE THIS BOOK

Chapter Files

In many exercises there will be a suggestion to use a provided file. You can download these from this book's companion website which is: focalpress.com/cw/Phillips

Download the files suitable for the Toon Boom program that you are using.

As well as downloadable files, you'll find supplementary videos to help you with features that we couldn't cover in the book.

THANKS

We've wanted a Toon Boom book for many years and most users agree that it's been a long time coming. I'm honoured to be the guy to finally write it. Thank you to David Bevans, Caitlin Murphy and the team at Focal Press for your patience, fantastic support and work on this title.

Thanks to all the excellent people at Toon Boom, particularly to Steve Masson, Lilly Vogelesang, Karina Bessoudo, Philip Greenstein and Stacey Eberschlag for responding to my emails and IMs.

Thanks to Wizards of the Coast art directors, Jon Schindehette and Daniel Gelon for help with the DUNGEONS & DRAGONS® image permissions process; to Bernard Derriman for answering my OSX questions; to Dan Forster for his wealth of information on the days of traditional animation camera; to Tom Olczyk for technical advice on OpenGL and software rendering. To all my family, friends and colleagues, past and present for putting up with me.

Lastly but absolutely mostly, thank you to my favourite person Jeanette Imer for keeping me alive and grinning. Oblong to you!

ILLUSTRATIONS

Every single illustration in this book I created with Toon Boom Animate, Animate Pro or Harmony.

CHAPTER 1

Interface

START YOUR ENGINES

I n this chapter you'll explore the Toon Boom interface and learn how to perform basic program actions. Traditionally, a software book might spend a few pages, or a chapter, going into detail about the directory structure, video codec, aspect ratio and file formats. That stuff is definitely good to know but first and foremost, this book is a practical guide for artists and animators to start creating great animation as soon as possible.

I've tucked the advanced and technical aspects tidily away in Appendix A and Appendix B where you can find them if you need them. Right now though, I know you're itching to use this program, so let's get you in the pool. Hey, look over there!

1.1

OPENING THE PROGRAM

Now to crack open the software and look around. A reminder that we'll start with the core features at the Animate level, with later chapters dedicated to advanced features.

Start Animate, Animate Pro or Harmony now and you'll briefly see the splash screen.

NOTE
After you install and run Toon Boom Animate for the first time, you'll get a popup message asking if you'd like to use Adobe Flash style shortcuts (see Figure 1.2). I strongly recommend you click 'No' here. First, because I believe it's better to learn Toon Boom as a new program, rather than try to make it conform to your Flash workflow and second, because throughout the book I'll list the Toon Boom shortcuts alongside each tool and function.

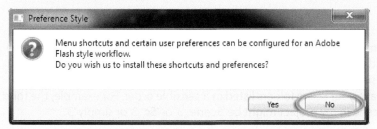

1.2

If you clicked 'Yes', don't panic. It's not that important right now and just ahead, on page 18, I'll show you how to change it back.

Assuming you have already activated the licence (see Appendix B), when the program opens, whichever one you're using, we should all now be seeing pretty much the same thing.

The **Create** button at the bottom is greyed out, making it impossible to start without first specifying a few parameters. Even if you check the 'Do not show this window at startup' checkbox, you'll be unable to start working in Toon Boom until you've completed this preliminary setup.

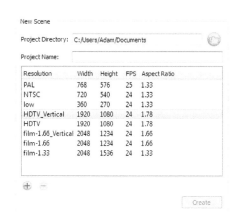

New Scene

Project Directory: C:/Users/Adam/Documents

Project Name:

Resolution	Width	Height	FPS	Aspect Ratio
PAL	768	576	25	1.33
NTSC	720	540	24	1.33
low	360	270	24	1.33
HDTV_Vertical	1920	1080	24	1.78
HDTV	1920	1080	24	1.78
film-1.66_Vertical	2048	1234	24	1.66
film-1.66	2048	1234	24	1.66
film-1.33	2048	1536	24	1.33

Create

1.3

SETTING UP A PROJECT

Our very first step is to set up project directories so that Toon Boom knows where to save our work. Throughout the book, we'll be doing a lot of short, quick exercises – scenes in which we can make an absolute mess and not worry about being careful or even saving. So in the first exercise below we'll set up one of those 'throwaway scenes' for use in this chapter.

New Scene

Project Directory: C:/Users/Adam/Documents

Project Name:

Resolution	Width	Height	FPS	Aspect Ratio
PAL	768	576	25	1.33
NTSC	720	540	24	1.33
low	360	270	24	1.33
HDTV_Vertical	1920	1080	24	1.78
HDTV	1920	1080	24	1.78
film-1.66_Vertical	2048	1234	24	1.66
film-1.66	2048	1234	24	1.66
film-1.33	2048	1536	24	1.33

Create

Do not show this window at startup

1.4

> EXERCISE 1.1
> CREATING A PROJECT FOLDER AND SCENE FILES

The first input field on the left is labelled *Project Directory* and it speci-fies where your file will be saved. By default, this should show a path to your documents folder.

> 1.   Click 'Choose' – or if you're using Harmony, the browse folder icon.

> 2.   Choose your Desktop and click 'OK'.

The next field is your *Project Name*. You can also think of this as a scene title, which can be any name you want to call that scene. I recommend using numbers in the title, so that as your movie comes together, you have your scene folders listed in a sensible order. For example, the third scene in my project might be 'Scene_3' or 'Sc_3' or simply '3'.

As this is just a scene for experimentation, we don't need to worry about numbering.

> 3.   In the Project Name field, type test scene.

NOTE
Note that as you type this, the space is replaced by an underscore, so you end up with *test_scene*. The reason is because this will become a folder name; generally in the uptight world of file and folder naming conventions, spaces are considered sloppy practice, so this merely autocorrects it for you.

Almost done. Now Toon Boom knows the name and location of your project. Unless you're using Harmony 10, the Create button here is still greyed out, so a final piece of setup required is to specify your movie's resolution and framerate. You can see a list of useful resolution presets.

For simple projects or throwaway exercises, you can choose whichever resolution you like. No need to concern yourself with it too much, as you can easily change at any time throughout your project (even right at the end) and everything in your movie will resize itself to fit. I normally use the *HDTV (1920 × 1080)* preset. We'll talk more about frame rates later.

If you're using Harmony, the *HDTV_Vertical (1920 × 1080)* resolution is selected by default, so you could click the Create button right after entering your project name. If you require a different resolution though, you can simply select another before creating the scene.

1.5

> 4.   Choose your resolution, click 'Create' and hold your breath.

… aaaand breathe. A new, blank scene is open and awaits your scribblings. Exercise complete. Hoorah!

THE WORKSPACE LAYOUT

Now we're here, let's quickly make sure we're all seeing the same layout.

> EXERCISE 1.2
  PREFERENCES AND SHORTCUTS

> 1.   In the top right part of the program you'll see the *workspace layout* list. If you've never touched this before, it should display 'Default'. Change it now to 'Animating'.

1.6

The workspace will shuffle and shift momentarily. When it comes back, the layout should have changed. Now cast one or more eyes over the interface. There are a number of sections, typically known as *panels* and *views*. We'll discuss each of these only briefly, but as you use them more and more, you'll get to know them better.

Now remember back on page 15 when I advised against the Adobe Flash shortcuts? I'll be using the Toon Boom shortcuts from here on, so if you chose the Flash style, let's switch that back to the Toon Boom shortcuts now.

> 2.   In the top menu, choose Edit → Preferences or press [Ctrl U] on Windows, [⌘] or [⌘ U] on OSX.

> 3.   The first tab here is Shortcuts. Simply choose Toon Boom Animate from the dropdown list, as shown in Figure 1.7.

1.7 For Harmony users, the option here will be Toon Boom Harmony.

> 4.   In the bottom right of the Preferences window, click 'OK'.

Let's get back to the Toon Boom interface. Figure 1.8 shows the 'Animating' layout with the main areas labelled.

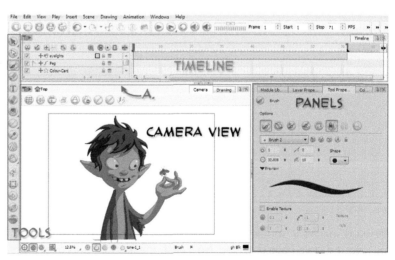

1.8

A WORD ON FOCUS

An *active* view or panel is indicated by a thin red outline. Usually when you first open the program, the Camera View has the thin red border (see Figure 1.8, arrow A), which indicates that this view 'has focus'. It works much like when you have multiple folders open on your computer; clicking one folder brings it to the front, allowing you to work in it.

> EXERCISE 1.3
> FOCUS AND WORKSPACE NAVIGATION

> 1. Tap anywhere in the Camera View to make sure it has the red border (see Figure 1.8, arrow A).

> 2. On your keyboard, press the [1] key several times to zoom out.

> 3. Press the [2] key to zoom back in.

> 4. Hold down [Spacebar] to activate the panning tool, which allows you to drag the workspace around.

> 5. Hold down [Ctrl/⌘ Alt] to activate workspace rotation, and drag in the view.

> 6. Press [Shift X] to reset rotation back to 0°, or [Shift M] to reset all (pan, zoom and rotation).

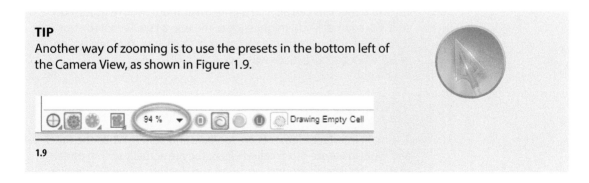

TIP
Another way of zooming is to use the presets in the bottom left of the Camera View, as shown in Figure 1.9.

94 %   Drawing Empty Cell

1.9

> 7. Click in the timeline to give it focus. Notice that the red border is now around the timeline.

> 8. Again, press the [2] and [1] keys to zoom in and out, respectively. Another way of zooming in the timeline is to use the magnifier slider as seen in Figure 1.10.

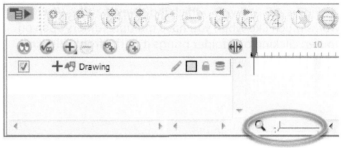

1.10

> 9. New in Harmony 10.3 is the ability to pan in the Timeline using [Spacebar].

Because the timeline now has focus, note how the zooming keys affect the timeline and not the Camera View.

TIP

A preference you might find handy is *Focus on Mouse Enter*, which makes the panels active when you hover over them, rather than needing to click. This happens to be my personal preference. You'll find it in: Edit → Preferences, or [Ctrl/⌘ U]. Then on the General tab there's a checkbox over on the right: Focus on Mouse Enter.

Be aware that this can also be a little frustrating if you're not used to it. For example, you might click to rename a layer or colour, but if your cursor strays outside the panel (usually into another) typing won't work because focus was lost.

TOOLBARS AND PANELS

The main interface elements are *toolbars* and *panels*. While the timeline and workspace are often called *views*, they're actually within panels that can be moved around, grouped and docked. As we get deeper into the program you'll encounter other views.

Toolbars are parts of the interface that hold the various tools and other icons. It's pretty obvious that the thin vertical bar on the left – packed with tools – is the main Toolbar, but almost every icon you see across the top of the interface is also in a toolbar.

> EXERCISE 1.4
CUSTOM LAYOUT

To avoid messing up the Animating layout, we're going to do two things. First we'll turn off layouts auto-saving so we can play around without ruining the defaults, then we'll create a new custom layout that we can personalise.

> 1. Go to Edit → Preferences, or [Ctrl/⌘ U], then click the General tab.

> 2. At the very top left, ensure 'Automatically Save Workspace' is *unchecked*. With this unchecked, you can make as many changes to the interface as you like, but none of them will be saved until you deliberately save it.

> 3. Click 'OK' to save the preference and return to the program.

> 4. At the top right of the Toon Boom interface, click the 'Workspace Manager' button on the top toolbar, as shown in Figure 1.11 (if you don't see this menu or button, you'll also find it in Windows → Workspace → Workspace Manager).

1.11

> 5. A window opens with two columns. On the left: *Available work-spaces* – while on the right: *Toolbar.*

> 6. In the left-hand column, click to select the *Animating* layout.

> 7. Click the small *add* ⊕ button at the bottom left.

> 8. You have just created a duplicate of *Animating* that's automatically named *Animating 2*. Give it another name using the *Rename* button if you wish.

> 9. Finally, load your custom layout onto the toolbar. Do this by selecting it in the list, then clicking the right-facing triangular icon button.

> 10. Click 'OK' to close the Workspace Manager.

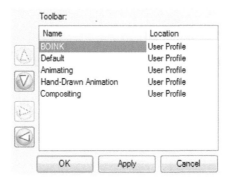

1.12

> 11. Now choose your new layout from the Workspace drop-down menu.

If you have any experience with digital graphics and animation software, much of what we've seen so far will feel familiar. The timeline, tools, main work area and panels can all be found in other programs, as well as the ability to customise your workspace layout. Let's now explore some of the toolbars.

> EXERCISE 1.5
  TOOLBARS

You could say the default interface is full of icons. Cluttered, even. Look closely and you'll see that one end of every toolbar has a grip handle, which enables you to move it.

Let's get minimalist and remove *all* the toolbars to see how much space we can free up.

> 1. Go to Window → Toolbars and *uncheck everything* in the list.

Most toolbars are just full of handy buttons and input fields that can be accessed elsewhere via menus or shortcut keys. So when you really need some elbow room, you might find removing them all is the way to go.

For some of these menu items, the toolbars are specific to certain views. For example, as you uncheck the Timeline View, notice it doesn't hide the timeline itself; just the toolbar of buttons on the timeline. Likewise, unchecking the Camera View will just remove the buttons toolbar from the Camera View.

> 2. Again in Window → Toolbars bring back the following toolbars:

- **Advanced animation** – this is off by default, but I recommend turning it on. When we start animating, we'll be using it a lot.

1.13

- **Playback controls** – again, when we start animating, this is a handy toolbar, not just for playback controls, but it also displays your scene's current frame, start/stop frames and frame rate.

1.14

- **Tools** – needs no explanation. Power users might leave it off and access each tool with its keyboard shortcut, but sometimes if you can't remember a tool's shortcut key, it's nice to just reach up and click the button. Note from Figure 1.15, you can place your Tools toolbar horizontally across the top, if you need that little bit more screen width. Likewise, you can move some horizontal toolbars into the vertical space, if that's how you like it.

1.15

- **Timeline View** – for beginners, there are some handy buttons here for common timeline tasks, like adding and removing keyframes.

> 3. Shuffle and reorder your toolbars however you like them.

A reminder that this is a practice workspace, so don't worry if it seems to be getting too messed up. Remember that if you followed Exercise 1.4, none of your changes will be saved unless you click the Save Workspace button (the tick icon, seen back in Figure 1.11). Until you do that, if it really gets out of hand, you can always reselect your custom layout, or any of the defaults from the Workspace Layout menu to reset everything.

> EXERCISE 1.6
  TOOLS AND THE TIMELINE

> 1. The brush tool [Alt B] is the third button in the main Toolbar. Select it now and write your name anywhere inside the Camera View, preferably within the rectangular border of the movie.

1.16

Beautiful work. Hey that's a nice name.

> 2. Now press the [.] key on your keyboard.

> 3. Hmm, your signature has disappeared from the Camera View... OK, let's try again. Rather than signing your name though, draw something else. No need for great art here. It's just a demonstration.

1.17

Let's pause here for a sec to look at the Timeline. Under the numbered strip, you see two little vertical 'blocks' on frames 1 and 2, with a red marker sitting above frame 2. You've done two drawings in this scene and here they are, represented by these small rectangles on the timeline.

1.18

> 4.   Press the [,] key on your keyboard. Your signature is back.

> 5.   Press the [.] key again and your second image reappears.

As you alternately press the [,] and [.] keys, watch the red marker in the Timeline. This marker is called the *playhead*. Wherever the playhead sits, the content for that frame appears in the Camera View. That is, when the playhead is on frame 1, your *first* drawing appears in the camera view. When it's on frame 2, your *second* drawing appears in the Camera View. As you press [,] and [.] you're stepping back and forward along the timeline, frame-by-frame.

You can also move along the timeline by dragging the playhead. This is known as *scrubbing* the timeline. Try it out now.

1.19

At its most basic, this is how to create animation in Toon Boom. You draw directly into the Camera View for one frame, then move to another frame and draw more. Eventually your timeline is filled with individual drawings that, when displayed at 24 frames per second, give the illusion of movement. Animation!

> EXERCISE 1.7
   PANELS

Every part of the interface with a named tab is a panel that can be moved, undocked and grouped with other panels. Figure 1.20 for example shows two panels docked together: the Colour panel and the Tool Properties panel.

1.20

The instantly recognisable title tab is the first clue that you're looking at a panel. The second clue is the two icons beside the title tab. The tiny arrow ⬇ is a menu list of all other panels. It'll come as no surprise that the ✕ icon – being a somewhat universal 'close' icon – closes the panel.

We'll be using the Drawing View later in the book so let's open it now.

> 1.   At the top of the Colour panel, click the ⬇ icon and choose Drawing from the list. If your colour panel isn't open, you can open it, or simply perform these steps in any other panel.

The Drawing View opens and becomes docked alongside your colour panel. You can show either of them by clicking their title tabs. There's one problem here: Drawing View is a drawing workspace much like Camera View, so really, it should be large. I've been a bit sneaky here and deliberately instructed you to open it in a small panel, just so I can show you how to move it.

> 2.   Click the Drawing view's name tab and drag it *onto* the Camera tab.

When you're hovered over the Camera tab (or any other tab) just before you release the drag you'll notice the *receiving tab* changes slightly: it gains a fine black border. This is saying 'if you drop that tab on me, we're going to be docked together'.

> 3.   In the Colour panel once more, click the ⬇. This time, choose *Top* from the list. We'll talk more about this particular view in a later chapter.

> 4.   Instead of docking it to another tab, drag your new Top view around the interface, noticing the outlines that preview where you can drop it.

> 5.   What if you don't dock it anywhere? Drop the new Top view in the middle of the Camera View (crazy, I know!)

Your Top view is now a separate floating window. This is especially useful for those of us using dual monitors. You can create whole panel groups floating independently of the main program window.

> 6.   If you do have a dual monitor setup and want to keep this separate floating window, I recommend adding the *Side* view panel, which is another useful view we'll talk about later.

> 7. Finish up this exercise with your own panel opening, docking and shuffling experiments.

> 8. Don't forget – if you're happy with your workspace, click the 'Save Workspace' button. It's a layout icon with a tick on the Workspace layout menu.

At this point, if you're curious about the other layouts and panels, take some time now to switch workspace layouts, either by the layout manager dropdown list, or the menu Windows → Workspace → Workspace. Explore the other panels in the list and get accustomed to shifting stuff around.

SAVING THE PROJECT

Before we end this chapter, remember the folder you set up in Exercise 1.1? If you go to your desktop and look inside that folder now, you'll see a few more folders.

Save your scene now and check again. There should now be some additional new files in there, including the file you'll use in future to open your scene. In the image below, this is the coloured icon with the name *test_scene*.

elements
environments
frames
jobs
palette-library
PALETTE_LIST
scene.elementTable
scene.versionTable
test_scene.aux
test_scene
test_scene.xstage.thumbnails

1.21

The rest of these folders and files all contribute to your scene in some way. Again, we cover some of these in greater detail towards the back of the book in Appendix B. Feel free to flip forward if you really want to know what it all means, but understanding it isn't crucial at this early stage. Needless to say, everything to do with your scene, whether audio, colour palettes, imported images or saved animation, they're all filed neatly away here.

Once saved, you can now close your file. In the next chapter, we'll get to know the interface with more exercises. Before that though, take a moment to read this brief list and come back to it if you need any reminders.

- Directory structure is set up when you hit the 'Create' button, but isn't actually created until you save the scene.

- The thin red border indicates which view has focus. Clicking in a view gives it focus.

- The timeline is a linear representation of frames in the scene.

- The scene can be shortened, or lengthened by dragging the end marker.

- The 'playhead' is the current frame indicator in the Timeline.

- 'Scrubbing' means dragging the playhead back and forth.

- See Appendix B on page 436 for information on technical aspects.

- Useful shortcut keys:

  » [1] and [2] – Camera and Timeline zooming

  » [.] and [,] – stepping forward and back one frame

  » [Ctrl/⌘ Alt] – workspace rotation

  » [Shift M] – reset view

  » [Shift X] – reset workspace rotation only.

CHAPTER 2

Tools

CREATING ART

I n later chapters you'll have the opportunity to animate a couple of simple movies, each consisting of several scenes with titles, credits, effects and audio. Of course, in order to create animation, you'll want to know how to get your art into the program – whether by scanning and vectorising drawings from paper, importing images from another program or by drawing and painting directly into Toon Boom.

In the first part of this chapter you'll learn all about the tools available to you for creating art. In the second part, you'll learn about colour management, layers and rendering. First let's briefly cover how to bring in images from outside the program.

IMPORTING ART

The art style of your project may require you to create backgrounds or animation in another program and import those images into Toon Boom. Generally throughout this book, we want to focus on the tools within Toon Boom, so the following is just a brief introduction to importing.

To import artwork, simply go to File → Import → Images. The Import Images window appears, giving you options to create new layers or add the imported images to existing layers.

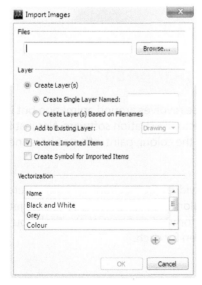

2.1

WARNING

Turn OFF Vectorise Imported Items – The Import Images window gives you an option to 'vectorise imported items'. If you're importing complex images with lots of colours and detail, or you're just importing sketches as reference images, you should turn vectorising off! It converts bitmap images into vector art, which can really slow down your computer when used on complex images like photographs or full-colour paintings. Don't worry at this stage if you don't know what bitmap and vector mean. You can learn more about scanning, importing and when to vectorise in Appendix B, page 436.

Before we move on, it's nice to note that you can import layered image files with their layering intact, for example, .psd and .tif formats. Just select 'All Layer Images' from the dropdown list in the Import Settings window (shown in Figure 2.2). This is extremely useful for scenes with multilayered backgrounds through which the characters can move.

2.2

ILLUSTRATING WITH TOON BOOM

The Toon Boom universe revolves around animation but it also happens to be excellent vector illustration software. Not just for the drawing tools, but also the colour, paint, effects filters and the built-in scanning interface.

In this chapter, the individual tool sections and their exercises have been written to stand alone. While I encourage you to get a feel for all of them, you can jump forward and back to the tools you want to learn, doing the exercises given for each.

2.3 ©Wizards of the Coast LLC.

To help you grow accustomed to using the tools, this chapter contains a number of exercises for each tool, an occasional tool challenge and then, at the end, a more substantial illustration project. All this will familiarise you not only with drawing and painting in Toon Boom, but also text, colour and rendering.

ILLUSTRATION PROJECT

The illustration project at the end of the chapter steps through making an example comic strip that I've already written for you. You should however feel free to get creative; use your own characters, text and colours as you see fit. The finished product will be suitable for print, online and whatever else you want to do with it. Let's prepare by looking closely at the tools and putting each into practice as we go.

TOOL PROPERTIES PANEL

2.4

As you may remember from the previous chapter, the Tool Properties panel is *context-sensitive*. That is, its contents change depending on which tool you have selected.

Go ahead and try it out; watch the panel update as you select different tools in the toolbar. Tool Properties is one of those panels you'll have permanently open, or at least within easy reach for calibrating each tool you use.

If you can't see it in your workspace, or you closed it in the previous chapter, you should open it now. Once again, you can access it from any panel with the ⬇ icon. I recommend putting it somewhere it can remain open at all times so you can change tool settings as you work without breaking your stride.

The panel is divided into sections, each of which contains different options, modes, fields and buttons depending on the tool you have selected. Figure 2.5 shows the Properties panel for the Brush tool.

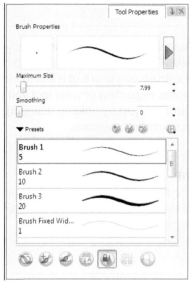

2.5
left: Animate 2 Brush properties;
right: Animate 3 Brush properties.

SHORTCUT KEYS

While all the tools are easily accessible from the toolbar, every tool can be activated by a shortcut key. Usually, the tool shortcut is holding down [Alt] while pressing the appropriate tool key, for example [Alt B] for the Brush tool.

WARNING
Shortcut keys are also context-sensitive! Before you use a shortcut key, be sure that the intended panel or view has focus. In the Camera View, the [D] key activates the Dropper tool, while in the Timeline [D] does something completely different.

In this chapter, unless specified otherwise, the shortcut keys listed are for the Camera and Drawing Views only.

If you take a look through Edit → Preferences → Shortcuts you'll find a lot of overlap on shortcut keys for different views and panels. We'll talk more about this when we get around to setting up a few custom shortcut keys later in the book.

OVERRIDE KEYS

As well as the [Alt] tool shortcuts, you'll also see mention of *override* keys. These usually correspond to the [Alt] key shortcuts. For example, the Brush tool shortcut is [Alt B] but its override key is [B]. In other words, regardless of what tool you have, you can temporarily activate the Brush just by holding down [B]. This is demonstrated several times in upcoming exercises.

TIP
The name of your active tool always appears in the bar at the bottom of the Camera View. When you activate an override key, you'll see its name displayed in red.

Shortcut keys are at the core of an efficient workflow. While I've emphasised them strongly in this chapter, nobody is expected to memorise each and every one from the start. It's recommended that you memorise just the one or two you use most and associate the mental image of the tool alongside its shortcut key.

THE TOOLBAR

As you know by now, the main toolbar is like a weapons rack from which you select the right implement for the task at hand. You've already had a chance to experiment with one or two of them in the previous chapter.

2.6

The tools can be loosely categorised for drawing, painting, selecting, transforming, editing and, of course, animation. So let's start off with the drawing and painting tools before moving on to selecting and editing. We'll look into animation tools later in the book.

BRUSH [ALT B]

2.7

The Brush tool is extremely versatile with a good range of adjustable properties. If you're the type of artist who draws everything directly into the software (rather than scanning) you'll find the Brush to be one of your most-used tools. When rendered, it's a beautiful line and with pressure sensitivity of your tablet, feels really nice to use. I have a feeling you two will get along just fine.

The underlying feature of a Brush stroke is that it isn't really a line. It's actually a long, thin *area* of paint contained inside a vector border. Figure 2.8 illustrates this.

2.8

This isn't important to understand right now but on page 83 we'll talk about manipulating that border for ultra-fine control. You can read more about vectors and points in Appendix B.

Looking at the Tool Properties panel with the Brush tool selected, you can see there are plenty of options to play with. Again, if you haven't got the Tool Properties panel open, you can do that using the ⬇ icon on any panel.

2.9

The Option buttons activate modes of the Brush. You won't need a tutorial exercise for every one of these. For example, Normal mode is pretty self-explanatory and certain others are beyond the scope of this particular chapter. Let's just look at the important ones right now.

NOTE
From this point onward, I'm going to assume you know how to start a new scene in your Toon Boom software. Please revise in Chapter 1, page 16 if you need a reminder.

Whether you use one file for many exercises, save separate files for each exercise, or whether you even save these exercises at all, I'll leave entirely up to you.

For the end of chapter project, I'll specify project setup, naming and saving in the steps.

> BRUSH EXERCISE 1
  RESIZING THE BRUSH

> 1. In a new scene file, click frame 1 in the Timeline. You should develop this habit of selecting the frame you're about to work in.

2.10

> 2. Ensure the Camera View has focus by clicking its name tab – again, more habit-forming. For a reminder of 'panel focus', see Chapter 1, page 19.

2.11

> 3. On your keyboard, press [Alt B] to arm yourself with the Brush. Right away you'll see that the Brush cursor is a kind of crosshair .

> 4. Again on your keyboard, this time hold down the [O] key and drag left to right in the Camera View. The [O] key is the interactive resizing shortcut for all drawing tools. In the Camera or Drawing Views, watch the cursor as you drag the Brush size smaller and larger. Release the [O] key and in the Brush tool properties, see how the value for the *Maximum Brush Size* has changed.

2.12

> 5. On your keyboard, this time hold down [Shift O] and again, drag in the Camera View.

> 6. In the tool properties, watch the Brush *minimum* size values changing.

[Shift O] is the shortcut for the *minimum* size of the Brush. When you use a graphics tablet with pressure sensitivity, you'll settle on a minimum size that you like and rarely change it. Mine is almost permanently set to 0.1 and I rarely use [Shift O] at all.

> BRUSH EXERCISE 2
>   SHORTCUTS OVERRIDE

If shortcut keys speed up your workflow, the *override* keys take it to the next level. Working with any tool, you can hold down another tool's key to temporarily arm it.

NOTE
Tool shortcuts and overrides, like the tools themselves, only work in the Camera and Drawing Views. The [O] shortcut has different functions in other views.

> 1. In the Timeline, select frame 1.

> 2. Resize your Brush with [O] to a good drawing size. Anything between 10 and 20 should be good. In the Brush properties, into the *minimum* size field, enter 0.1.

> 3. In your Camera View with the Brush tool active [Alt B], start sketching. Some primitive shapes will do.

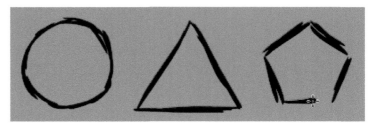

2.13

> 4. On your keyboard, hold down [E] to temporarily activate the eraser tool.

> 5. Without releasing [E], erase parts of your sketch.

> 6. Release [E] and the Brush returns.

> 7. Sketch more things!

> 8. Hold down [S] to temporarily activate the Select tool. Notice while holding [S] the cursor has changed to the select tool.

> 9. While holding [S], drag a selection area around parts, or all, of your sketch.

> 10. On your keyboard press the [Delete] key to delete the selected strokes.

> BRUSH EXERCISE 3
  MIXING A COLOUR FOR ROUGH SKETCHING

We're taking a brief detour here to better understand a couple of other Brush modes.

> 1. In your colour panel, locate the black colour swatch. In Animate and Animate Pro, this is named *Default Line*, while in Harmony it's simply named *Black*.

> 2. In the colour panel, double-click the black rectangular swatch itself (*not the name*) and the Colour picker will open.

> 3. Enter the HSV (Hue, Saturation, Value) values as shown in Figure 2.14. I'm using a very dark blue for the purpose of these screen-shots, but I would normally use a much paler blue. You may use whatever values work for you.

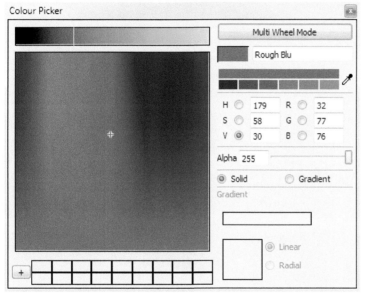

2.14

> 4. Move the Alpha slider to about a third of the way, or simply type 85 into the Alpha value field.

2.15

> 5. In the Name field at the top, rename this colour by replacing *Black* (or *Default Line*) with *Rough Blu.*

> 6. Close the Colour Picker and your new *Rough Blu* colour should now be at the top of the Colour panel.

2.16

> BRUSH EXERCISE 4
  SHOW AND FLATTEN STROKES

> 1. In the Timeline, select frame 1.

> 2. Give the Camera View focus then take some time to sketch a few random shapes. Use the Brush tool with the new *rough* colour you created in the Brush exercise 3.

2.17

Because the *rough* colour is semi-transparent, you can see layered opacity where the strokes overlap. You can also see how each stroke remains separate from the others. While this makes it easier to select, edit, move or delete each individual stroke, you can always flatten your strokes together so they form a single line.

> 3. In the top menu, go to View → Show → Show Strokes. Alternatively you can simply press [K] on your keyboard.

4.   Zoom in using the [2] key and drag-pan with [Spacebar] to get a good close up look at the Brush strokes. If you zoom in too far, press [1] to back out.

Notice that, even though you may have many strokes in your sketch, the blue vector outline defines the border around them as a whole, rather than outlining each one individually.

Show Strokes is useful in many ways, but one particularly handy application is revealing areas of difficult-to-see colour, or even hidden colour. For example, suppose one of your colours was almost the same grey as the Camera View background. It would be difficult to see. Similarly, if you were using white in the Drawing View, which has a white background, Show Strokes will reveal the outline.

2.18

WARNING
Use Show Strokes with caution. On a very complex sketch, showing strokes can lock up your computer momentarily. The program may become unresponsive for anywhere from a few seconds to several minutes, depending on the power of your computer and the complexity of the sketch.

> 5.   On your keyboard, press [K] again to hide the strokes.

> 6.   In the Brush tool properties, activate the *Auto-Flatten* button.

2.19

> 7.   In the Camera View, zoom out if necessary using the [1] key and then continue your sketch.

As soon as you lift your pen after the first stroke, all the existing strokes merge to become one. There's no longer any visible overlapping of strokes.

While this Brush option flattens your strokes as you draw, you may find it removes detail or nuances you prefer to keep. For example, in

2.20

my sketch above, the slightly darker parts of the eyes lose their appeal when flattened.

For this reason, I usually leave the Auto-Flatten option turned off, and only flatten drawings when I need to, by selecting it, then Drawing → Optimise → Flatten [Alt Shift F].

> BRUSH EXERCISE 5
  PAINT BEHIND MODE

> 1. Ensure Auto-Flatten is turned off.

> 2. With the default black paint, draw some Brush strokes in the Camera View.

> 3. From your colour panel, choose any other colour.

> 4. In the Brush tool properties, activate the *Paint Behind* option.

2.21

> 5. In the Timeline, select frame 1.

> 6. In the Camera View, the Paint Behind cursor looks like this ⁙. Draw some strokes over the top of your sketch. When you release the pen, your colour strokes will appear behind your sketch.

There are many uses for this mode. You might later find it useful for filling in tiny holes in paintwork, or perhaps drawing a shirt collar behind a character's neck.

2.22

> BRUSH EXERCISE 6
REPAINT BRUSH

One exceptionally useful Brush mode is the *Repaint* Brush. It allows you to repaint any existing painted areas with another colour.

2.23

> 1.   Start by choosing a solid dark blue from the colour panel.

ANIMATE PRO HARMONY ONLY
Animate users have 120 existing colours to choose from but Animate Pro and Harmony users might like to create a completely new colour.

> 1a. In the colour panel, click the ➕ button.

> 1b. Double-click the new colour swatch to mix a solid dark blue. If you need guidance, revisit Brush exercise 3 (on page 40).

> 1c. Input HSV values as shown in Figure 2.24.

There will be more on colour mixing and management later in this chapter starting on page 101.

> 2.   In the colour panel, ensure this new colour is selected.

> 3.   In the Timeline, select the frame with your shape sketches from exercise 4.

> 4.   Select the Repaint Brush using the shortcut [Alt X]. Alternatively you can activate the Repaint Brush in the Brush tool properties panel, as shown in Figure 2.23.

> 5.   In the Camera View try sketching in an empty part of the scene.

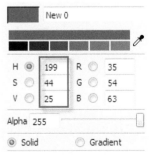

2.24

Repaint mode only repaints existing colour. It won't sketch like the normal Brush mode because it only works on already-painted areas and strokes.

> 6. With the Brush holding the new colour, paint over your existing sketches.

Here you can see how the sketch strokes, and nothing else, are repainted with the new colour you chose in step 2.

2.25

> BRUSH EXERCISE 7
  CUSTOM BRUSHES

I've intentionally skipped the remaining mode buttons as they're linked to more advanced concepts and will be covered later in the book.

2.26

In the Brush properties panel, we have the list of Brush presets. In earlier versions of the software, this is a drop-down list that, by default, shows 'Brush 1'. In the most recent version, large Brush previews take up most of the panel. This is a list of saved *Brush and texture styles* (note: Brush textures are not available in Animate 2).

Custom Brush styles store the sizes, texture, shape, and smooth/optimise information. They do not save colour information.

> 1. Select each Brush preset in turn, note the Preview stroke and test it out by drawing in the Camera View.

Any texture file in .psd format, including your own custom textures, can be applied to your Brushes via the Brush Properties:

- **Animate Pro 2** and **Harmony 10.3** – textures are accessed at the bottom of the Tool Properties panel as shown on the left in Figure 2.28.

- **Animate 3**, **Animate Pro 3** and **Harmony 11** – textures are accessed from the *Extended Brush Properties* window, which you can find by clicking the large triangular icon in the Brush Tool properties, shown in Figure 2.28.

The list of preset brush styles may be the only ones you'll ever need. Then again, you might like to continue this exercise to create your own.

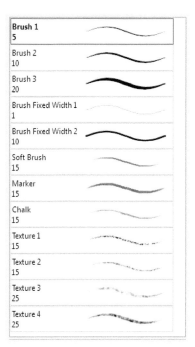

2.27

> 2. In the Brush tool properties, click the New Brush icon 🖌. A new Brush style is now in the list with a default name like *Brush 7*. You may need to scroll down the list to find your new style.

> 3. With your new Brush style selected in the list, rename it.

- **Animate 2**, **Animate Pro 2** and **Harmony 10.3** – Click the Rename Brush icon: Ⓐ.

- **Animate 3**, **Animate Pro 3** and **Harmony 11** – Use 🗐 to access the 'Rename Brush' menu item.

> 4. Name your Brush style whatever you like and click 'OK'. I've called mine *roughs*.

2.28 (left) Animate Pro 2, Harmony 10.3 Enable texture;
(right) Animate 3, Animate Pro 3 and Harmony 11 Brush properties

2.29

Earlier Toon Boom versions don't allow you to change the Brush order. Each new Brush is created at the bottom of the list. However, the latest versions of Toon Boom software allow you to shuffle the ordering of your Brush presets. You can drag your favourite, most frequently used brushes to the top of the list.

Brushes can be resized on-the-fly so why not just use the same Brush and resize it with the [O] key as needed? If that's what you're thinking, there's nothing stopping you from deleting some of them using the Delete Brush button .

On the other hand, custom styles can be useful for common tasks. For example, you may have your 'roughs' style and a separate 'cleanup' style for cleaning up your character sketches.

With the release of Animate 3 and Animate Pro 3, users have access to an awesome feature called Dynamic Brushes, which were previously available in Harmony only. You can learn more about textures and dynamic Brushes in Appendix A.

In the Brush tool properties, we can see numerical fields for minimum and maximum thickness, smoothing and optimising, and Brush shape. In the most recent versions, you will find these in the Extended Brush Properties window, accessed by clicking the big triangle (see Figure 2.28). Go ahead and experiment with each of fields and settings, and watch the Preview stroke in the panel (see Figure 2.29). If you create something you like, why not save it using what you've learned from this exercise?

> BRUSH EXERCISE 8:
BRUSH SHAPES

We have a selection of Brush shapes to choose from, each offering a unique line for a range of tasks. For example, you may find the flat styles useful for calligraphic pen effects, or perhaps something as simple as drawing a ribbon. These shapes aren't available on texture brushes.

> 1. In the Timeline, select frame 1.

> 2. In the Brush Properties panel, choose an angled Brush shape.

> 3. Type in a minimum Brush size of 80 and a maximum of 80.

> 4. In the Camera View, draw a flowing length of ribbon.

> 5. Experiment with other angles, sizes and Brush shapes for different effects.

2.30

2.31

PENCIL [ALT /]

The Pencil draws a *central vector* – rather than a vector border filled with paint, as you saw with the Brush tool. It's built like a strand of electrical wire: a central core with a coating of colour.

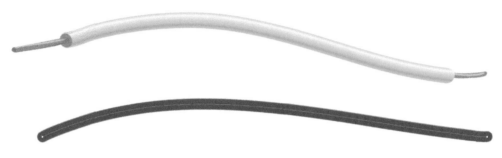

2.32

Harmony users and those with Animate 3 or Animate Pro 3 will find that the Pencil is super powerful and rivals the Brush in many ways. The first two exercises will cover the basic version then we'll see what's so great about its new features.

Once again, you can learn more about vector strokes and lines in Appendix B towards the back of this book.

The Pencil tool behaves much like the Brush and its options are very similar to those you saw in the Brush tool exercises. We have modes for Paint Behind and Auto-Flatten, as well as the now-familiar style presets list where custom values can be saved and renamed.

Just as you learned in the first Brush exercise on page 38, the Pencil can also be resized using the [O] key.

> PENCIL EXERCISE 1
  PENCIL LINES

> 1.   Arm the Pencil now by using the shortcut key [Alt /] and let's take it for a spin.

> 2.   In the Timeline, select frame 1.

> 3.   In the Camera View, draw a line, a triangle and a circle.

> 4.   Hold down [Shift] to draw straight lines. Even in the middle of a stroke, you can hold [Shift] to draw straight and then release [Shift] to return to freehand mode. If you're using Animate 2 or Animate Pro 2, right away you'll notice that the Pencil line has no pressure sensitivity, so it has a consistent width from end to end. This may be desirable for some tasks, especially for mechanical or architectural lines. For organic shapes though, it's definitely a hard, wiry, almost-too-perfect look.

> 5.   Press [K] to Show Strokes.

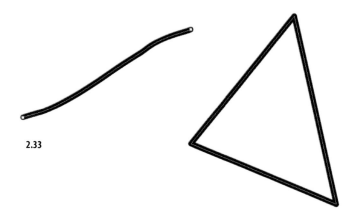

2.33

Unlike the blue outline of the Brush stroke, the blue line you see in Figure 2.33 is the *central vector*. A single, central line is much lighter and faster for the computer to process than the Brush stroke's vector outline.

The triangle is fully closed, but the yellow and red squares represent unconnected points and are designed to show up gaps in your line-work. If you haven't carefully closed the circle and triangle, these little end markers will reveal the gap, at a glance.

PENCIL EXERCISE 2
CLOSING GAPS

> 1. Ensure you have the Pencil [Alt /] selected.

> 2. In the tool properties panel, for the purpose of this exercise, make sure the Auto Close Gaps button is off.

2.34

> 3. In the Camera View, deliberately draw a square without quite closing the gap at the end, as shown below.

2.35

> 4. On your keyboard, press and hold [Y] (paint unpainted tool) and try to flood the square with colour by clicking in it. The gap in the square doesn't allow you to fill it.

> 5. Important: Ensure Show Strokes is *on* using [K] on your keyboard. The thin blue central vector will appear in your Pencil lines.

> 6. Now hold down [C] (close gaps override) and draw an invisible line across any gaps to close them. Once the gap is closed, the end markers should disappear.

2.36

> 7. On your keyboard, hold down [Y] once again and click inside the square to fill it with colour.

> 8. Hide Strokes now with [K]. Step 2 of this exercise instructed you to turn off the Auto Close Gaps button. Now let's turn it on and see how it affects things.

> 9. In the Pencil tool properties, turn *on* the Auto Close Gaps button (see Figure 2.34).

> 10. Click the Camera View's name tab to give it focus.

> 11. Show Strokes with [K].

> 12. In the Camera View, draw a circle or square.

With Auto Close Gaps turned on, you don't need to be so precise. You will certainly find this to be a huge time-saver when you're drawing frame after frame of character animation.

> PENCIL EXERCISE 3
  VARIABLE WIDTH

The new advanced Pencil is available only in Animate 3, Animate Pro 3 and all versions of Harmony. It has *minimum* and *maximum* size input fields in the properties panel. This means it can have variable width, just like the Brush tool, yet all the CPU-friendly economy of a central vector line.

> 1. Select the Pencil [Alt /] and in the Tool Properties panel choose 'Pencil 1' from the styles list.

> 2. In the Extended Pencil Properties (the big triangle button), enter the values shown in Figure 2.37.

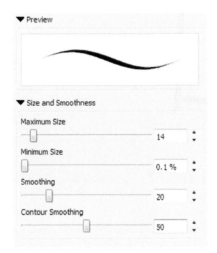

2.37

> 3. In the Timeline, select frame 1.

> 4. Draw some strokes. Just like the Brush, the Pencil lines are variable depending on the tablet pressure you use.

> 5.   Show Strokes using [K], or View → Show → Show Strokes.

2.38

Regardless of the width, the Pencil is still just a central vector with the line built around it.

Try out some of the styles provided in the list and note their settings. You can create your own custom styles here, in much the same way as you did in Brush exercise 7, back on page 46.

> PENCIL EXERCISE 4
  LINE BUILDING MODE

Line Building mode is an incredible feature, originally Harmony-only, but now in Animate 3 and Animate Pro 3. Like the Auto Close Gaps button, it eliminates the need for meticulous precision and tedious manual gap-closing.

> 1.   In the Timeline, select frame 1.

> 2.   In the Pencil properties, activate Line Building mode. It's the button with a hammer icon.

2.39

> 3.   In the Camera View, begin sketching a simple shape using multiple strokes, just as you might do with a real pencil.

Right away it'll become apparent just how awesome this is. You can 'sketch' an entire outline and at the end, have a beautiful clean drawing.

The only slight downside of this mode is that you're handing over some control, so occasionally you'll have a situation where the line building mode merges the wrong lines, or otherwise produces unwanted results. After a bit of experience with it though, you will get a feel for the drawing tasks that are best suited for this mode and find yourself toggling Line Building on and off.

> PENCIL EDITOR EXERCISE 1
  PENCIL EDITOR TOOL

As well as the Pencil tool properties, the Pencil Editor tool gives you an ultra-fine level of control over how your Pencil lines look. Once again, this was previously a Harmony-only feature but is now available in Animate 3 and Animate Pro 3 as well. If you use Animate 2 or Animate Pro 2, you unfortunately won't have these features.

> 1.   In the Timeline, select frame 1.

> 2.   With the Pencil, draw some lines in any colour or style.

Obviously I've drawn the handle lines way too thick giving me a convenient excuse to use the Pencil Editor!

> 3.   Press [Alt W] to select the Pencil Editor. Alternatively click-hold the Contour Editor in the Toolbar and choose the Pencil Editor from the list that appears.

2.41

> 4.   Press [K] to Show Strokes

> 5.   With the Pencil Editor, click on, or drag across the central vector of any Pencil stroke. A red outline with solid square points surrounds the Pencil stroke.

> 6.   Drag any point to widen or thin the stroke.

> 7.   Hold [Shift] then drag any point to uniformly widen the stroke on both sides of the vector.

> 8.   Hold [Ctrl] and click the *central* vector to add more control points.

> 9.   Draw a selection around any point, or group of points to reveal tangent handles (also known as Bezier handles). Experiment with the tangent handles to adjust the curvature of the stroke.

> 10.   Hold [Alt] then drag any tangent handle to break the connection with its opposite handle.

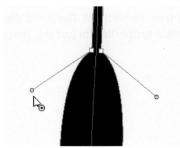

2.43

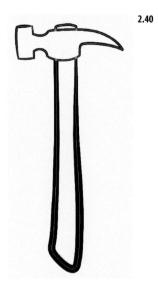

2.40

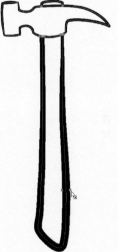

2.42

> PENCIL EDITOR EXERCISE 2
  PUMP AND SHRINK

> 1. With the Pencil Editor [Alt W], drag across any Pencil stroke to
     select it.

> 2. Drag a region around any point, or group of points to reveal the
     tangent handles on those points.

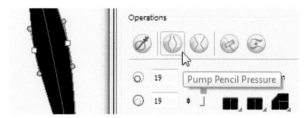

2.44

> 3. In the Pencil Editor properties, click the Pump Pencil Pressure
     button a number of times to watch the line widen.

Experiment with Pump as well as the next button, Shrink Pencil Pressure, and take note how each affects twin points or group selections.

> PENCIL EDITOR EXERCISE 3
  MERGE LINES

2.45

The Line Building mode, as you saw back in Pencil exercise 4, joins lines
together as you draw. But sometimes you'll want to join lines up after
you've drawn them. You'll find the Merge Lines button in the Pencil
Editor properties for just this purpose.

> 1. In the Timeline, select frame 1.

> 2. Select the Pencil tool [Alt /] and a colour of your choice.

> 3. In the Pencil tool properties, ensure Line Building mode is turned
     off.

> 4. Sketch a simple shape with a number of individual strokes.

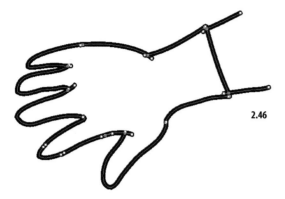

2.46

> 5. Select the Pencil Editor [Alt W] and drag a selection area around all of the Pencil strokes.

> 6. In the Pencil Editor properties, click the Merge Lines button.

This heavy-handed approach to merging everything at once can create problems. Chances are the merge has created gaps or merged too much.

> 7. On your keyboard, press [Ctrl/⌘ Z] to undo the merge.

> 8. Now try again by selecting just a few strokes at a time and merging them.

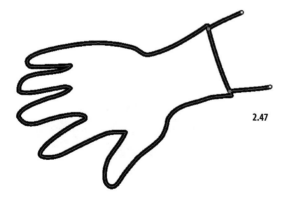

2.47

Later we'll talk about manipulating the lines to smooth out any undesirable curves.

> PENCIL EDITOR EXERCISE 4
  PENCIL TEMPLATES

Similar to Brush and Pencil presets, Pencil templates allow you to save line styles that you've created using the Pencil Editor.

> 1. In the Timeline select frame 1.

> 2. With the Pencil [Alt /] hold down [Shift] and draw a short, straight line.

> 3. With the Pencil Editor [Alt W], drag across the line to activate the red handles.

> 4. Create a new pair of manipulator points by holding down [Ctrl] and clicking the central vector as shown in Figure 2.48. As you add the new point, a pair appears; one on either side of the vector.

2.48

> 5. Select individual points and manipulate them and their handles to create a pair of lips in the line. A reminder that [Alt] breaks the connection between tangent handles.

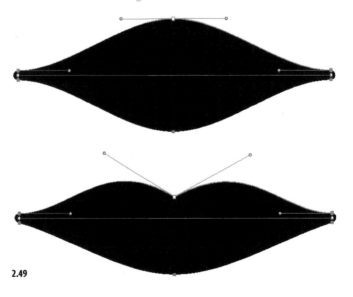

2.49

> 6. When you're happy with the lips, making sure that the red manipulator envelope is still up, click the New Pencil Template button in the

Pencil Editor properties. Figure 2.50 shows the Pencil Template
button in previous versions of Toon Boom (left) and the latest (right).

2.50

You'll now find your new template at the bottom of the templates list,
named 'Pencil Template 1'.

> 7. Select 'Pencil Template 1' from the list and use the Rename menu
      to call your template 'smile'.

2.51

Now it's time to use your first Pencil template!

> 8. Grab the Pencil [Alt /].

> 9. In the tool properties, select 'smile' from the bottom of the styles
      list. You'll probably need to scroll the list to find it, but you can drag
      it to the top of your list if you like.

> 10. In the Camera View, draw some short strokes until you can't help
      but smile back.

NOTE
A couple of things to note as you experiment with this:

• You can curve the line up like a smile, or down to make it more
  pouty.

• If the line is longer, the smile will be stretched.

• If you draw the line from right-to-left, the smile will be
  upside-down

• Templates might be fun for short strokes like smiles, leaves and
  bats but the general idea is to create interesting line styles with
  longer sections for entire character outlines.

Finally, you can apply this template to any existing Pencil stroke. In earlier versions of Animate Pro and Harmony, you would first need to select the stroke using the Pencil Editor tool [Alt W], and then click the Apply Pencil Template ☻ button. It's much simpler in Animate 3, Animate Pro 3 and Harmony 11, as follows:

> 11. Select any Pencil stroke with the Select tool [Alt S].

> 12. Simply select any of the Pencil Styles in the Pencil Properties to change the style of the selected stroke.

> 13. Experiment further by applying Pencil templates to various Pencil strokes.

For a bit of fun you can practice creating various shapes with the Pencil Editor, as illustrated in Figure 2.52. Some of them might even turn out to be useful!

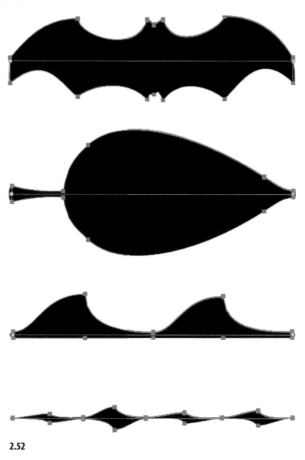

2.52

ERASER [ALT E]

Right after learning about the Brush and Pencil tools, it makes sense to talk about erasing. The Eraser is as simple as it gets though, so this will be brief.

It's an eraser, so it erases. It works like a negative paint Brush – simply drag to erase.

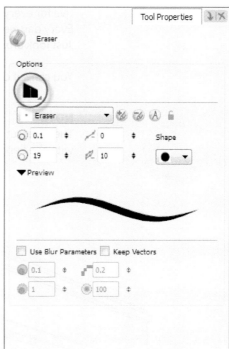

The Eraser options are the same as we've seen for the Brush and Pencil, although there are no mode buttons in the eraser's properties panel. It includes the familiar *minimum* and *maximum* size fields, which means you can use the [O] key to resize the eraser as you work in the Camera view. There is also a list of Eraser styles just like that of the Brush and Pencil.

The eraser in Animate 3, Animate Pro 3 and Harmony gives you one option button, which is circled in Figure 2.53. This applies specifically to erasing Pencil or any other central vector line. When you use the Eraser to break up Pencil or Shape tool strokes, Harmony provides three options for how the line ends are capped. As you saw in the Pencil tool properties, lines drawn can be capped with rounded, square or bevelled ends. In the eraser properties, simply enable the option for how you want your lines to be cut as you erase them.

2.53

2.54

SHAPE [ALT \]

 The Shape tool has three modes: Line, Rectangle and Ellipse.

For traditional artists and animators, these tools may seem too primitive for everyday use, but they are in fact extremely useful in practice. Every day we are surrounded by mathematically solid lines and arcs. Just look around you.

You can set options for each Shape tool mode in the properties panel.

NOTE
The shortcut for this tool is Alt + back slash [Alt \], not to be confused with the Pencil's forward slash [/].

When used in conjunction with the Contour Editor (we'll talk about that later on page 83) each line can be manipulated with great precision, providing excellent control when drawing architecture, machinery, perspective grids and more.

By now, most of the buttons in the Shape properties panel will be familiar to you, with just a couple of exceptions.

2.55

> SHAPE EXERCISE 1
  LINE SNAPPING

If you're new to software, it might help to know that the term 'snapping' has nothing to do with breaking. It refers to the magnet-like snapping together of line ends to other objects.

> 1.   In the Timeline, select frame 1.

> 2.   Select the Shape tool with [Alt \]. The tool properties show that it's in *Line* mode.

> 3.   In the Camera View, click-drag and release to create lines of various angles. You can hold down [Shift] to snap lines to 15° angles.

> 4.   Click the Snap to Contour button in the tool properties.

2.56

NOTE
Snap to Contour has a shortcut key. Simply hold down [Alt] when drawing with the Line, and your line ends will snap together.

It's not necessary to keep [Alt] held down while dragging the line. Once the line sticks, you can release the [Alt] key throughout the drag and the start of the line will remain snapped.

If you've released the [Alt] key while dragging, you can simply hold it again to snap the end of your line to another Pencil line or Brush stroke.

> 5.   Draw some polygons and see how the line ends snap together as if magnetic. This is useful for ensuring your linework has no gaps, when it comes time to paint.

> 6.   Press [Ctrl/⌘ '], or go to View → Grid → Show Grid.

> 7. In the Shape tool properties, turn the Snap to Grid button on.

2.57

> 8. As the cursor hovers in the Camera View, notice that a tiny circle jumps around the grid.

> 9. Click-drag to draw some new lines and you'll see how the start and ends of your line are aligned perfectly to the grid intersections.

> 10. You can turn off grid snapping by toggling the button off. The grid itself can be turned off simply by pressing [Ctrl/⌘ '] again.

> SHAPE EXERCISE 2
> RECTANGLE AND ELLIPSE

> 1. From the toolbar, select the Rectangle tool from behind the Line tool, or press [Alt 7].

> 2. You'll notice that the tool properties panel is barely distinguishable from the Line tool settings.

2.58

> 3. In the Camera View, draw a rectangle by dragging diagonally in any direction. You'll see the rectangle preview stretch and distort as you move the cursor around.

> 4. While dragging, hold down [Shift] to constrain the Rectangle tool to a perfect square, and [Alt] to create the rectangle from the centre. You can also use [Shift Alt] together to create a perfect square from the centre.

The Ellipse options are exactly the same as the Rectangle. Select it as you did the Rectangle in Step 1, or press [Alt =], and repeat the above steps.

> SHAPE EXERCISE 3
AUTO FILL

2.59

The Rectangle and Ellipse shapes have the Auto Fill option. Activate this button to automatically fill your rectangle or ellipse with the chosen colour. Alternatively you could simply fill the empty rectangle or ellipse using the Paint tool, which we'll talk about after this exercise.

> 1. In the Shape tool properties, turn the Auto Fill option on.

> 2. In the Camera View, draw rectangles and ellipses.

If you have solid black chosen as your colour, your rectangles and ellipses will be filled with solid black.

NOTE
If your lines and fills are different colours, don't worry for now; at least you know the Auto Fill works. Later, in the Colour Management section starting on page 101, we'll look at linking and unlinking colours so that your outlines can be a different colour to the fill.

From this day forward, whenever you need to fill the screen with blue for a sky background, or whenever you need to draw a filled white circle for the moon, chances are you'll be using the Shape tool.

> SHAPE EXERCISE 4
NO OUTLINE

To create a rectangle, circle or any other closed shape without an outline, simply set the line thickness to zero and ensure that Auto Fill is turned on (see exercise 3). You may receive a popup message that your strokes are invisible, but simply click OK and then you can Show Strokes with [K] to see your invisible lines.

PAINT [ALT I]

With the paint bucket you can flood-fill closed areas with colour. Considering most 2D animation consists of outlines filled with colour – from a simple background rectangle filled with sky blue, to a crowd scene with potentially hundreds of individually coloured areas – you'll quickly grow familiar with this tool.

The fantastic thing about Toon Boom paint is its ease of application. To fill tiny areas like eyes, jewellery and buttons, it's not necessary to painstakingly click inside those empty spaces (even though you can, if that's what you like to do). The paint bucket has marquee and lasso modes, so to paint a closed area no matter how small, you can simply drag your lasso through or around it. The paint bucket detects which areas are closed and fills them. This makes painting *very* fast. No more zooming in 1200 percent to delicately click in a small area!

In the tools properties, you'll find several Paint modes which we'll see in the upcoming exercises.

2.60

As you may have already seen in the Pencil exercises, paint cannot exist without a vector border around it. Just like a real life paint can, it won't hold any paint if there's a hole in it. Similarly, if there's a gap anywhere in your vector border, the Paint tool simply doesn't work. Hence this constant emphasis on closing gaps in your linework.

2.61

The beginning part of each exercise below will require you to use those drawing tools you've already learned (Brush, Pencil, Shape) to create various outlines for filling.

> PAINT EXERCISE 1
  CLICK, LASSO AND MARQUEE

> 1.   In the Timeline, select any frame you'd like to draw on.

> 2.   From the toolbar, choose the Brush or press [Alt B].

> 3.   In the Camera View, draw any closed shape you like. Carefully ensure the linework is completely closed, leaving no gaps.

2.62

> 4.   Choose the Paint (bucket) tool from the toolbar, or use the shortcut [Alt I]

> 5.   With the Paint tool, click once inside the closed shape.

If the area hasn't been flooded with paint, you may have gaps in your linework. In this case, we can take advantage of the Auto Close Gaps option in the Paint tool properties. Alternatively, you can revisit Pencil exercise 2 on page 52 for a refresher on finding and closing them.

TIP
Does your paint bucket seem to be painting with the wrong colour?
It may be that your tool colours are unlinked. Skip ahead to page 115
and see how tool colour linking works, then skip back here.

Next, we'll look at the lasso mode of the Paint tool.

> 6. In the Timeline, select the frame you'd like to work in.

> 7. Using the Pencil or Brush with black paint, draw a character's head
and eyes in linework. Ensure each of these is a closed shape, and
notice in Figure 2.63, even the shirt has a line closing the area.
Incidentally, in animation, this is called a cutoff line. It's usually just
outside the border of the movie where it won't be seen, and exists
purely to close the area for paint.

> 8. Select the Paint tool from the toolbar, or press [Alt I].

> 9. From the colour panel, now choose a colour for the character's
skin.

2.63

NOTE
If you're using Animate Pro or Harmony, feel free to mix a new skin
colour. Refresh your memory if necessary by revisiting Brush exercise
3 on page 40. There is a substantial section dedicated to Colour Management coming up on page 101.

> 10. In the Paint tool properties, make sure the mode is set to Lasso.

2.64

> 11. With your Paint tool now, 'draw' a stroke across the hair.

As long as your stroke passes through the hair, it'll be filled with hair colour. But we have a problem: the black outline has also been painted. Let's undo the last step and fix that.

> 12. Press the shortcut key [Ctrl/⌘ Z] to undo the Paint fill.

> 13. Try the exact paint motion again but this time, hold down [Y] as you do so.

[Y] is the shortcut for the Paint Unpainted mode of the tool. When held down, your Paint cursor changes to this icon ⠐PU. It means that anything that is already painted (such as the black character outline) won't be painted again. It only works on empty, *unpainted* areas. Rather than hold the override key down every time, you can equip the Paint Unpainted tool with [Alt Y].

> 14. Repeat the above steps to fill his skin and shirt colours in the same way.

Now that he has a shirt on, a full head of hair and a skin colour, let's finish with the eyes.

> 15. Choose another colour for the eyes. For this exercise, no need to bother with pupils, irises, eyelashes or bloodshot capillaries. Just a typical cartoonish blue-white will do.

> 16. With the Paint tool, again hold down [Y] and draw a lasso area around the eyes.

2.65

Because you have *Paint Unpainted* mode active, the other colours are left untouched. Only the eyes have been filled, because they were the only unpainted, closed areas.

Like a lot of things in this software, once you get used to it, this method of painting is remarkably efficient. To watch an adept user apply complex colouring with flicks and swishes is very impressive.

Finally, the Marquee mode of the Paint tool is simply a rectangular area, rather than the Lasso's freehand area. You can enable it in the properties panel or by holding down [Alt] while the Lasso mode is enabled.

2.66

> PAINT EXERCISE 2
  REPAINT AND UNPAINT

You've already seen the Paint Unpainted mode so let's look at two others: Repaint and Unpaint.

> 1. In your colour panel, select or create a completely different skin colour.

> 2. Choose the Paint tool in Repaint mode with [Alt R].

In the tool properties panel, you could also have used the Repaint mode button.

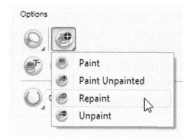

2.67

> 3. In the Camera View, click anywhere on the character's skin to repaint it with the new skin colour.

The reason we clicked, instead of using Lasso or Marquee is because we don't want to repaint the black outline. Repaint works on existing paint, which includes the outline. Later you'll see how to protect colours so they can't accidentally be repainted or erased.

Now let's look at Unpaint.

> 4. Hold down [U] and click in the character's eyes to unpaint them. Alternatively, you could activate Unpaint mode in the Paint tool properties.

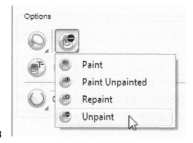

2.68

> 5. Choose another colour and then hold down [Y] to fill the eyes with Paint Unpainted mode.

NOTE

If all these modes and their shortcut keys are confusing you, don't worry. You don't need to memorise them all right away. They'll become second nature for whatever modes and tools you use most. Even after several years of using Toon Boom software, I often find myself dipping into Edit → Preferences → Shortcuts to learn some new keys.

TEXT [ALT 9]

Text is all around us in our everyday lives, whether on signposts, clothing, computer screens or poster prints. It makes sense that when adding realism to your scenes, you'd make frequent use of the Text tool.

> TEXT EXERCISE 1
  ADDING TEXT

> 1.   Select frame 1 in the Timeline.

> 2.   Choose the Text tool from the toolbar, or just press [Alt 9].

> 3.   In the Text properties, set a size, font and colour of your choice.

> 4.   In the Camera View, click to place the text cursor.

> 5.   Type your pet's name.

> 6.   If you'd like to start a new line, press [Enter/Return].

> 7.   Press your [Esc] key to finish typing and deselect your text.

2.69

> 8.   Keep this text here for the next exercise.

Although made up of several characters, your text can be manipulated as a single object.

> TEXT EXERCISE 2
  REFORMATTING TEXT

To change your text after it has been typed, you can use the Text tool to click and drag-select characters, just as you would in any word program or internet browser.

> 1.   If you deleted your text from the previous exercise, grab the Text tool and type something in the Camera View.

> 2.   Deselect the text by clicking a blank area of the Camera View, or press [Esc].

> 3.   With the text tool selected, hover over your text to see the text edit cursor I.

> 4.   Click and drag across some of the characters to select them.

2.70

You can now change the selected characters in the text properties panel, or type new characters. If you'd like to change the colour of the selected characters, simply choose any other colour in your Colour panel.

> TEXT EXERCISE 3
  BREAKING TEXT APART

While text is initially created as a single object, you have the option break it down into individual characters, allowing you to reposition, recolour and animate them independently. Broken down just once, characters will retain their text properties, allowing you to select and retype the individual characters. However, you can break them down even further to a vector art level, so you can paint, morph and manipulate them. Beware, however, that once you've broken it down all the way, you've destroyed the font information and it can no longer be changed with the Text tool.

> 1. With the Select tool, drag a selection around your block of text.

> 2. Go to Drawing → Convert → Break Apart Text Layers.

This step has broken the text from a single text object, down to individual characters. You can still use the keyboard to retype or reformat these characters individually.

> 3. Using the Text tool, drag-select any character and retype it.

> 4. Equip the Select tool [Alt S] and move the individual characters around. If you're a bit confused by the selection handles, there's no harm skipping forward to the Select tool on page 78.

As you can see, the words no longer exist as a single text object. It's a scattered collection of individual characters.

2.71

Now let's break it down even further by turning it into raw vector art. This step is identical to the previous steps 1 and 2.

> 5. Once again, drag a selection around your text.

> 6. In the top menu, choose Drawing → Convert → Break Apart Text Layers.

The result looks like text, but you won't be able to format it with the Text tool, nor will you find text options in the tool properties panel. This is now vector art.

> 7. Choose or create a new bright colour in your Colour panel.

> 8. Equip the Brush in Repaint mode. The shortcut for the Repaint Brush is [Alt X].

> 9. Paint a few strokes through your text. I've added a few more words too.

2.72

Breaking text apart allows you to customise it fully, removing the constraints of the font and adding your own touches. An example is my Brackenwood logo (Figure 2.73), which uses two fonts fully broken down, then painted and manipulated to the point that it's unique.

2.73

STROKE [ALT V]

Now and then your work might call for a colour separation without any visible linework. For example, the colour of a character's lips might look a little nicer if there is no outline. You could use the Pencil with a thickness of zero, or you could use the Stroke tool, which was made for jobs like this.

> STROKE EXERCISE 1
DRAWING INVISIBLE LINES

> 1. Get the Stroke tool by pressing [Alt V].
      The cursor looks like ⁚⁝⁚.

2.74

> 2. In the Camera View, draw a stroke.

Gotcha! Right away, there's a popup warning that says you won't be able to see your stroke. You may have seen this earlier if you used the Pencil or Shape tools with zero line thickness. Personally I find this warning a bit intrusive but it's a handy reminder for beginners.

2.75

> 3. Feel free to check 'Don't show this message again' if you like, then click 'OK' to close the warning.

> 4. On your keyboard, press [K]. The line you drew in step 2 is now revealed as a blue hairline vector with red and yellow points, or 'vertices'.

> 5. Now that you can see what you're drawing, make a few simple closed shapes. The Stroke tool properties panel has options for straight lines and end-snapping. Using both of them together makes for some very fast polygon drawing.

> 6. Hold down [Y] and trace a line through all of the shapes to fill them.

> 7. Hide strokes now by pressing [K] again.

2.76

You've created some filled shapes with no visible outline! Lovely.

SELECT [ALT S]

You've already used the Select tool here and there in other exercises. It has pole position at the top of the Tools toolbar. There are a few aspects to the Select tool that we will need to cover later, but the following exercises will demonstrate the basics of selection.

The properties panel for the Select tool presents two sets of properties. There are the properties for *the tool itself*; then there are properties for *any currently selected objects*. For example, if you use the Select tool to select text, the tool properties will display Select tool options at the top of the panel, then Text options down lower, as shown in Figure 2.77.

Likewise, selecting Brush or Pencil strokes will display options for altering them in the Select tool properties.

> SELECT EXERCISE 1
OBJECT SELECTION

2.77

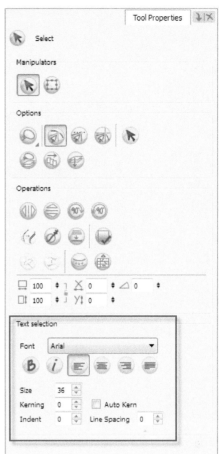

> 1.   In the Timeline, select any blank frame to work on.

> 2.   Using the Brush or Pencil, draw something simple in the Camera View.

> 3.   Choose the Select tool from the toolbar, or just press [Alt S].

> 4.   In the Select tool properties panel ensure the Lasso mode is active.

> 5.   In the Camera View, trace a freehand selection area around your new drawing.

2.78

This orange box around the selected object indicates your object is selected. Dotted around the orange outline are a number of white squares and a circle in the middle. These are the manipulation handles. Let's take a closer look.

> SELECT EXERCISE 2
PIVOT, POSITION, ROTATION AND SCALE

> 1.   Mouse over any of the corner handles to see the ↗ scale cursor.

> 2.   Drag this handle around to scale your object. Hold down [Shift] while scaling to constrain the proportions.

> 3.   Mouse over any of the side handles to see the ↔ *squash* and ↕ *stretch* cursor.

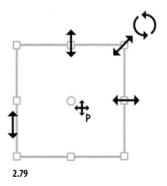

2.79

> 4. Experiment with the squash and stretch handles for different sizes and effects.

> 5. Mouse over any of the side rails to see the skew cursors ⇌ and ⇕ .

> 6. Drag the side rails to skew the drawing.

> 7. Hover the mouse just outside any corner handle until you see the rotation cursor ↺ .

> 8. Drag the handle to rotate your object and note that object pivots around the circular handle in the centre.

> 9. Hover the mouse over the circular centre handle and note the ✛ cursor. This is the selection pivot.

> 10. Drag the pivot just outside of the object and use the rotation handles again.

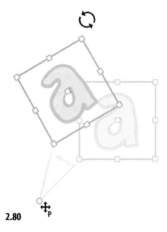

2.80

> 11. Deselect the drawing now using the [Esc] key.

> 12. Again, using the Select tool draw a selection area around the object.

Note how the pivot has returned to the centre. The Select tool pivot will always reset every time you reselect a drawing object. Later, you'll see other types of pivot that remain fixed wherever you place them.

> 13. Drag the pivot aside and note the square handle that remains in the centre. This is the position handle.

> 14. Hover your mouse over the square translate handle and you'll see the cursor ✛.

> 15. Drag this handle to move the selection around.

You can also drag using any part of the drawing itself, which is fine for large objects but what if your drawing is too small and fiddly for click and drag? Consider a snowflake, star or – as in Figure 2.81 – an eye. When selected it's obscured by the selection handles themselves. The position handle you saw in step 13 is the cure for this very situation.

> 16. Finally, deselect using the [Esc] key.

2.81

SELECT EXERCISE 3
TOOL PROPERTIES

We've already seen how the Select tool properties will change depending on what you have selected. For example, selecting text will give you text options at the bottom of the Select tool properties. Likewise, selecting a Pencil stroke will allow you to manipulate its properties, such as size, colour and texture.

> 1. Press [Alt 9] to arm the Text tool.

> 2. Click in the Camera View to place a cursor.

> 3. Type any word or short phrase.

> 4. Choose the Select tool and then select the text.

2.82

Text options are now available at the bottom of your tool properties panel as you saw back in Figure 2.77. You may need to use the panel scrollbar to see these options.

Here you have formatting options, as well as size, colour and font styles. As long as your text is selected in the Camera or Drawing Views, any changes will update the text as you make them.

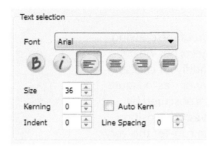

2.83

> SELECT EXERCISE 4
  PENCIL STROKES

Any existing Pencil strokes can be selected and have their properties manipulated in the Select tool properties panel.

> 1. In the Timeline, select frame 1.

> 2. In the Camera View, draw a few simple shapes with the Pencil tool.

> 3. Select one or more strokes with the Select tool [Alt S].

> 4. In the Select tool properties, adjust the width, colour and texture of the stroke.

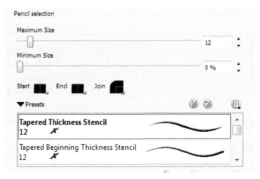

2.84

CONTOUR EDITOR [ALT Q]

The Contour Editor is very much like the Select tool but rather than selecting whole objects, it allows you to select the components that make up that object; that is, the sub-objects. You may have noticed that I've mentioned 'vector points' a few times. These are the sub-objects known as vertices. They define the vectors (lines) that make up all vector art.

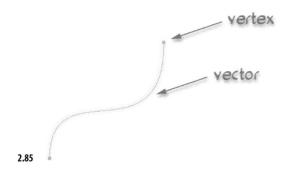

2.85

The Contour Editor allows you to manipulate each and any individual vertex of your strokes and fills, which gives you ultra-fine control over how your art looks. If one of your strokes is not quite where you want it, or perhaps it's just a little too thick, you can use the Contour Editor to manipulate it all the way down at the vertex level to get it looking perfect.

> CONTOUR EDITOR EXERCISE 1
  CURVING LINES AND MANIPULATING VERTICES

> 1. Press [Alt \] to select the Shape tool in Line mode. Note that Line mode is shown in the toolbar and in the Shape Tool Properties panel.

> 2. Anywhere in the Camera View, drag out a straight line.

> 3. Now select the Contour Editor tool from the tools panel, or press [Alt Q].

> 4. Hover the cursor over the line and you'll see it change to a small ⌐ .

> 5. Drag the middle of the line to curve it in any direction.

Immediately upon clicking, the points on each end are suddenly revealed. There's one vertex on each end of the line. You'll also see a preview curve as you drag. When you stop dragging, the curve is created.

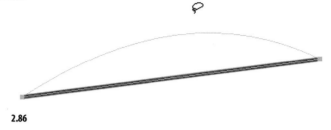

2.86

> 6. Hover your cursor over the vertices on each end. The vertex cursor is a square.

> 7. Draw an ellipse and a rectangle in the Camera View. A reminder that these tools can be found in the Toolbar behind the Line tool, or with [Alt =] and [Alt 7].

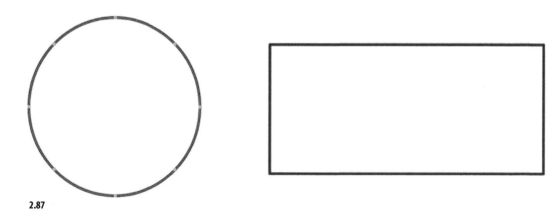

2.87

> 8. Now with the Contour Editor [Alt Q], click on your new ellipse. Note that it's made up of eight vertices.

> 9. Trace a selection around the ellipse's top three vertices, and then drag them up to deform it into an egg shape.

> 10. Experiment with reshaping your rectangle by moving vertices and curving the lines.

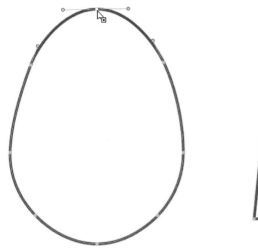
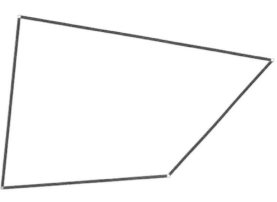

2.88

Later in the book, you'll be creating morph sequences where one shape is animated into another. You'll think back to this exercise and hopefully gain a little insight as to how it works behind the scenes.

> CONTOUR EDITOR EXERCISE 2
  MANIPULATING CURVES

Each vertex has one or two handles with which you can manipulate the curve. In Figure 2.89, the end vertices have only one handle, but the middle vertex has twin handles; one on either side.

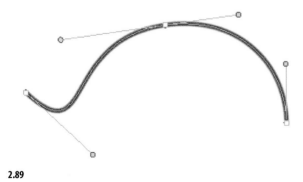

2.89

Twin handles are usually locked at 180° to one another, so that when you move one, the other responds; but you can break that connection.

> 1. Create a new ellipse in the Camera View then touch it with the Contour Editor.

> 2. Trace a selection around the topmost vertex to show its tangent handles.

> 3. Hover your cursor over a handle and note the handle cursor is different to the vertex cursor you saw in the last exercise It's helpful to know the difference when you're working in a cluster of vertices and their handles.

> 4. Hold [Alt] while dragging the left handle to break the connection between the two.

> 5. Drag the left handle upwards and then do the same with the right.

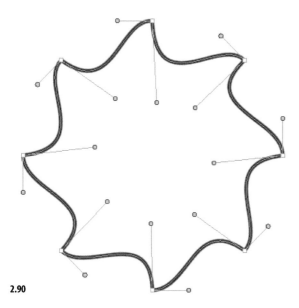

2.90

Breaking the connection allows you to create sharp corners and more interesting shapes. The shape in Figure 2.90 was created, starting with an ellipse and simply [Alt] dragging every other handle in toward the centre.

This fine level of control may or may not be something you use a lot, but it's nice to know that you can tweak every vertex to this extent.

NOTE
After breaking the connection between handles, if you release the [Alt] key and continue dragging, they will realign when one of them is dragged 180° to its twin.

> CONTOUR EDITOR EXERCISE 3
  DELETING, ADDING AND CHANGING VERTICES

Vertices have corner or curve behaviour – or both. You may have noticed that the ellipse has tangent handles on every vertex but the rectangle doesn't. That's because the rectangle has no curve information; the lines are all straight. Tangent handles only show up when the vertices have curve information. If you want tangent handles on a rectangle, you first need to add them – which we'll do in just a moment – or drag-curve the lines, as you saw in the first exercise.

In this exercise, we'll look at changing the behaviour of vertices, as well as deleting and adding new ones.

> 1.   Create an ellipse in the Camera View.

> 2.   Use the Contour Editor and click the ellipse to reveal the vertices.

> 3.   Trace a selection around the top three vertices then press [Delete].

> 4.   Do the same for the bottom three so your ellipse has only two vertices, as shown in Figure 2.91.

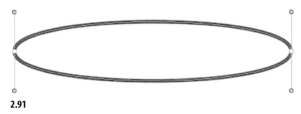

2.91

As you can see here, an ellipse really only requires two vertices. If you really wanted to, you could fiddle with the tangent handles on these two to make it more circular.

We've just removed six vertices for the sake of the exercise, but let's now add two of them back.

> 5.   Hold down [Ctrl] and your cursor will gain a little add icon

> 6.   Click on the curve at the top of the ellipse and a new vertex will be placed on the path.

> 7.   Do the same at the bottom to place a new one.

2.92

> 8.   Hold down [Alt] and note the cursor shows a negative sign 🔸 [Alt click] the bottom vertex to remove the curve information from it. It becomes a corner point, rather than a curve point.

> 9.   Do the same with the top vertex, turning it into a corner point as well.

> 10. By moving vertices around and using the tangent handles on the two side vertices, reshape this thing into a love heart.

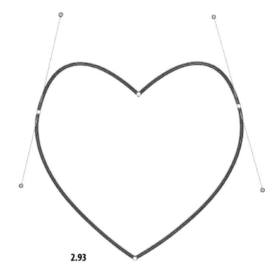

2.93

To add handles to a corner point, you can simply [Alt drag] the vertex.

> 11. Create a rectangle in the Camera View.

> 12. Using the Contour Editor, hold down [Alt] and drag any vertex.

> 13. Release the handles to finish the curve.

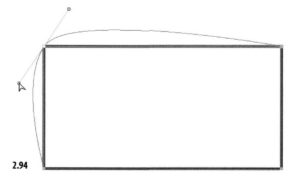

2.94

Smoothing makes your curves more graceful and efficient by reducing the number of vertices. This can be especially useful for smoothing out ragged linework.

> 1. Choose the Brush tool and in the Tool Properties, set it to Auto Flatten.

> 2. In the Camera View, sketch something fairly simple.

> 3. When you're done, select the Contour Editor and click on your sketch.

2.95

Depending on your complexity, you may now be seeing a lot of vertices, but we turned on Auto-Flatten for a good reason: it flattens many individual strokes into one, so right away we avoid having a ridiculous number of vertices. Revealing the vertices on a really complex, unflattened sketch can slow down or even crash your computer, so be careful. Try to avoid using the Contour Editor on anything with extreme detail.

You can see that the chair in Figure 2.96 is actually a rough sketch, which is why it has so many vertices, as opposed to the clean lines in the previous figure. I've also shown the handles here (overleaf) just to give you an idea of how a full screen sketch might lock up your computer if you use the Contour Editor on it.

2.96

> 4. With the vertices of your sketch showing, make a mental note of how many there appear to be.

> 5. In the top menu, go to Drawing → Optimize → Smooth. Note that its shortcut key is [Alt Shift S].

If your sketch is relatively simple, you may see an immediate reduction in the number of vertices. In a more complex sketch though, it may be hard to see any difference right away. You can hit [Alt Shift S] a number of times to watch the number of vertices gradually recede.

Smoothing multiple times will eventually result in your strokes having a more angular appearance. Of course, it's possible to smooth a sketch into oblivion; removing more and more vertices, creating gaps and cutting off corners until it bears little resemblance to the original linework.

This is sometimes a heavy-handed solution, so you may occasionally find it necessary to zoom in and manually remove or manipulate the vertices. Although fiddly, this level of control can become quite addictive.

2.97

PERSPECTIVE [ALT 0]

This handy tool is in the sub-menu of the Contour Editor. You can select your art with the perspective tool, then use its manipulator handles to distort into a perspective simulation.

2.98

2.99

When you're working with this, you may notice that it's not exactly true perspective. The Perspective tool merely distorts, whereas in true perspective, distant detail is squashed more. Still, it's a decent distortion tool with many uses aside from faking perspective on walls, doors or signs like the one in Figure 2.99.

CUTTER TOOL [ALT + T]

You'll find the Cutter tucked neatly away behind the Select tool. The way you use it is just like the Select tool but rather than simply selecting objects, you're slicing up the artwork. This is particularly useful for segmenting characters in preparation for cut-out style animation.

Suppose you have a character drawing and want to cut the head off to put it on a separate layer. With the cutter tool you'd trace a selection around his head in the same way you might use the Select tool.

Once cut, the affected area has a washed-out appearance with green manipulation handles. From here you can alter the area in the same way as you would with the Select tool's manipulator handles, with rotation, skew or scaling. You can also move, delete or cut and paste this segment.

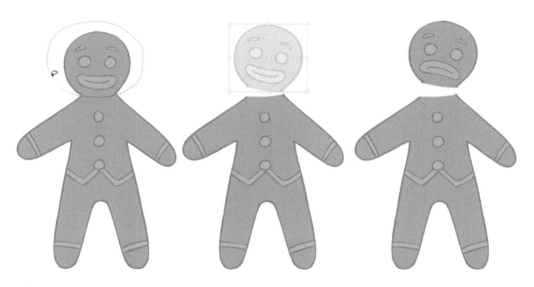

2.100

Sometimes when animating frame-by-frame, the best of us can fall victim to 'volume change'. This is where something, for example the character's head, gradually becomes too large or too small over the course of the scene. The cutter tool is very handy for tweaking things like that, so you don't have to redraw the head, simply cut and then, with the Perspective tool (see Figure 2.99) tweak it to the right size on each frame.

> CUTTER EXERCISE 1
  REMOVING OVERHANGING LINES

One fantastic feature of the Cutter allows you to cut off overhanging lines with a click or swipe. It really speeds up your workflow, removing the need for tedious drawing or erasing precision.

> 1. In the Timeline, select a blank frame to work in.

> 2. Using the Shape tool in rectangle mode [Alt 7], draw three tall, thin rectangles, placing them fairly close together as shown in Figure 2.101.

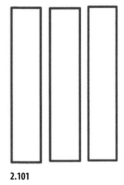

2.101

> 3. Using the Select tool, click on the middle rectangle.

> 4. Now hold [Shift] and drag a corner point to rotate the selection 90°.

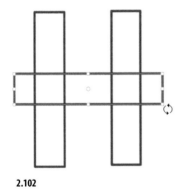

2.102

This is almost a letter H but there are some overhanging lines. Let's get rid of them with the cutter tool.

> 5. On your keyboard, press [2] to zoom in and view the lines at a comfortable size.

> 6. If you don't already have the Cutter, press [Alt T].

> 7. As shown in Figure 2.103, click the overhanging part on the left end of the middle rectangle to select it.

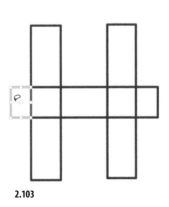

2.103

Toon Boom has detected where the lines intersect and isolates the overhanging lines for you.

> 8.   Press [Delete] on your keyboard to remove those overhanging lines.

> 9.   Repeat the process to do the same on the other end, and you should have something that looks more like a H.

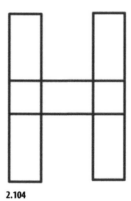

2.104

Before you go ahead and remove the other unwanted lines, I wanted to introduce you to another feature of the Cutter. Enabled by default, there's a 'mouse gestures' feature in the Cutter tool properties. It allows you to quickly swipe a line to remove it.

2.105

> 10.   With the Use Mouse Gestures mode activated, swipe across the remaining unwanted lines to complete the H.

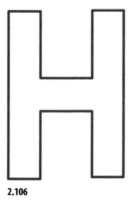

2.106

POLYLINE [ALT SHIFT -]

Just like the Shape tool, Polyline draws by plotting points. However, while the Shape tool *automatically* plots points (vertices) for lines, rectangles and ellipses, Polyline lets you create more complex objects by placing vertices *manually*.

As I mentioned earlier in the book, if you're using a mouse, this tool may even become your best friend. Though it takes some getting used to, combined with the Contour Editor it grants ultimate control, even if you are a tablet user.

> POLYLINE EXERCISE 1
  PLOTTING POINTS

Let's draw a pentagon by plotting five points.

> 1. In the toolbar, you'll find the Polyline behind the Shape tool. Alternatively you can press [Alt Shift -].

> 2. In the Polyline tool properties, activate the Snap to Contour option. This will make it easier to close the shape leaving no gaps.

> 3. In the Timeline, click any blank frame to work in.

> 4. In the Camera View, click to create the first point. This red vertex is the point from which your first line will be drawn. Red is always the colour of your most recently placed vertex.

> 5. Mark out the pentagon by placing the other vertices. Note that these are created as corner points, resulting in perfectly straight lines.

> 6. Hover over the first point you created and your cursor becomes a 🖋+ icon. Click to close the shape.

> 7. To finish the job, now click the red vertex.

2.107

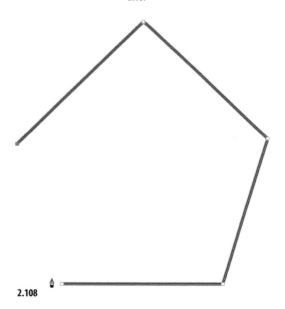

2.108

TIP
Clicking the red vertex will finish the shape regardless of whether the shape is closed or open. Holding [Ctrl] and clicking anywhere has the same effect.

Once your line or shape is finished, you can tweak it using the Contour Editor, or fill it with colour. With your Polyline tool's contour snapping on (as shown back in step 2), you should have no trouble closing the shapes.

> POLYLINE EXERCISE 2
  PLOTTING CURVE POINTS

In the previous exercise you plotted corner points. That's good for angular shapes, but if you're drawing more organic stuff, like characters, you'll need to know how to make curves.

> 1.   If you don't already have the Polyline tool, choose it from the toolbar, or press [Alt Shift -].

> 2.   On a new blank frame in the Camera View, click, drag and release.

This has created a vertex with a tangent handle. The length of your drag equates to the length of the handle.

> 3.   Elsewhere in the Camera View, click and drag in any direction to create your second vertex.

The curve appears and now you get to see how the handle lengths affect the curve. Don't worry if it all seems too much like guesswork at this stage. You'll grow accustomed to it the more you use it.

> POLYLINE CHALLENGES

Here are a few challenges to help you get used to the Polyline tool. Try to recreate each shape in Figure 2.109, attempting to draw the curved lines with as few vertices as possible.

2.109

TIP
Don't necessarily concern yourself with getting each shape right the first time. The Polyline is made to be used alongside the Contour Editor. Place your vertices and curves as best you can, then tweak them with the Contour Editor.

When you've finished drawing the shapes, fill them with colour using the Paint tool. Remember that if your paint isn't working, you may need to activate the Auto Close Gaps option in the Paint tool properties.

DROPPER [ALT D]

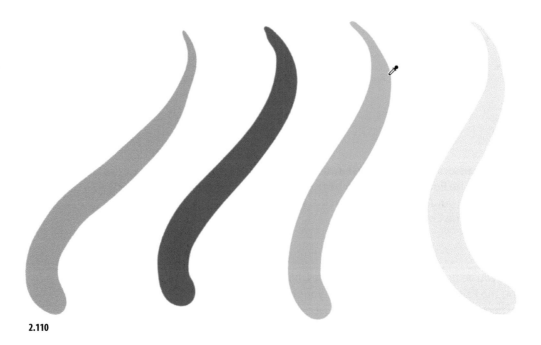 No art software can be taken seriously without an eyedropper tool for picking colours. Because of the way colour works in Toon Boom, its Dropper only picks colours that you've already created and used in your drawings. It can't pick colours from the interface icons, imported images or the desktop.

Later on page 106 you'll learn about creating new colours, including using a separate type of eyedropper that lets you pick colours from the desktop, interface or imported images and save them as new colours in your Colour panel.

> DROPPER EXERCISE 1
  PICKING COLOURS

> 1.   In the Timeline select a blank frame.

> 2.   Using the Brush, draw several strokes of various colours in the
         Camera View.

2.110

> 3. Select the Paint tool in Repaint mode with [Alt R].

> 4. Hold [D] and click one of the coloured strokes.

NOTE
Note that while using the [D] override, your cursor changes to an eyedropper ✐ and the red text at the bottom of the Camera View shows 'Dropper'.

> 5. Confirm that the colour you just picked is now selected in the Colour panel.

> 6. When you release [D] your Repaint tool returns to the cursor ⊹ᵣ (see step 3). Trace a line through any of the coloured strokes to repaint it with the selected colour.

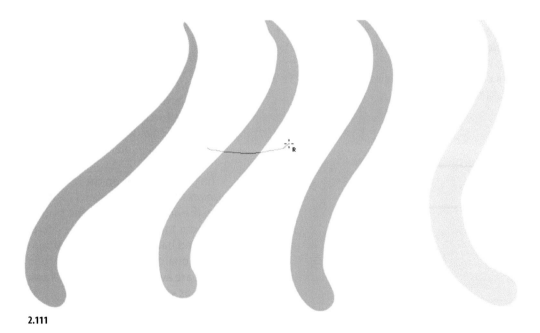

2.111

> 7. Hold [D] and pick another colour, then release [D] and repaint another stroke.

From this exercise, you can probably see now how the override function of each tool, in this case [D], can really help speed things up.

MORE TOOLS AND WHERE TO FIND THEM

So far, because we've mostly been focusing on drawing and painting, we haven't covered tools pertaining to animation. We'll look at those in the animation chapters.

HARMONY ONLY – TOOL PRESETS

Generally, switching tools and constantly tweaking their properties as you work is par for the course. However, there will always be one or two tools that you'll use more than others, with special settings for certain tasks.

Suppose, for example, that in every project, one of the first things you do is to draw a sky for the background. In the Shape tool options you'd choose the rectangle mode, resize the line thickness, set the mode to Auto Fill, choose a colour and drag out your rectangle shape in the Camera View.

With Tool Presets, you can save these custom settings, assign a shortcut key and even create your own icon for it! Thereafter, you'd simply select your 'sky' Tool Preset and draw the rectangle without manually setting those options. In Figure 2.112, I have created a Brush tool preset with its own icon and colour settings. If it was a real brush, it would be my most-used and probably worn and filthy, which is why I named it 'oldFilthy'.

2.112

The Harmony documentation has a thorough walkthrough on creating your own tool presets, so I won't clutter the chapter by rewriting it here. In the Harmony Help file [F1], you'll find it under Stage User Guide → Drawing Chapter → Drawing → Tool Preset View.

Additionally there are one or two advanced tools that we will use in the course of future exercises, such as a gradient manipulator which you'll see in the Gradient Colour section up ahead.

CAMERA VIEW VERSUS

DRAWING VIEW

Up until now we've mostly been working in the Camera View, which displays all layers of the scene together; for example, in Figure 2.113 we see sky, smoke, effects and characters. It's the ideal overview of your scene coming together as a whole.

The Drawing View, on the other hand, *isolates* a layer. In Figure 2.113, it's helping the animator see just the smoke without the distraction of the characters and background layers. Certain traditional animation tools and functions are available only in the Drawing View, as you'll later see.

When it comes to drawing and painting though, if you can do it in the Camera View, you can do it in the Drawing View, and vice versa.

2.113

BASIC COLOUR MANAGEMENT

Toon Boom's colour management system is legendary. Behind the scenes, all colours have a unique colour ID that can be named, saved, selected and grouped into palettes. You can even have several identical colour values – say, three identical reds – each unique by their ID.

One of my personal favourite features is the way entire projects can be painted with temporary colours and changed later. This means if you decide at the end of a project that your blue-skinned characters should instead have green skin, it takes mere seconds to apply that change across the entire project!

The basics of colour management are covered here, while the more advanced colour concepts will be covered in Appendix A.

> COLOUR EXERCISE 1
  TWEAKING USED COLOURS

> 1. Select any colour in your Colour panel.

> 2. With any of the drawing tools, draw something simple in the Camera View.

> 3. Now back to the Colour panel, on the colour you used, double-click the rectangular swatch, or right-click → Edit.

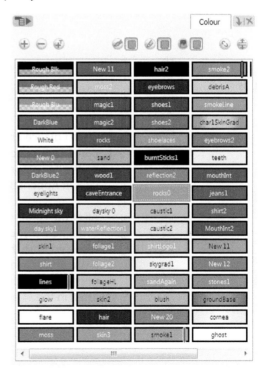

2.114

> 4. Shift the Colour Picker window aside so you can see your drawing in the Camera View.

> 5. In the Colour Picker window, change the colour values, watching it update in your Camera View as you do so.

This is an incredible feature, allowing easy colour tweaks right into the 11th hour of a project.

2.115

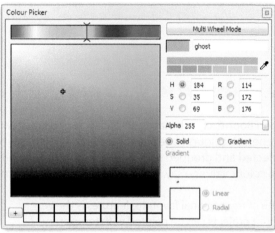

THE COLOUR PANEL

At first glance, there doesn't seem to be a lot going on in the Colour panel, but scratch the surface and you'll find more layers of functionality. We'll postpone some of the advanced stuff for now and cover it later in Appendix A.

All of the colours and palettes contained in your project are accessed from the Colour panel. If you don't already have it open, you'll find it (as always) listed in the ↓ panel menu.

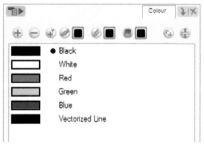

2.116

> COLOUR EXERCISE 2
  PARTS OF THE COLOUR PANEL

This panel consists of two main parts: *palettes* are listed at the top, and the *colours* themselves are listed below.

> 1. Expand the palette list with the ⬥ button. In a file with multiple palettes, selecting one in this list will display its colours below.

> 2. Right-click a palette and choose Display Colour Values. This toggles the RGBA (red, green, blue, alpha) values of each colour in the panel.

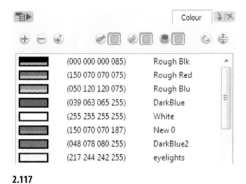

2.117

> 3. Right-click in the colour palette and chose Swatch mode to see the colours as larger swatches with their names. The colours form a grid that, with very large palettes, is much tidier than a long list.

PALETTES

If you're using Animate, there are 120 colours in your starting palette. Animate Pro and Harmony palettes, however, have just six; the idea being that advanced users create colours as needed.

A new scene will have a default palette with the same name as the scene file. That is, if your scene file is called 'Scene_1', then the starting palette will have the same name.

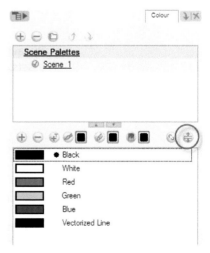

2.118

> COLOUR EXERCISE 3
  CREATING A NEW PALETTE

> 1.   If it's not already open, expand the palette list by clicking the ⊕
      button (see Figure 2.118).

> 2.   Click the New Palette ⊕ button and name your new palette
      'foliage'.

> 3.   With the foliage palette selected in the palette list, move down to
      the colour list and you'll see a single Default black.

2.119

> 4.   Save the scene with [Ctrl/⌘ S].

By saving your scene now, foliage.plt becomes one of the saved scene
assets. You'll find it there in your scene's palette-library folder.

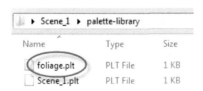

2.120

Your main scene palettes are saved as a .plt file in your scene's palette-library directory, as shown in Figure 2.120. You can send it to

colleagues, link to or import this palette into any other scene using the Colour panel's menu. This is useful when you have a character palette that you want to reuse in other files or projects, or send to colleagues to use in their scenes. Once again, you can learn more in Appendix A.

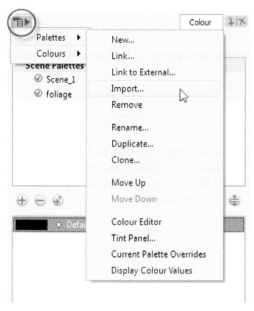

2.121

SOLID AND GRADIENT COLOURS

A *solid* colour is a single colour value, as opposed to a transition between two values, which is otherwise called a *gradient*. A gradient swatch may consist of several colours with transitions between them, as shown in Figure 2.122

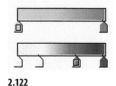

2.122

The first gradient bar here shows a single transition between two flat colours. Underneath that is a four-colour gradient.

You've created some colours in previous tools exercises, so in the following exercise you'll be mixing more, including gradients.

COLOUR EXERCISE 4
CREATING SOLID COLOURS

> 1.   From the previous exercise, select your 'foliage' palette in the
       Colour panel.

> 2.   Select the Default black swatch and click the Add Colour button ⊕.

**A new swatch is created with the same values as Default and the name
'New 0'.**

> 3.   Double-click the rectangular swatch of this new colour to open the
       Colour Picker window.

**The Colour Picker window contains everything you need to mix your
New 0 colour. There are controls here for HSV (hue, saturation and
value), RGB (red, green and blue), Alpha (transparency) and gradients
(linear and radial). First though, let's rename it.**

> 4.   In the Name field, replace 'New 0' by typing 'bushes'.

NOTE
**If you press [Enter] and your colour mixing window expands into
Multi Wheel mode, feel free to look around but we'll be using the
Single Wheel mode for its simplicity. If you like the Multi Wheel mode
though, there's no harm in staying. Otherwise, return to Single Wheel
mode with the button that says … uh … Single Wheel Mode.**

> 5.   Click the Hue (H) radio button so the top colour bar changes to a
       hue slider.

> 6.   I'm moving the slider along to somewhere green.

2.123

> 7.   Click the Value (V) radio button and the top bar changes to a
       brightness slider.

> 8.   Move the slider about halfway along.

> 9. Click the Saturation (S) radio button. The top bar changes to a saturation slider.

> 10. Move the slider back to about one-third of the way.

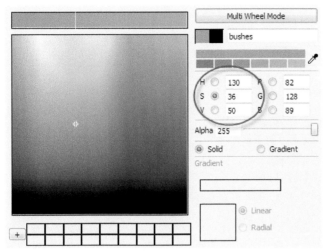

2.124

> 11. With 'bushes' selected in the Colour panel, once again click the Add Colour button.

Notice that new colours are created with the same values as the colour you have selected. This is useful for making variations on a selected colour. In this case we want to make a shade of the same green by simply adjusting the V (value) slider.

> 12. Double-click the new green swatch to open the Colour Picker.

> 13. Rename this new one to 'bushesDark'.

> 14. Let's leave the Hue and Saturation fields alone. Click the V (value) radio button and drag the slider slightly to the left so it's a little darker than 'bushes'.

2.125

You now have two shades of the same green colour for light and dark bushes. Mixing from a selected colour is an easy way to create a bunch of colours with similar values. You could use the same method for mixing skin tones, for example.

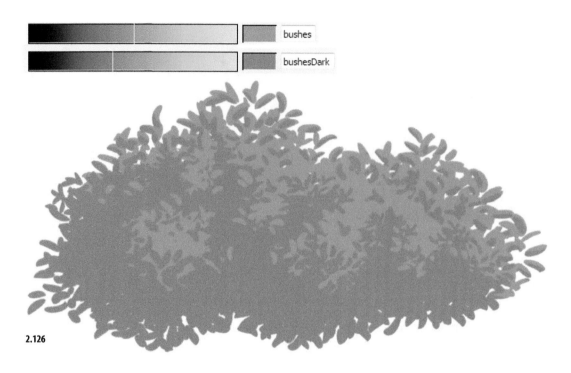

2.126

> COLOUR EXERCISE 5
CREATING GRADIENTS

> 1. Click the New Palette button and call the new palette 'skies'.

> 2. In your new 'skies' palette, select the Default black and click the New Colour button.

> 3. Double-click the new swatch to open the Colour Picker window.

> 4. Rename your new colour 'skyGrad'.

Just below the Alpha slider, you'll see that the colour is currently set to Solid, with the gradient section below greyed out.

> 5. Click the Gradient radio button to activate the gradient mixer.

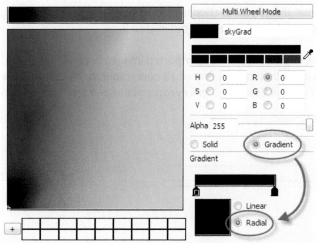

2.127

> 6. As shown in Figure 2.127, select the Radial gradient type.

Immediately after step 5 you'll see the gradient bar below has two swatches that look like tiny houses. These pointer swatches, sometimes called 'chips' or 'tacks' can be moved along the bar to vary the transition.

Notice that the first tack 🏠 has a small square inside it, indicating that it's selected. The bar at the top of the mixer window is black to reflect this.

> 7. Start moving HSV sliders around to give this tack a colour. Mine is a light sky blue.

> 8. Select the tack on the right (Figure 2.128, step 1).

> 9. Click the Colour Picker's own eyedropper (Figure 2.128, step 2) and then pick the same blue directly from the left-hand tack (Figure 2.128, step 3).

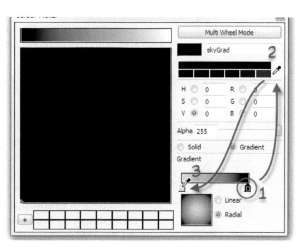

2.128

This particular eyedropper is different to the Dropper tool. While the Dropper tool only selects saved colour values, the Colour Picker eyedropper allows you to choose colours from any part of the program interface, which is what we just did in step 9.

Therefore, to pick colours from imported images or photographs, or the program icons themselves, first add a new colour in the Colour panel and then use the Colour Picker's eyedropper to pick the values you need.

> 10. With the left-hand tack selected now, raise the V slider up and/or bring the S slider down to make the colour brighter.

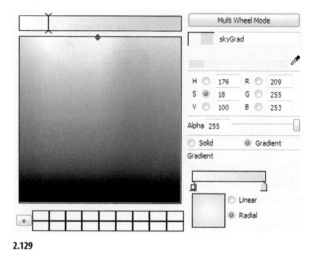

2.129

Once you're happy with your sky gradient, close the Colour Picker. In the Colour panel now, your skies palette contains a nice radial gradient ready for painting. Now go ahead and try it out using the Rectangle tool with the Auto Fill option turned on.

ADDING AND REMOVING TACKS

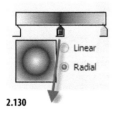

2.130

If you click anywhere on the gradient bar, you'll add more tacks. New tacks added will be the colour of the one currently selected. Therefore if your currently selected tack is white, a new white tack is created.

Click the tacks to select them, slide them to the desired position, use the sliders or eyedropper to assign colours, or remove any unwanted tacks simply by dragging them away and off the gradient bar. This is the process for creating a swatch with multiple gradients.

MANIPULATING GRADIENTS

Once applied to your drawing, gradients are centred on the artwork. For example, if you draw a box filled with a radial gradient, that gradient will be centred on each surface of the box, as shown below. The gradient can then be manipulated using the Edit Gradient/Texture tool [Shift F3]. Equip this tool and click on the gradient to be manipulated.

2.131

NOTE
The size of the manipulation envelope is proportional to the artwork. To adjust the gradient for a large area – a sky for example – you will need to zoom out to see the handles. For a tiny area like an eyeball, you may need to zoom in to manipulate the gradient.

Depending on what type of gradient or texture you're manipulating, the manipulation handles will be slightly different. Figure 2.132 shows the manipulation handles for Linear and Radial gradients.

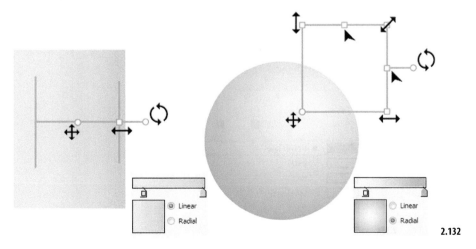

2.132

In the same way we can move a gradient around on the drawing, we can also position, rotate and scale textures. There's more texture info later in Appendix A.

PROTECTING COLOURS

Once you've painted something, for example a character, you can protect certain colours so that they can't be erased or repainted. Protect Colour allows you to freely paint or erase some colours while leaving others untouched.

> COLOUR EXERCISE 6
  PROTECT AND REPAINT

> 1. In the Colour panel, select your Default black and click the Add Colour button.

> 2. Rename the new black 'flower line'.

> 3. Select frame 1 in the Timeline.

> 4. With the 'flower line' colour and the drawing tool of your choice, create some line art of a flower similar to the one in Figure 2.133. Be careful to leave no gaps in the linework.

> 5. Add five new colours to the palette and name them as follows: 'petal', 'face', 'faceTone', 'stem' and 'stemTone'.

> 6. Colour mixing time! Adjust the colour values of each to suit the parts of the flower. 'stemTone' should be the same hue (H) as 'stem', but a lower value (V) to make it darker. Likewise, 'faceTone' should be the same hue as 'face', but darker.

2.133

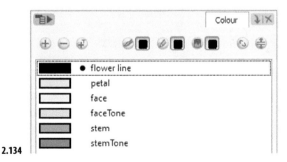

2.134

> 7. In the Colour panel, select the 'stem' colour.

> 8. Using Paint Unpainted [Alt Y], fill the flower stem with the colour called 'stem'. Fill the petals with 'petal' and the middle of the flower with 'face'.

Remember to use one of the Gap Closing options in the paint tool properties if you're having trouble with gaps. At the end of it, your flower should be painted with flat colours.

> 9. In the colour panel, select your 'flower line' colour, then while holding [Shift] select the last colour in the panel. All of the flower colours should now be selected.

2.135

> 10. Right-click any of the selected colours and, at the bottom of the menu, choose Protect Colour. You can also use the Colour panel's own menu ⬛▶ → Colours → Protect Colour.

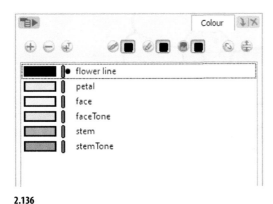

2.136

All of the selected colours will have a red bar indicating that they are all protected.

> 11. In the Colour panel, press [Esc] to deselect all of the selected colours.

> 12. Using the Eraser in the Camera View, try to erase the flower.

If your colours are all protected, the eraser will have no effect.

> 13. In the Colour panel right-click the 'face' colour and choose Protect Colour once again, to *unprotect* it, so that we can paint onto the face.

> 14. In the Colour panel, select the 'faceTone' colour.

> 15. In the Camera View press [Alt X] to equip the Brush in Repaint mode.

> 16. Scribble wildly over the flower and notice how the tone colour only works on the face. This is because face is *unprotected* while all other colours are protected.

> 17. Press [Ctrl/⌘ Z] to undo the wild scribble.

> 18. Resize the maximum Brush size using [O] to around 30.

> 19. Paint a tone on the underside of the face as shown in Figure 2.138.

2.137

2.138

Just as the 'flower line', 'petal' and 'stem' colours were protected from the eraser, they're also protected from being repainted. This makes it very easy to paint tones without any concern for accidentally painting the petals, or the line art.

NOTE
Colour protection is not drawing protection. In other words, colour protection doesn't stop the colours from being selected or manipulated with the Select tool. You can select a piece of colour with the Select tool and then simply delete it using your keyboard's [Delete] key. You can protect the drawing and you'll see how in the upcoming Timeline section.

> 20. In the Colour panel, deselect any colours by pressing [Esc].

> 21. Right-click and protect the 'face' colour.

> 22. Right-click and *unprotect* the 'stem' colour.

> 23. Select 'stemTone' and paint a tone in on the stem, once again using Repaint mode.

You may find yourself protecting and unprotecting colours very frequently throughout a project. As of this writing, there's no shortcut key for Protect Colour, so the quickest way is to right-click and protect.

2.139

COLOUR-TO-TOOL LINKAGE

In the Colour panel at the top of the colours list, you'll find three colour buttons with Brush, Pencil and bucket icons. This allows you to assign colours to these tools. For example, when *unlinked*, you can assign black to the Pencil and red to the Paint bucket. When you draw a rectangle with the Shape tool, it'll have a black outline with a red fill. Then if you're using the Brush, you can choose new colours at will without losing the chosen Pencil and Paint colours.

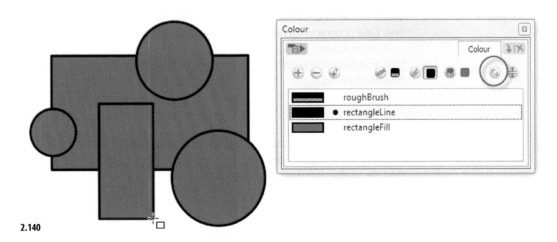

2.140

While very useful at times, this feature can be a little confusing for a beginner. If you switch tools and suddenly find you're painting with an unexpected colour, it's possible that the colour buttons are *unlinked* and the tool you're using has a colour assigned to it.

Alongside those colour buttons, the next icon to the right is a chain link ⊕. This toggles the linkage between the three colour buttons. When linked, the chosen colour will be applied to all tools. This is the setting I would recommend for beginners to avoid confusion. Simply toggle the chain on ⊕ and choose your colour.

TIMELINE LAYERS

Like most digital art and animation programs, Toon Boom has a system of layers that allows you to separate elements from one another – for example, having a background held for 60 frames on its own layer, while a character moves on another layer over the top.

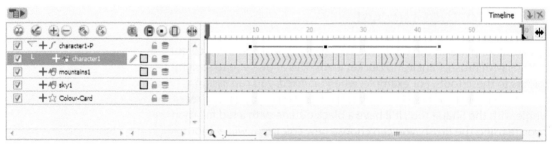

2.141

When it comes to drawing scene elements on layers, we use the Timeline. One common technique is to make rough sketches on one layer and clean linework on another. In the upcoming project, you'll do just that: use Timeline layers to separate your rough drawings from your finished line art.

NOTE
In Toon Boom there is another type of layering that occurs *within* a drawing. It's a much more advanced concept though, so we'll save that discussion for the next chapter.

There are many types of layers in the Timeline. Right now we're only concerned with Drawing layers, into which we can create art with the drawing tools. At the start of a new scene file, as you know by now, there is a single layer in the Timeline called Drawing.

LAYER PROPERTIES

In the same way that the Tool Properties panel lets you control tools, so the Layer Properties panel gives you information and options for the selected layer. You'll find it in the panel menus ⬇.

At first glance it may be a bit daunting with all its numerical input fields. Indeed, it's a little advanced and not something you'll use a lot at first. But we'll use it briefly in the upcoming exercise and I recommend keeping it handy for later.

> LAYERS EXERCISE 1
  ADDING AND RENAMING TIMELINE LAYERS

> 1.   In the Timeline, hit the ⚇ Add Drawing Layer button.

2.142

> 2.   Select the bottom Drawing layer and look at your Layer Properties panel. Again, if it's not open, you'll find it in the panels menu.

At the top left you have the Enable/Disable checkbox (see Figure 2.143). This does the same job as the layer checkboxes in the Timeline; it simply hides, or unhides the layer.

On the top right is a padlock. As mentioned in the Colour Protect exercise, you can protect your drawing from accidental editing. The padlock here in the Layer Properties panel does the same job as the padlock on each Timeline layer.

Next is the Name field. You'll see that the name corresponds to that in the Timeline. Select each layer and see the Name field update.

2.143

Below the Name field, if you're using Animate, you'll see two tabs. If you're using Animate Pro or Harmony, there are three tabs. Each of these tabs has a handful of useful options and settings. Go ahead and browse if you feel so inclined, but we're only concerned with the Name field for now.

> 3.   In the Name field, remove the default name and type 'rough'. Note that it updates in the Timeline.

> 4.   Select the second layer you added.

> 5.   In the Layer Properties, rename it 'clean'.

You could go nuts and add a hundred layers if you like, giving them all names of what you expect to put in your scene, like sky, sun, cloud, mountain, city, flagpole and so on. Although, like colours, you might simply add them as you need them.

> LAYERS EXERCISE 2
  HIDING AND DELETING LAYERS

On the left-most side of the Timeline are checkboxes for every layer. To hide layers, you can uncheck these visibility checkboxes one by one. You can also hide/show all layers by clicking the 👀 eyes.

> 1.   In the Timeline, select the 'rough' layer and click the checkbox on the far left. This hides the layer.

> 2.   Look at the Layer Properties to see that 'rough' is disabled.

If you disable a layer, it remains in the scene with everything intact. It is simply hidden and can be enabled at any time. Disabling layers will come in handy when you want to render your final scene and hide any rough sketches.

> 3.   Still with the 'rough' layer selected, delete it using the ⊖ Delete Layers button. You'll get a confirmation popup window in which you can click 'OK'.

The layer has been deleted completely from the scene, taking with it any drawings or animation it contained, hence the confirmation popup window in step 3.

> LAYERS EXERCISE 3
SHUFFLING LAYER ORDERING

The bottom layer on the Timeline represents the bottom layer in the scene. So as an example your sky would be on the bottom, while foreground scene elements will be on top.

2.144

As you create new layers, they are added *above* the layer you currently have selected, but sometimes you just want to add a ton of layers, rename them and then put them in order. Let's do that now.

NOTE
This is just a layer ordering exercise, so you won't need to actually draw anything here. In fact, you could maximise your Timeline to fill the workspace if you really wanted to.

> 1. As you learned in Layers exercise 1, add five layers to your scene and name them 'sky', 'mountain', 'flower', 'cloud' and 'bee'.

> 2. Click and drag the topmost layer downwards. You'll see a preview line between other layers.

> 3. When the preview line appears *between* two other layers, drop it.

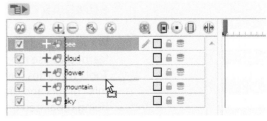

2.145

> 4. Now instead of dropping between layers, drag any other layer *onto* another layer.

2.146

When you drop a layer onto another, the dropped layer will be indented underneath the other. This means you've just created a hierarchy. The indented layer has become a *child* of the upper. This is known as *parenting* one layer to another – the upper layer being the *parent*.

Hierarchies are an essential part of Toon Boom workflow, especially when it comes to cutout character animation. We don't need it for this particular exercise though, so let's *unparent* it. Don't worry, there'll be a lot of parenting to be done in the next chapter.

> 5. Drag the child layer away to unparent it and drop it *between* two others.

> 6. Using what you've just learned, reshuffle the order of the layers so they make sense – and ensure there is no indenting or parenting – as shown in Figure 2.147.

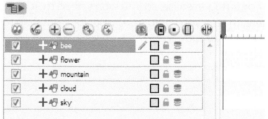

2.147

SUMMARY

We've covered a massive amount of information in this chapter. You've learned to use most of the tools and how to control them using the Tool Properties panel. You've seen how to create and name palettes, mix colours and gradients, as well as protecting certain colours from being repainted or erased.

You've visited the Timeline and seen the basics of layer ordering and how adding, naming and order shuffling are done.

All that's left to do in this chapter is put what you've learned into practice with an illustration project! Each step of the way will have page numbers for reference, so you can revisit earlier exercises if you need to revise.

PROJECT 1: COMIC STRIP

It's time to put all those tools and techniques into action and create a comic strip. By the end of this project, you'll have some practical experience as well as a fully rendered image that you can post online, set as your desktop image or even print for your wall.

Throughout this project you'll learn more about colour management, rough construction, Timeline layers and rendering.

> PROJECT 1 – TASK 1
  SET UP THE SCENE

You can revise scene setup in Chapter 1 starting from page 16.

> 1. Open your Toon Boom program to create a new scene with the name 'comic'.

> 2. Choose the HDTV resolution.

> 3. Click 'Create' and a fresh scene opens.

> 4. In the top menu, go to Scene → Scene Settings…

> 5. Instead of 1920 × 1080, change the dimensions to 2480 × 1748 (see Figure 2.149).

> 6. Click 'OK' to close the Scene Settings window.

At 300 dots per inch (a standard minimum print resolution) these pixel dimensions equate to an A5 print.

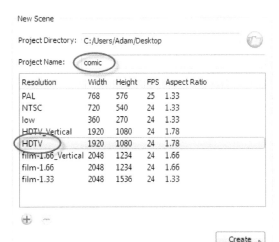

2.148

If your work happens to involve making a lot of A5 prints, you could save these dimensions as a custom preset by clicking the Save icon, as shown in Figure 2.149.

(custom)

Resolution		Field of View	
	2480	◉ Horizontal Fit	
	1748	○ Vertical Fit	
Aspect Ratio: 1.419		○ Custom Fov	38.827 ‡

Frame per seconds 24

2.149

> 7.   Once again in the Scene menu, this time choose Scene Length...

> 8.   Set the value to 1 and click 'OK'.

> 9.   Press [Ctrl/⌘ S] to save this scene file.

Now the scene is just one frame long. It'll contain no animation so we'll only need a single frame in the Timeline.

TIP
Another way to reduce or extend the scene length is to drag the red end marker in the Timeline. This may be awkward on very long scenes though.

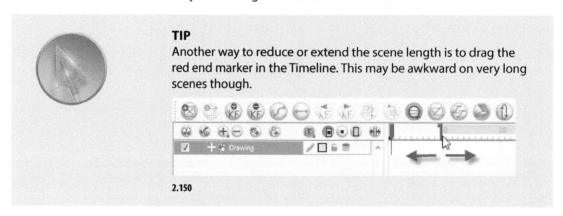

2.150

> PROJECT 1 – TASK 2
  CREATE A NEW PALETTE

Revise palettes starting on page 103.

> 1.   If the palette list isn't already open in the Colour panel, expand it using the ⊕ icon.

> 2. Create a new palette and name it 'sketching'.

Your new palette is added with a single Default colour.

New Palette Name sketching

OK   Cancel

2.151

> 3. Select the new 'sketching' palette to prepare for mixing some new colours in the next task.

> 4. Press [Ctrl/⌘ S] to save your scene.

> 5. On your computer, open up the scene folder. If you followed along in task 1, the folder is on your desktop, called 'comic'.

> 6. Inside that folder, you'll see the palette-library folder. Open it up to find two palette files. One is called comic.plt and the other, sketching.plt.

These are your scene's palette files. Like most scene files, they can be stored, emailed, linked, imported and updated in any other scene. There's much more colour management to come in Appendix B.

2.152

> PROJECT 1 – TASK 3
CREATE A COLOUR FOR ROUGH SKETCHES

Revise how to add new colours starting on page 106.

Whether we're talking about design, sculpture, painting or animation, one of the very first steps towards creating art – and one that any good art teacher will emphasise – is to start rough. It's essential to loosely define the major volumes and lines of your subject before adding any level of detail. And if you've ever seen a pencil test, you'll know that rough sequences of animation are beautiful in their own way and can be just as mesmerising as a finished scene.

2.153

Traditionally in 2D animation, animators used a *non-photo blue* pencil for preliminary roughs because light blue wasn't detected by the Xerox copier and, later, the digital scanner. For this reason, light blue was also used for notes, labelling and timing grids on each drawing. After constructing animation roughly with this light blue pencil, they later sketched over with the black/lead pencil.

Of course, in this digital age, using blue or red is just tradition but hey, it looks nice and makes sense, so let's go with it all the same and create a new light blue and a red for rough sketching.

> 1.   In your Colour panel, be sure your 'sketching' palette is selected. This ensures the colours you're seeing belong to the 'sketching' palette.

> 2.   Select the Default black and add two new colours.

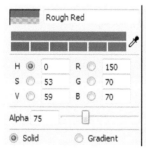

2.154

> 3.   Edit the colours with the values shown in Figure 2.154, including alpha. Don't forget the names.

Close the Colour Picker window and in your Colour panel now, you'll see Rough Blu and Rough Red waiting, just begging to be splashed around.

> 4.   Save your scene with [Ctrl/⌘ S].

> PROJECT 1 – TASK 4
  SKETCH THE PANEL LAYOUT

Revise brush sketching starting on page 37.

Before you do any sketching, it might help to have a written descrip-
tion of what happens in the comic strip then break it down to what
happens in each panel.

Retelling a favourite joke in comic strip form is an excellent exercise
in panel-based storytelling. Go ahead and use your own story if you
prefer. I'm proud to announce that the world-class joke below was
plumbed from the depths of my own comic genius.

Man sitting on the hood of his car, says 'hey, baby'.

Pretty lady is pushing a baby carriage. The baby says 'hey, man'.

I know, right? Comedy gold. Once you've recovered from your giggle
fit, we'll sketch up just two panels with a rough composition for each.
In film and animation terms, this process of composing shots, or
scenes, in sketch form is known as the *storyboard*.

> 1.   In the Timeline, select the Drawing layer by clicking on it.

> 2.   Click the name and rename this layer 'sketch'.

> 3.   Click frame 1 of the sketch layer and begin your rough sketching.

If you don't find the Camera View's grey background very pleasant to
sketch against, you can add a Colour-Card to your scene. You can do so
in the Timeline by dropping down the Add Layers menu .

2.155

By default the Colour-Card is a white background, but you can change
it to any colour you like in the Layer Properties panel.

If you add a Colour-Card, be sure to reselect frame of the sketch layer
to resume your sketch.

2.156

In my own sketch I've used the Brush with the Rough Blu colour. For the composition, I've carefully considered how to convey all of the information in just two panels. The first panel composition is only wide enough to show this overconfident fellow trying to get a pretty lady's attention, while not yet revealing the baby carriage. I've also factored the speech bubbles into the composition.

2.157

Panel 2 is a reversed camera angle, so it's a wider shot of the woman with the baby sitting up in the pram and the guy silhouetted in the foreground. Again, the speech bubble is an important composition consideration.

> PROJECT 1 – TASK 5
ADD NEW LAYERS FOR CLEAN LINEWORK

Revise adding timeline layers starting on page 116.

In the Timeline, there are several ways to add a new layer. You've already seen the Add Drawing Layer button . The menu path is Insert → Drawing. The quickest way though, as if your mind wasn't already overflowing with shortcut keys, is to use [Ctrl/⌘ R].

> 1. Select your 'sketch' layer name in the Timeline.

> 2. Add a new drawing layer by any of the above methods.

> 3. Rename the layer 'panelBorders' either in the Timeline or the Layer Properties panel.

> 4. In the Timeline, select frame 1 of the new 'panelBorders' layer and draw the borders, either with the Shape tool in rectangle mode, or using the Brush. Remember you can hold down [Shift] to constrain a Brush stroke to straight lines, and hold [Alt] as well to snap it to 90° angles.

2.158

> 5. In the Timeline, add four more drawing layers. Figure 2.159 shows the names.

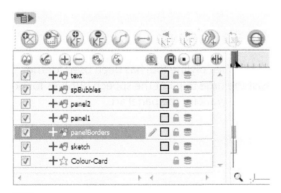

2.159

> 6. Once you've added these new layers, reorder the layering if necessary (see page 119).

> 7. Finally, save your scene with [Ctrl/⌘ S].

> PROJECT 1 – TASK 6
  ADD THE LINEWORK

Revise your chosen tool: Brush on page 37, Pencil on page 50, Polyline on page 95.

Everything's falling into place. Looks like you're ready to start drawing your linework!

> 1. Select and configure your chosen drawing tool, including colour and size.

> 2. Select frame 1 of the spBubbles layer.

> 3. Using your rough sketch as a guide, clean up the speech bubbles with closed line art.

2.160

As shown in Figure 2.160 the Polyline tool has been used for the speech bubbles. Resist the urge to paint the speech bubbles for now. They will only obscure the work for the panel art.

> 4. Select frame 1 of the panel1 layer.

> 5. Using the rough sketch as a guide, create the clean line art for this panel.

> 6. Select frame 2 of the panel2 layer.

> 7. Using the rough sketch as a guide, once again create the clean lines.

> 8. Save with [Ctrl/⌘ S].

2.161

In Figure 2.161 you might have noticed I've used a lighter line for the car. This is so the characters with their heavier lines are the focus of the scene.

> PROJECT 1 – TASK 7
MIX AND PAINT WITH NEW COLOURS

Revise Colour exercises 4 and 6 (pages 106 and 112).

You now need to create new colours for every area of linework that needs filling.

> 1.   In the Colour panel's palette section, create three new palettes. Name them 'man', 'woman', 'baby'.

> 2.   Select the 'man' palette and create a few colours for him. He'll need 'skin', 'pants', 'hair', 'shirt' and so on.

> 3.   Do the same for the 'woman' and 'baby' palettes.

If you'd like to add additional palettes for the car and baby carriage, feel free to do so, otherwise you can simply add car and carriage colours to the existing 'comic' palette.

> 4.   In the main 'comic' palette, add colours for text and speech bubbles.

How many colours you create will depend on the complexity of your line art. Have you zoomed in and drawn buttons and zips on the character's clothing? Will you need colours for shoelaces and watch buckles? The finer the detail, the more colours you're likely to need.

NOTE
Of course, if you want to go all the way, you could even mix two variations for each, having a dark tone for some colours.

If you'd like to paint tones like these, revisit the Protect and repaint exercise on page 112.

2.162

> 5.   Select frame 1 of the panel1 layer.

> 6.   Use the Paint tool in Paint Unpainted mode [Alt Y] to fill in the colours. Remember that if the Paint tool isn't working, it could mean you have small gaps in your linework. In that case, the easiest thing to do will be to turn on Auto Close Gaps to help you.

> 7.   Repeat steps 5 and 6 for the panel2 layer.

TIP
A reminder: you needn't adjust the colours to perfection just yet. Go ahead and paint with temporary colours for now. You can always tweak them at the end.

> 8.   Finally, select frame 1 of the spBubbles layer, then fill them with the speech bubble colour, using [Alt Y].

> PROJECT 1 – TASK 8
  ADD THE TEXT

Revise this topic starting on page 73 with the Text tool exercises.

> 1.   In the Timeline, select frame 1 of the text layer.

> 2.   Choose the Text tool and adjust its properties, such as font, size,
       colour and alignment.

> 3.   Place a cursor in the first speech bubble and type the text.

> 4.   Get the Select tool and select the text.

> 5.   In the Select tool properties (you may need to
       scroll down) adjust the text properties some
       more if necessary, to better align the text.

> 6.   Repeat steps 1–5 for panel 2.

2.163

> PROJECT 1 – TASK 9
  HIDE THE ROUGH SKETCH LAYER AND PREVIEW THE RENDER

> 1.   Select the rough sketches layer

> 2.   At the top of the Layer Properties panel, *uncheck* the Enable/dis-
       able box. You could also do this by *unchecking* the layer's visibility
       box in the Timeline.

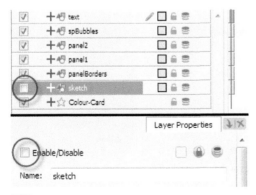

2.164

> 3.   At the bottom left of the Camera View, press the Render button ✹ to see how the finished image looks.

> 4.   If you need to go back and do some more work, you can switch out of the Render view and back to your workspace with the ✹ button.

> PROJECT 1 – TASK 10
  EXPORT TO AN IMAGE

We haven't covered exporting yet, so consider this task a brief, step-by-step introduction.

The export process in Animate Pro and Harmony gives you a wide range of customisable export options. In Animate, however, it is simplified.

ANIMATE ONLY

> 1.   Render your comic image via the top menu: File → Export → Images…

> 2.   Choose your favourite format as the file type. I usually go with PNG because of its overall quality and reasonable file size.

Take note of the export directory. It will be the scene's *frames* folder, but you can change that by hitting the Browse button and choosing any location on your computer.

2.165

> 3.   Leave all other settings as they are and hit 'OK'.

> 4.   Navigate to your scene directory and into the frames folder where you'll find the rendered image.

ANIMATE PRO & HARMONY ONLY

In the next chapter you'll get a proper introduction to the Network view. While daunting at first, it's an advanced and extremely sensible visualisation of your scene structure.

> 1. If it's not already open, you'll find the Network view in the panel menus.

> 2. In the Network view you'll see a cluster of *modules* and connecting wires. The module we want is named Write. Pan around in the network using the [Spacebar] if necessary.

> 3. On the Write module, click the yellow box to open its Layer Properties.

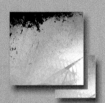

2.166

These settings tell Toon Boom how to 'write' your output. In other words, these are your export settings.

> 4. Set the output directory to any location on your computer, or simply leave it set to your scene's frames folder.

> 5. Into the Drawing Filename field, type 'comic'.

> 6. In the formats list, select whatever format you'd like your comic image to be. I usually go with PNG because of its overall quality and reasonable file size.

> 7. Close the Layer Properties.

> 8. In the top menu, go to File → Export → Render Network, or use its shortcut key [Ctrl/⌘ Shift Y].

2.168

2.167

> 9. Leave these settings as they are and click 'OK'.

> 10. Navigate to the location you specified in step 4 to find the exported image.

CONCLUSION

This concludes the comic strip project and this chapter. Feel free to go ahead and experiment more with all of the tools and settings you've learned so far. In the next chapter, you'll be creating more advanced art and making it move!

2.169
Don't forget your signature!

CHAPTER 3

Animation

Toon Boom is advanced software technology, but many of the tools are directly descended from those used by traditional animation pioneers. The traditional animation disc, peg bars, X-sheets and light table all have their software equivalents.

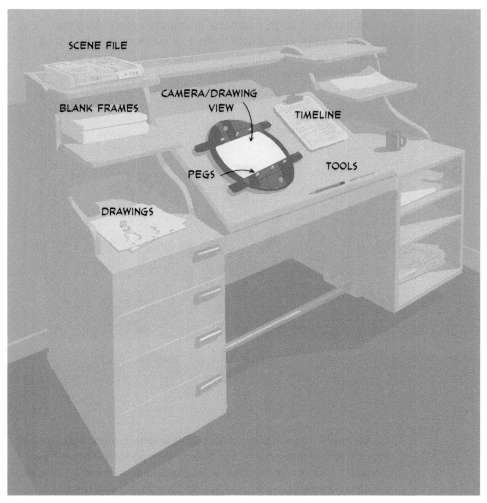

3.1

These links are often lost on the modern-day animator who may have never peered into a lightbox, never 'rolled' drawings, filled in an X-sheet or understands just how funny it is to hit your funny bone on a peg. These connections to traditional tools can be a bit puzzling and take some getting used to.

On the flip side though, traditional animators – particularly the dinosaurs – while at ease with traditional methods, may be just as bewildered by some of the technological advances, like particles, deformation, inverse kinematics and node-based compositing.

3.2

Toon Boom brings the two worlds together with just enough for each, not only to feel comfortable, but also to learn about the other. If you consider yourself a modern-day animator and don't know much about traditional animation, you'll reap huge benefits from learning about the techniques and tools of the original craft. Likewise, if you're a traditional animator, you're probably already discovering how advances in technology have made animation tasks quicker and easier with amazing new tools.

WHAT'S IN THIS CHAPTER?

In the previous chapters we touched lightly on frames and layers in the timeline. But with all those drawing and painting exercises of Chapter 2, most of what you've learned so far has to do with single frame images. Here in the animation chapter we'll learn all about using the Timeline (and various other views) for animation.

FPS

Animation is a series of still images, or frames, flashing by at high speed. The rate at which frames are displayed, commonly known as the *frame rate*, is measured in frames per second (FPS). The standard frame rate for cinematic film is 24 fps. This means that in every second, 24 images are rapidly displayed in sequence. At this frame rate, you need 72 frames for just 3 seconds of animation.

Being the traditional standard, 24 fps is the default frame rate in Toon Boom. However, you can change the scene's frame rate at any time in the FPS field of the top toolbar, as shown below.

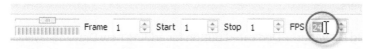

3.3

Frame rates vary wildly, from 10 fps in web banner ads, right up to 60 fps in some games. While certain video formats require 24, 25, 30 or even 48 fps, generally while learning Toon Boom animation, you'll get by just fine working at the default 24 fps.

THE TIMELINE

The annotated image shown as Figure 3.4 (overleaf) is followed by a list of the various Timeline parts. Although most of these may be new to you, we'll certainly cover them all before this chapter's through.

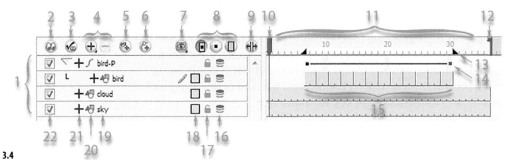

3.4

1. Layers: There are many types of layer. You may think of Drawing layers as individual flipbooks, each with their own pages.

2. Visibility of all layers: Toggles visibility of all layers on or off.

3. Show selected layer only: Shows the selected layer, hiding all others.

4. Add and Delete layer buttons: Add various layer types; Delete layers.

5. Add Drawing: Dedicated button for adding new Drawing layers.

6. Add Peg: Adds a peg for moving the selected layer. Must have a layer selected first. Pegs are discussed ahead on page 177.

7. Visibility modes: Choose to show only certain layer types, e.g., only show drawings in the Timeline.

8. Paste modes: Choose to paste only certain frame types, e.g., keyframes.

9. Data view: Expands layer and keyframe data.

10. Playhead, (sometimes called the scrub bar): Current frame indicator.

11. Frames: The playhead travels along the timeline displaying frames as it crosses them.

12. End Scene marker: Drag this to mark the end of the scene.

13. Loop markers: Drag these to define the start/finish frames for Timeline playback.

14. Motion Keyframes: Points marking the beginning or end of a movement.

15. Drawings: Displayed as the playhead passes over them.

16. Layer onion skin: ⬓ Toggle the onion skin for the layer.

17. Layer Lock: 🔒 Enable/disable editing the layer contents.

18. Layer Colour: ⬡ Define the colour of the layer shown in the Timeline.

19. Layer Name: Rename the layer by clicking the name.

20. Layer Type Icon: ⬛ ∫ ☆ Indicates the type of layer, e.g., Drawing ⬛, Peg ∫, Effect ☆.

21. Function Expand: ＋－ Scroll out the layer's transform values (pan, rotate, scale).

22. Layer Visibility checkbox: Enables/disables the layer visibility.

FRAMES

As you probably know, traditional animation was drawn by hand onto individual sheets of paper. Each of these sheets represents a single frame in a strip of film.

If you're new to digital animation software, it's often helpful to think of frames in the timeline as a stack of these drawings. The drawings in the timeline are individual pieces of paper, each on a single frame that, when flipped like a flipbook, contributes to the illusion of movement. You may have noticed that the book you're reading right now has flipbook images at the top. Try it out!

3.5

Looking at the Timeline now, your layer named 'Drawing' is like a flip-book. You create your animation on those individual frames, just like pieces of paper.

> FRAMES EXERCISE 1
FRAME-BY-FRAME ANIMATION

> 1. Create a new scene with a name and resolution of your choice.

> 2. In the Timeline, drag the red scene end marker back to frame 36. Alternatively you can set the scene length to 36 in the top menu: Scene → Scene Length…

> 3. In the timeline, rename your default Drawing layer 'ant'.

> 4. In the Colour panel, choose the Default black.

> 5. Select frame 1 in the Timeline.

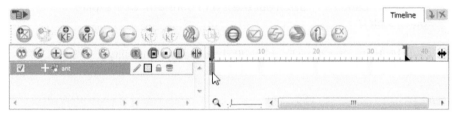

3.6

> 6. Select the Brush tool and give it a max size setting of around 10.

> 7. In the lower left corner of the Camera View, paint a very short diagonal stroke.

If anyone asks, this is an ant! You'll now animate this ant frame-by-frame across the scene.

> 8. Press your [.] key to go to the next frame. Alternatively you can select the blank frame 2, in the Timeline.

> 9. In the Camera View, make the second drawing of your ant. It should be about a body-length forward of the first drawing. In Figure 3.7, all of the drawings are faded to illustrate the distance between them.

> 10. Continue drawing your ant on each frame up to and including frame 12. Feel free to make him wander in any direction, or walk in a straight line.

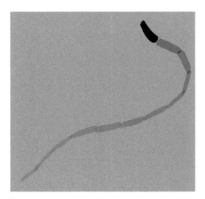

3.7

This has been a simple exercise in the 'straight ahead' method of frame-by-frame animation. Later in the chapter we'll talk much more about this and other frame-by-frame methods.

> FRAMES EXERCISE 2
  LOOPING PLAYBACK

Let's test this piece of animation. If it's your first, you may like to crack open the biscuit tin and gather your friends and family around.

In the program's top toolbar, you'll see four numeric input fields, two of which are labelled Start and Stop (see Figure 3.8). The names for these fields also happen to be clickable buttons.

> 1.   Position the playhead on frame 12, or whichever frame is your last ant drawing.

> 2.   Click the *name* of the Stop field. It's not very obvious that it's a button.

3.8

Looking at the timeline now, you'll notice that frame 12 has a black triangular marker like a tiny bookend. This is a *playback marker* (see Figure 3.4, number 13). Instead of clicking the buttons, you could enter a specific frame number or simply drag these markers along the time-line to define the frames that you want to be played.

> 3.   As shown in Figure 3.9, set your playback to loop.

> 4.   Press Play or [Shift Enter] to watch the ant scramble across the scene repeatedly.

> 5.   To stop the playback, press [Shift Enter] again, or click anywhere in the Timeline.

3.9

> 6.   Press [Ctrl/⌘ S] to save your progress. You'll be using this file in the next exercises.

ONION SKIN TOOL

You may have seen a real world light table or lightbox before. Used by many artists, from architects to graphic designers, from book illustrators to animators, it's a glass topped table with a bright light underneath. It allows the artist to see through several layers of paper, which is essential in animation.

3.10

In traditional terms, 'onion skin' is actually a type of translucent tracing paper. In software though, it simulates the tracing paper effect. When turned on, it reveals your previous drawings underneath, just like tracing paper, or a lightbox.

> **NOTE**
> Incidentally, the circular disc of an animator's desk (shown back in Figure 3.1 at the start of this chapter) allows the animator to freely rotate the drawing to a comfortable working angle. As you saw earlier in the book, this is activated in Toon Boom with the [Ctrl Alt] key combination, so now you know what the onscreen disc icon represents.

>FRAMES EXERCISE 3
THE ONION SKIN

Now let's look at the ant animation with the onion skin to see how it works.

> 1. In the Timeline, select frame 5 of your ant layer.

> 2. Turn on the layer's onion skin using the onion skin button 🥞. You can also right-click the playhead and choose Show Onion Skin [Alt O].

3.11

In the Camera View you should now see two faded red and two faded green ant images. Also shown in Figure 3.11 are two blue markers on the playhead showing that you can see two frames behind and two frames in front of your current drawing. These blue markers can be dragged, just like the looping playback markers you saw in the previous exercise.

> 3. In the Timeline, drag the onion skin markers out on each side of the playhead until you can see all of your animation from frames 1 to 12.

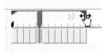

3.12

I like to think of red and green as past and future. In the Camera View, the number of past (red) ants corresponds to the number of frames under the left onionskin marker. Likewise the number of future (green) ants corresponds to the number of frames under the right handle.

Before we wrap this exercise up, one final thing to note is how the intensity of these green and red ants is gradually faded to illustrate how far those drawings are away from the playhead. In Figure 3.13, note the frame numbers and how the ant is more faded, the further it gets from the current frame.

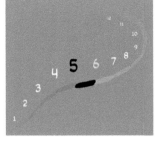

3.13

> 4. Finally, in the Timeline, hide the ant layer by unchecking its visibility checkbox.

> 5. You can safely close this file without saving as you won't need it from here on.

> FRAMES EXERCISE 4
FIREBALL ANIMATION

Now let's put what you've learned into practice. In this exercise you'll animate a simple magical fireball projectile; the kind a magician might throw in battle.

> 1. Create a new scene called 'fireball' with the HDTV_Vertical resolution.

> 2. Set the Scene Length to 36.

> 3. In the Timeline, rename the default layer 'rough'.

> 4. In the Colour panel, choose the Default black for sketching.

> 5. Get the Brush and set its max size to somewhere between 5 and 10.

> 6. In the Timeline, select frame 1.

> 7. Sketch a *horizontal* fireball in the Camera View, as shown in Figure 3.14.

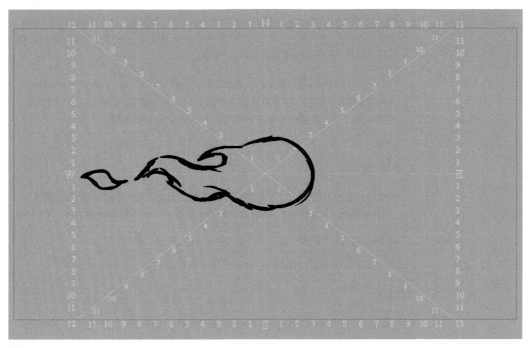

3.14

> 8. In the Timeline, on the fireball layer, turn on the onion skin using
> the 🝱 button.

> 9. Still in the Timeline, select frame 2 of the fireball layer or just press
> [.] to step forward one frame.

NOTE
As this is a flying projectile, the general idea is to make the flames
flow away from the ball. We're animating this fireball in place because
later, you'll learn a special way of moving it across the scene.

> 10. Draw two more frames of the fireball for a
> total of four.

> 11. Now might be a good time for a break. Save
> your scene here with [Ctrl/⌘ S].

3.15

If you'd like to test your fireball animation, position the playback markers as demonstrated in Frames Exercise 2, make sure the loop playback button is on, and press [Shift Enter].

This is four drawings at a rate of 24 fps which, as you can see, makes the flames frighteningly fast (that's one-sixth of a second). In the next exercise we'll learn about timing to slow it down a bit.

TIMING

The animation is very fast because you have animated it on 'singles' or 'ones', meaning there's a drawing on every single frame in the timeline.

3.16

In the next exercise, we'll be 'timing' these drawings so we can control the speed of the animation.

> FRAMES EXERCISE 5
  TIMING METHOD 1

When you animate something on singles, as you've just done with the ant and fireball, you may need to add time to your drawings so that they play slower. On the other hand, it's possible that occasionally you may want to speed up parts of the animation by removing drawings or frames.

Each fireball drawing is currently 'exposed' for just one frame. We'll now slow the animation down by exposing each drawing for two frames. In animation terms, we're about to put this animation 'on doubles', also called 'twos'.

NOTE
If you'd like a starting file for this exercise, open up fireball_rough from the download files for this chapter. You'll find it in the 'fireball' scene folder.

> 1. In the Timeline, [Shift]-select all the drawings in your fireball layer. That is, with the first frame already selected, hold [Shift] and then click the last frame as shown in Figure 3.17.

3.17

> 2. Right-click any of the selected frames and choose Exposure → Set Exposure to 2.

Each drawing of your fireball should now be exposed for two frames. The length of this animation should now be eight frames.

> 3. Position the playhead on frame 8.

> 4. In the top toolbar, press the Stop field name. The little triangular *loop end* marker should now be braced against the back of frame 8 like a little bookend.

> 5. Ensure looping playback is active and press Play, or hit [Shift Enter].

3.18

In step 2 you may have noticed that there are more timing options in the right-click menu. Go ahead and experiment with other timings for these frames if you get the urge. Just repeat the above exercise.

NOTE
At 24 fps, exposures greater than 2 will appear jerkier, because each drawing is held for longer. Jerky animation can always be smoothed out with inbetween drawings, which you'll see later in this chapter.

CYCLES

You've seen how to loop a few frames using the playback markers, but what if you want to loop these four drawings repeatedly for the full 36 frames of the scene? This is a very easy process with several ways of doing it so let's look at one of those right now.

> FRAMES EXERCISE 6
  CYCLES

> 1. In the Timeline, [Shift]-select all eight frames of your fireball animation.

3.19

> 2. Right-click the selected frames and choose Create Cycle.

A cycle window opens prompting you for a number. We have eight frames that we want to cycle to the end of the scene.

> 3. Enter 5 and click 'OK'. The Timeline is instantly populated with your eight frames cycled to the end of the scene.

> 4. Drag the playhead to the end of the scene. Then, in the main toolbar, press the Stop field's label.

3.20

> 5. In the top toolbar, turn *off* the playback loop.

> 6. Now reposition the playhead at frame 1.

> 7. Press Play or hit [Shift Enter] to watch the playback.

You've only done four drawings, but that sequence of four drawings is now looping over 36 frames. Being able to cycle a few drawings, rather than redrawing each frame over and over, is a huge time-saver, particularly for more complex animation like a character walk cycle.

> 8. Before we finish this exercise, I recommend you repaint all of your rough drawings with a lighter rough sketch colour. This will make it easier to clean up the linework, a few pages from now.

> 9. Finally, save the scene with [Ctrl/⌘ S] and close it. We'll come back to it later in the chapter.

DUPLICATING DRAWINGS

Sometimes you'll want to use one drawing as the basis for a new drawing. Take for instance a seedling growing in time lapse. You might redraw the sprout on every frame working carefully to keep the stem consistent as more leaves sprout from it. An easier way would be to duplicate each drawing and alter it on the next, as we'll see now.

> FRAMES EXERCISE 7
  DUPLICATING DRAWINGS

> 1. Start a new scene with a name, location and resolution of your choice.

> 2. In the Timeline, rename the default Drawing layer to 'seedling'.

> 3. In the Timeline, select frame 1 of the seedling layer.

> 4. Using the Brush tool with any colour, draw a narrow shoot coming from the ground.

3.21

> 5. In the Timeline, select frame 5 of the seedling layer

> 6. Press [F5] to extend the drawing one exposure up to this frame.
>   You could instead right-click frame 5 and choose Extend Exposure.

So you have one drawing *held* for five frames. To start animating this seedling, you obviously want a second drawing.

> 7. Select frame 2 of the seedling layer

> 8. Click the Duplicate Drawings button at the top of the Timeline (see Figure 3.22). Another way of doing this is to right-click frame 2 and select Drawings → Duplicate Drawings or simply press [Alt Shift D].

This has added a duplicate of your first drawing, indicated by a small

3.22

NOTE

If you don't see the buttons across the top of the Timeline as shown in Figure 3.22, you can turn them on with Windows → Toolbars → Timeline View.

separation line between frames 1 and 2 of the seedling layer.

> 9. Alter the drawing on frame 2 by adding a tiny leaf shoot.

> 10. In the Timeline, select frame 3.

> 11. Again, click the Duplicate Drawings button.

> 12. Turn on the onion skin for the seedling layer using the 🥣 button.

> 13. Using the Eraser or Cutter tool, remove the small leaf. Through the onionskin, you can now see your previous leaf drawing on frame 2.

3.23

> 14. Redraw the leaf slightly larger in this frame.

> 15. Repeat the process for frames 4 and then 5; erasing and redrawing the leaf growing slightly larger on each frame.

> 16. Now that you have five individual drawings, go back to the drawing on frame 2 and add another tiny leaf.

> 17. On frames 3, 4 and 5 you won't need to duplicate the drawing or erase the new leaf. Simply animate this new leaf growing on the existing drawings.

3.24

This short, simple sequence of animation demonstrates how useful Duplicate Drawings can be in frame-by-frame animation. As you get into more complex projects, you'll find Duplicate Drawings useful in other ways.

> FRAMES EXERCISE 8
TIMING METHOD 2

Now, just like in exercise 5, let's slow down the animation of the seedling by increasing the exposure of the drawings. Back in exercise 5 you saw how to put your drawings on *doubles* (that is, expose each drawing for two frames each) by right-clicking the frames and choosing Exposure → Set Exposure to 2. You could do the same here, but let's step through a different method.

If you'd like a starting file for this exercise, you'll find it in the download files for this chapter. It's called seedling_timing.

> 1.   In the Timeline, select your first seedling frame.

> 2.   Now right-click the frame and take note of the shortcut keys for Increase [+] and Decrease Exposure [-].

NOTE
If you have a numeric keypad on your keyboard, these are straight-forward shortcut keys and easy to remember. If you don't have a numeric keypad though, you'll need to press [Shift =] for Increase; that is to say, type [+].

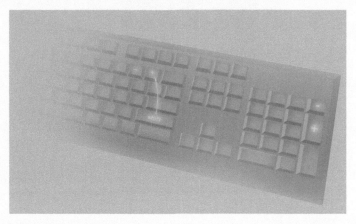

3.25

> 3.   In the Timeline, select the first seedling drawing and press [+] now.

This has increased the exposure of the selected drawing by one frame. You could continue pressing [+] a number of times to add more exposure to this frame, or press [-] to reduce the exposure of any drawings. I've exposed the first seedling drawing for four frames.

> 4.   Using the same method, increase the exposure of the other seedling frames.

3.26

> 5. When you've timed each frame, watch how it plays with [Shift Enter].

Is it too fast? Too slow? Experiment with different timings to get the speed you think works best. If you wanted to give, say, 12 frames exposure to each drawing, you may need to lengthen the scene. Feel free to do so to accommodate the seedling speed you want.

> 6. Close the scene with File → Close. As this has been a throwaway scene, you don't need to save it if you don't want to.

The timing method in this exercise has done exactly the same job that the right-click → Set Exposure method would have; but this is a little quicker for timing individual frames.

DRAWINGS AND FRAMES: THE DIFFERENCE

Cast your mind back to the beginning of the chapter, when I mentioned that at 24 fps, there are 24 frames flashing by every second. As you've seen though, that doesn't necessarily mean 24 drawings. The frame rate remains constant, regardless of how many drawings you use.

Working on *doubles* (each drawing exposed for two frames) there are only 12 drawings per second. If you're animating on 4s (each drawing exposed for four frames), you'll only need six drawings per second. Timed on 8s, you only need three drawings per second, and so on.

Once again though, the longer the exposure of each drawing, the more jerky the animation will appear when played back.

FRAMES SUMMARY

It may surprise you, but what you've learned so far is almost all you need to know about animating frame-by-frame in Toon Boom. With what you've learned, you could safely go ahead and animate any linework and any scene, from a wandering ant to a smoky explosion. Of course, there is so much more to Toon Boom; so many professional tools and time-saving features that we've yet to cover.

DRAWING SUB-LAYERS

Before we talk about Timeline Layers, there's another type of layer that's built into every drawing; a kind of *sub-layer* for different types of artwork *within* the drawing. Let's look at these and see why you might use them.

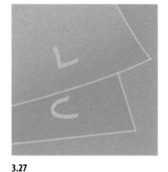

Imagine you have clear sheets called cels. You do all your work on these clear cels until one day on closer inspection, you discover that each cel is actually two thinner sheets pressed together; let's call them L and C.

You soon find that you can draw your linework on the L sub-layer and then apply your colour to the C sub-layer, keeping them separate. You can even hide L so just the colour art is visible, or hide C so you only see the line art. And yet to the casual observer, it's still just one cel. Magical, right?

3.27

3.28

In the Camera or Drawing views, look at the icons on the bottom left. If you're using Animate, your drawings have these L and C sub-layers. Animate Pro and Harmony though, have O, L, C, U – Overlay, Line, Colour and Underlay sub-layers.

NOTE
For the Animate user: if you don't see these buttons in your Camera and Drawing views, you can turn them on via Edit → Preferences → General tab. In the middle of the window towards the bottom, check the box Use Advanced Art Mode. It requires you to close and restart the program. Upon restarting, you'll see those L and C buttons shown in Figure 3.28.

TIP
The reason they're disabled in Animate by default is because they're designed for an advanced workflow. How you use these sub-layer levels, or whether you even use them at all, is entirely up to you and the needs of your scene.

The great thing about sub-layers is that your *line* art can be kept separate from your *colour* art, even though they're actually counted as the same drawing. The whole idea is to make it easy to colour and treat your lines separately from your paint fills.

3.29

As for the U and O layers (Animate Pro and Harmony only), I usually use the Underlay for my rough sketches/animation and then clean up on L. Where Toon Boom is used in animation studios, Overlay is often reserved for notes, corrections and timing charts.

Each of these sub-layers can be hidden from the final render too, so that notes and rough animation don't need to be deleted from the scene – just hidden. There'll be more on how to do this, starting on page 227.

When you open a scene, the L sub-layer is selected by default. Everything we've done throughout the book so far has taken place on the L sub-layer. Let's now explore the others.

> DRAWING SUB-LAYERS EXERCISE 1
  LINE AND COLOUR ART

Thus far in the book we've been drawing everything on the L sub-layer.

> 1. Open your fireball scene, if it isn't already open. If you'd like a start-
      ing file for this exercise, open up fireball_cycle from the chapter
      files, and skip to step 3.

> 2. In the Timeline add a new Drawing layer using the button 🌑, drag
      it to the top and rename it 'cleanFireball'.

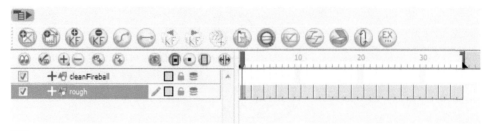

3.30

We'll now create clean linework for the fireball. The Line Art button ○
should be active by default. If not, activate it now.

> 3. In the Timeline, select frame 1 of the cleanFireball layer.

> 4. Clean up only the first four drawings. Later you'll cycle them to the
      end of the scene, just as you did with the rough fireball.

3.31

> 5. Expose each drawing for two frames using the [+] keyboard
      shortcut.

> 6. In the Timeline, select the fireball layer and then click the ⬤ button
      to switch to the Colour Art sub-layer.

If you were to try erasing some fireball lines, you'll find that you cannot, because you're currently on the Colour sub-layer, while the linework is on the Line sub-layer. Also, trying to fill the linework with colour won't work for the same reason: on the Colour sub-layer there are no lines to fill.

It means that we need to create invisible borders to fill with paint. So maybe now you're dreading the thought of creating invisible duplicates of your linework. You'll be relieved to know that with a shortcut keystroke, Toon Boom can automatically generate those for you.

> 7.   Get the Select tool [Alt S] from the toolbar.

> 8.   Make certain that you're currently on the Colour sub-layer. Press [Shift 8] or, in the top menu, go to Drawing → Create Colour Art from Line Art.

You should now be seeing those invisible vector borders as wiry blue lines. If not, toggle strokes on with [K], or go to View → Show → Show Strokes. Also, if you switch over to the Drawing view and click the ⬤ button, you'll see the wiry blue vector border as shown in Figure 3.32.

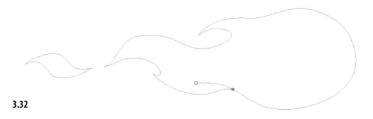

3.32

> 9.   Choose, or mix up, a fiery orange colour and then, using the Paint Unpainted tool [Alt Y], fill the closed flames on all drawings. Again, be sure you're filling the invisible strokes on the Colour sub-layer and *not* filling the linework on the Line sub-layer.

> 10. Hide strokes with [K] at any time to see the coloured areas without lines.

TIP
If you're working in the Drawing view, you may not be able to see the Line Art level while working in the Colour Art level. However, using the Preview Line and Colour Art button ⬤ you can see both levels together while working in one of them.

>DRAWING SUB-LAYERS EXERCISE 2
REPAINTING LINES

Let's repaint the fireball's linework with a second fiery colour.

> 1. At the bottom-left of the Camera View, click the ◎ Line sub-layer button.

> 2. Select the Paint tool in Repaint mode [Alt R].

> 3. In the Tool Properties panel, hit the 'Apply current tool to all drawings' button. This useful function lets us repaint all of the drawings at once!

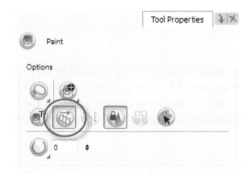

3.33

> 4. Using a new fiery colour with the Repaint tool, draw an area around your fireball.

> 5. Step through the frames with [,] and [.] to confirm that the lines have been repainted on every frame. For any that were missed, simply trace an area around them with the Repaint tool.

> 6. In the Timeline, select all of your clean drawings and cycle them to the end of the scene (right-click → Create Cycle).

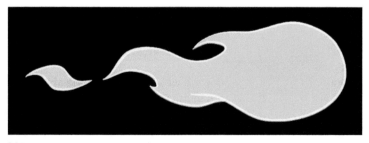

3.34

> 7. Finally, loop the playback and hit play to watch the animation.

> 8. Save your progress now because you'll use this file later to make the fireball fly across the scene.

While considered an advanced concept, you've just seen how keeping your lines separate from colour keeps your art highly organised and makes it easier to repaint, treat or otherwise change parts of it.

LAYERS

Timeline Layers have a variety of types and uses. So far we've really only explored the Drawing layer type, which happens to bear a resemblance to a flipbook. Other layer types include Effects, Groups, Cameras and, one of the most fundamentally useful layer types, Pegs.

SELECTING AND DESELECTING LAYERS

Each time you select a frame in the Timeline, you're also activating that Layer for editing, or drawing. This is indicated by the edit pencil ✏ icon, which tells you you're now working on this layer.

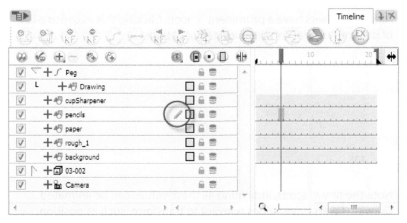

3.35

Because each layer is covered in buttons, boxes and labels, the best way to select a layer without clicking any buttons is to simply click the layer name, any of its frames or any blank part of the layer. You can also use the keyboard shortcuts [H] and [J] to move up and down the layers.

NOTE

Should you click the name of a layer that's already selected, you'll be prompted to rename the layer. If this happens and you don't want to rename the layer, simply press [Enter] or just click a blank part of the layer.

To deselect any selected layers, ensure the Timeline has focus and press your keyboard's [Esc] key. You can also click any of the blank areas above or below the Timeline layers.

LAYER PROPERTIES

Just like the tools, every type of layer has properties to mess with. As you go through the Layer exercises, keep the Layer Properties panel close by. I suggest docking it with the Tool Properties so you can switch easily back and forth between the two.

> LAYERS EXERCISE 1
EXPANDING AND COLLAPSING

Almost all layers have a prominent + icon. Clicking this expands a list of parameters that can be animated over time.

> 1. On any layer, click the Expand Function + icon.

3.36

Note the tiny ∿ icons, indicating all these values can be animated. Drawing layers have values relevant to transform, such as position, scale, rotation and skew. We'll see other values as we explore other layer types in the exercises that follow.

> 2. To collapse the layer back into itself, click the Collapse — icon and the list rolls back up.

FUNCTION CURVES

All throughout the Timeline and Layer Properties panel, you'll see the function curve 𝄐 icon. Whenever you see this, it means a parameter can be animated. For example, the *Position* attribute of a bird layer is what you animate to make the bird fly across the sky. The *Scale* value can make a boat gradually shrink as it sails into the distance. The *Transparency* effect module (seen in the next chapter) can be animated to make a cloud of smoke fade off over time.

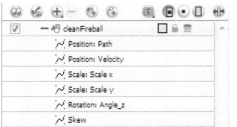

3.37

Whenever you see this 〰 function icon in the Timeline, you can double-click it to open up that parameter's function curve, which is essentially a motion graph for fine control over the animation timing. We'll use this much more in later exercises.

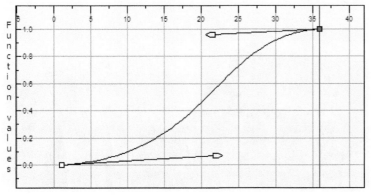

3.38

In any scene, simply click the ＋ button on any Timeline layer to roll out the layer attributes.

None of these will be clickable until animation keyframes are added; for now we're just browsing, but we'll animate these later. Drawing layer attributes are specifically for transformation: position, scale, rotation and skew. Notice also that you can add 𝄐 function curves for each attribute.

DUPLICATING LAYERS

There are many reasons you might need to clone or duplicate a layer. Here are a few examples.

- Crowds, flocks, schools and swarms.

- Waves, flames and clouds.

- Glows, shadows and other filters.

Duplicate and *clone* each have their own special uses.

DUPLICATE

A duplicate may be altered in any way without affecting the original. This is useful for the above crowd example. Suppose you have animated three incidental crowd members. If you duplicate these three, you can alter each character with different colours or clothing to make the crowd appear larger and more varied. You've probably seen this technique in television animation where you can see several versions of the same guy in the crowd, each with different coloured skin or clothing.

3.39

CLONE

When you clone a layer, any changes you make to the clone will also alter the original, and vice versa. One example where the technique may be useful is for creating a character shadow on a wall. The character can be cloned and the clone used as a Shadow matte. Any changes you make to the character will also be made to the shadow.

3.40

>LAYERS EXERCISE 2
  DUPLICATING AND CLONING

In this scene we'll animate a raindrop ripple and duplicate it a number of times for an effect of rain on a pond surface.

> 1.   Create a new throwaway scene.

> 2.   In the Timeline, rename the default layer *ripple* and then select frame 1.

> 3.   Using drawing tools and colours of your choice, animate a four-drawing sequence of some ripples growing outward from the centre and dissipating, as shown in Figure 3.41.

> 4.   Add exposure to each drawing so they're on doubles/twos (see page 149).

3.41

> 5.   Right-click the ripple layer's name and choose Duplicate Selected Layers.

The duplicated layer is automatically named with '_1' appended for you, but like any layer, you can rename it if you prefer. At this point, the layers should appear as shown in Figure 3.42.

3.42

> 6.   In the Timeline, [Shift]-select the first *four frames* (two drawings) of the *duplicated* ripple.

> 7. Press [Ctrl/⌘ X] to cut them from the Timeline. The blank frames should still be selected.

3.43

> 8. Making sure the blank frames are still selected, on your keyboard, press [Z]. This pulls the remaining drawings back to frame 1, leaving a gap at the end.

NOTE

The [Z] key function in the Timeline is known as *Clear and Pull*, which can also be accessed by right-clicking drawings or blank frames Exposure → Clear Exposure and Pull.

> 9. In the ripple_1 layer, select frame 5 and then press [Ctrl/⌘ V] to paste those frames you cut in Step 7, onto the end.

> 10. Move the playhead to frame 8 and click the Stop Frame label in the top toolbar.

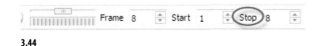

3.44

> 11. Activate playback looping and press [Shift Enter] to watch the playback.

In this exercise you've created two ripples from one, in a fraction of the time it'd take to animate two. For rain on a pond surface, you could fill the scene with these ripples, offsetting each by a different number of frames.

In the next exercise I'll set you on the path to do this yourself, where you'll reposition all the drawings of your duplicated ripple layer.

> LAYERS EXERCISE 3
> REPOSITION ALL DRAWINGS

In the previous chapter we skipped some of the tools because they are animation tools. Now that we're animating, let's revisit the toolbar and check out the Reposition All Drawings tool.

> 1. In the Timeline, select frame 1 of the ripple_1 layer.

> 2. In the toolbar behind the Select tool you'll find the Reposition All Drawings tool (Figure 3.45).

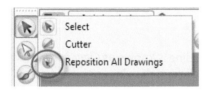

3.45

Once the Reposition All Drawings tool is selected, your drawing is automatically selected ready for repositioning, scaling and rotation.

> 3. Using the middle handle of the Select tool (a reminder to move the pivot point aside to access the reposition handle) move the drawing to the other side of the scene.

> 4. Scrub the Timeline and you'll see that all your drawings have been moved together.

> 5. We'll use this scene in the next exercise.

DRAWING LAYERS

By now you have plenty of experience working with Drawing layers. The *ant*, *fireball* and *ripple* animation you've done along the way, as well as all the drawing tools exercises in the previous chapter, have been done on Drawing layers.

DRAWINGS IN THE LIBRARY

Every drawing you do is automatically stored in the Library. Even if you delete a drawing from the Timeline, it remains in the Library and you can put it back on the Timeline quickly and easily at any time. Later we'll work more in the Library but the quick exercise below is a brief introduction.

> DRAWING LAYER EXERCISE 1
  THE LIBRARY

We're still working in the ripple scene for this exercise.

> 1.   If the Library panel isn't already open, choose it from the 🔻 panel menu.

> 2.   In the Timeline, [Shift]-select four drawings in your ripple layer and delete them using your keyboard's [Delete] key.

> 3.   Select frame 1 of the ripple layer, which should be now blank.

With frame 1 of the ripple layer selected, your Drawing Substitution window will show the layer name, while the preview pane is blank.

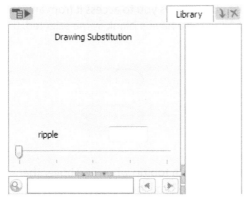

3.46

> 4.   In the Library, move the Drawing Substitution slider back and forth to see previews of all your ripple drawings. Each ripple shows in the preview pane.

> 5. Position the slider on your first ripple drawing (Figure 3.47).

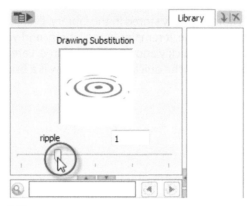

3.47

When you position the slider on the first ripple drawing, it appears in the Drawing Substitution preview, the Timeline and the Camera View. You can move the slider to whichever drawing you want to show on frame 1.

NOTE
When a Drawing is selected in the Timeline, also take note of the Drawing name at the bottom of the Camera or Drawing View. This name is a unique identifier that allows you to access it from any frame in the ripple layer. When you have a blank frame selected, the name here will say so.

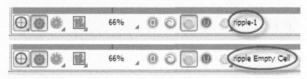

3.48

Drawing names will also appear in a tooltip when you hover the mouse cursor over drawings in the Timeline.

> 6. In the Timeline, select frame 3 of the ripple layer which should currently be blank.

> 7. In the Library, as shown in Figure 3.49, move the slider along to the *second* drawing.

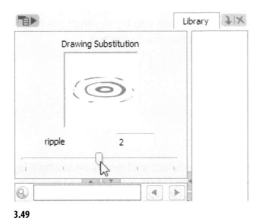

3.49

As you release the slider, ripple drawing 2 appears on the Timeline. Notice that the first drawing is exposed for two frames, filling the gap between 1 and 3.

> 8. Select frame 5 in the Timeline.

> 9. Move the Drawing Substitution slider to the third drawing.

This process of quickly inserting specific drawings at specific frames is called *drawing substitution* and is perfect for lip-sync animation. There's a whole project dedicated to drawing substitution near the end of this chapter.

NOTE
Now and then in the Drawing Substitution window, you'll find your numbers aren't perfect. For example, if you draw something on frame 3, delete it and draw something else on the same frame, the deleted one will be named 3, but the new one will be named 3_1. If you ever want to correct your drawing names, you can do so individually with [Ctrl/⌘ D]. Alternatively, you can venture into the X-sheet view. Select all drawings in the layer column, then right-click and choose → Drawings → Rename by Frame.

LIMITING DRAWING SELECTION

When you have several layers in your scene – let's say a separate bird and sky layer – it can be annoying when you try to select the bird in the Camera View, and the sky also becomes selected.

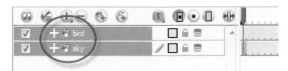

3.50

By default, in the Camera View the Select tool works on *multiple* layers at once. This has its uses but you can set the select tool to only work on your currently selected layer. To make the change go to Edit → Preferences → Camera tab → Select tool works on single drawing (Figure 3.51).

Shortcuts	General	Camera	Network	Exposure Sheet	Drawir

Tools

Initial Animation Mode   On

☐ Show Locked Drawings As Outlines

☑ Bounding Box Selection Style

Nudging Factor: 1

☑ Set Keyframes on all Functions with the Transform Tool

☑ Set Keyframe at Frame One with First Application of the Transform Tool

☑ Paste/Drag &Drop adds keyframes at beginning and end

☑ Select tool Works on Single Drawing

☐ Use Rotation Lever with transformation tools

3.51

When this preference is *unchecked*, the select tool will select anything in the Camera View, on all unlocked layers. My personal preference is to have this preference *checked*, so that the Select tool only works on the currently active layer.

ANIMATING A DRAWING LAYER

Earlier you saw the various parameters that you can animate with function curves. On a Drawing layer, these parameters are position, scale, rotation and skew. Let's animate some of these parameters.

> DRAWING LAYER EXERCISE 2
LAYER ANIMATION

The *Transform* tool is another animation tool we skipped over in the last chapter. Now you'll get to use it.

> 1. Create or open a throwaway exercises scene file.

> 2. In the Timeline, add a new layer named 'propeller'.

> 3. Select frame 1 of the propeller layer.

> 4. With your choice of drawing tools and colours, draw a propeller in the Camera View.

This propeller can be as simple or complex as you like. Mine is a simple polyline drawing of a triple-bladed marine-style propeller (Figure 3.52).

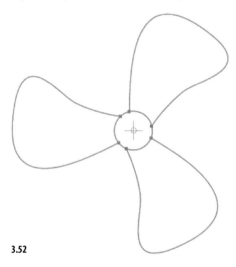

3.52

> 5. In the Timeline, extend the exposure of the propeller drawing to the end of the scene. The quickest way to do this is to select the last frame of the propeller layer, then press [F5].

> 6.   Return to frame 1 of the propeller layer by selecting it in the
>   Timeline.

> 7.   In the Tools toolbar ensure Animate Mode is on (Figure 3.53).

3.53

When the Animate button is active, any transformation you make to a
Drawing layer will automatically create a keyframe in the Timeline, as
demonstrated in the following steps.

> 8.   Directly below the Animate Mode button in the toolbar, choose the
>   Transform tool. The manipulator handles appear on the propeller
>   drawing.

As you can see, the Transform tool has similar handles to the Select
tool manipulation handles you're already familiar with. You'll also see a
pivot point.

> 9.   Get the Drawing Pivot tool [Shift P] and click the centre of the
>   propeller to place the pivot there.

> 10. Using the Transform tool, rotate the propeller now.

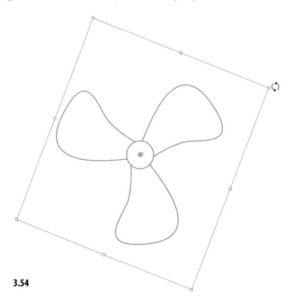

3.54

When you finish rotating the propeller, you'll notice in the Timeline
that a keyframe has been created on frame 1, indicated by a tiny black
square. The reason this keyframe was created is because Animate
Mode is on (see Step 7 and Figure 3.53).

> 11. In the Timeline, expand the propeller layer's function parameters by clicking the **+** button. You'll find that the keyframe has been created on all parameters.

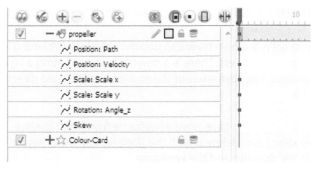

3.55

> 12. Move the playhead to the end of the scene, or simply select the last frame of the propeller layer.

> 13. In the Camera View, again with the Transform tool, rotate the propeller around one complete revolution.

A second keyframe has been created in the Timeline and on all parameters a line is drawn between the two, indicating changing values between keyframes.

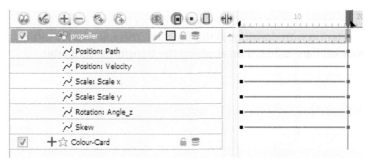

3.56

> 14. Drag the playhead or press play to watch the propeller animating on the Timeline.

Congratulations! You've just animated the rotation value of this propeller. You could go ahead and animate with position and scaling parameters in just the same way: position the playhead where you want a keyframe, then use the Transform tool on the drawing.

To finish up this exercise, why not challenge yourself to refine the propeller rotation for a seamless cycle?

KEYFRAMES

As you've just seen, a whole layer can be animated by keyframing its transformation parameters. There is a downside to animating a layer in this way however. The keyframes of the motion are attached directly to the drawings.

For example, if you want to remove a keyframe from the Timeline, you can't simply select and delete it with the [Delete] key, otherwise it'll delete both the drawing and the keyframe.

As another example: when you want to drag a keyframe in the Timeline it will drag the drawing with it. Sometimes you want to move keyframes independently of drawings. The solution for this is coming up soon when we talk about the Peg layer type. For now, let's look at how to add and remove transformation keyframes effectively.

> DRAWING LAYER EXERCISE 3
  ADDING AND REMOVING KEYFRAMES

Let's look at some shortcut keys that allow you to add and remove keyframes without transforming the object in the Camera View, or interfering with drawings in the Timeline. This is useful for setting out your keyframes first, then applying the transformations later.

> 1. In the Timeline select any frame of the propeller layer.

> 2. Press [F6] to create a keyframe. The tiny black square appears on that frame.

> 3. In the Timeline, select an existing keyframe.

> 4. Press [F7] to remove that keyframe.

In summary, animating the transformation values of a Drawing layer has its uses, but it's often more efficient to keep the motion separate from the Drawings themselves, as you'll see next.

PEG

The Toon Boom documentation defines a Peg as *a trajectory onto which you can hook your drawings*. You can also use a Peg for static or non-animated transformations without trajectories.

Rather than transforming the Drawing layer as you've just seen, you can attach it to a Peg. The Peg is a *dedicated* layer type that holds the Drawing layer transformation, keeping the motion separate from the Drawing layer itself.

Additionally, if you ever need to rework the Drawing layer after you've animated the transformation values, you can temporarily disable the Peg to 'hide' all of the motion and transformation.

In the propeller exercise you learned to animate the Drawing layer. However, this time it's the Peg that is keyframed.

> PEG EXERCISE 1
  PEG ANIMATION

In this exercise, you'll send your fireball flying across the scene by attaching it to a Peg layer. If you'd like to use a starting file, you'll find fireball_Peg in the 'fireball' directory.

> 1. Open the fireball scene and scrub the Timeline to watch the fireball animation flaming away on the spot for 36 frames.

> 2. Select the cleanFireball layer.

> 3. Add a Peg using the ⊕ button.

3.57

Now you have a dedicated movement layer for your fireball. It has been automatically named cleanFireball-P and has the original cleanFireball Drawing layer 'nested' underneath it.

NOTE

Nested layers indicate a *hierarchy*. In this little hierarchy the Peg is the *parent* and the Drawing is the *child*. Essentially it means that however you transform the Peg, whatever the Peg does, the Drawing follows.

3.58

Hierarchies are the basis for building puppet-style characters as you'll see towards the end of this chapter. A character's arm, for example, would be a child of the torso. Wherever the torso layer goes, there-fore, the arm layer follows.

Now you're ready to keyframe the transform parameters of this Peg. It'll keep all that movement separate from the Drawing layer.

> 4. In the Timeline, select frame 1 of the fireball's Peg layer.

> 5. Ensure Animate Mode is on.

> 6. Select the Transform tool.

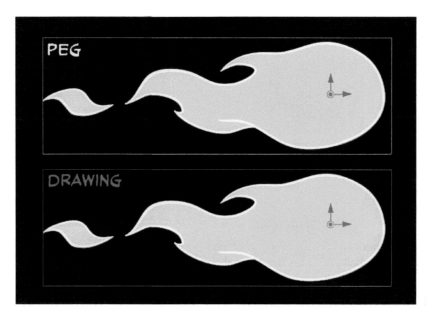

3.59

At this point, you will notice either that the Transform manipulator has a *yellow* border, or the fireball itself is washed with *yellow*. Yellow is indicative of a Peg with Animate mode on, whereas when you transform a Drawing layer, it's a pinkish-purplish border or wash.

NOTE
You can choose to show selected elements with the bounding box style (the border) or the tint style (the wash). At the bottom of the Camera View, open the Camera Display menu and toggle Box Selection Style.

> 7. Using the Move handle of the Transform manipulator, drag the fireball to a starting position on the screen.

> 8. Select the last frame of the Peg layer.

> 9. Once again using the move handle, move the fireball to its finish position.

In the Peg layer, there's now a line joining the two keyframes, indicating there's motion. And that's it! The Peg is animated from one side of the scene to the other, taking the fireball with it. Hit the play button or press [Shift Enter] to watch the fireball flying across the scene.

Now if you need to move keyframes around in the Timeline, you can simply drag them back or forward in the Timeline without interfering with any drawings.

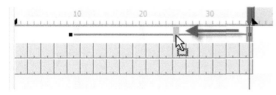

3.60

If you need to change the fireball's animation drawings, you can disable the Peg (in the Layer Properties panel, uncheck the Enable/Disable box) to remove the transformation. Make your changes and then re-enable the Peg.

> 10. Save the fireball scene now and leave it open for the next exercise.

CAMERA

The Camera layer type is exactly what its name implies. When you add a Camera to the scene, you can add a Peg to it, then keyframe its position, zoom and rotation for quick and easy camera moves.

Cameras in Toon Boom are incredible. There's a whole chapter dedicated to the Camera later, but let's quickly add one to the scene and see how it works.

> CAMERA EXERCISE 1
  ADDING A SCENE CAMERA

If you want a starting scene for this exercise, open up fireball_Camera from the chapter files.

> 1.   In your fireball scene add a new layer, name it 'background' and drag it to the bottom of the layer order.

> 2.   On this layer, draw a simple background sketch. No need to add colour or detail if you don't want to, as this is just for demonstration purposes. Also note in Figure 3.61 that I've extended the sketch beyond the scene border to accommodate a camera move.

3.61

> 3.   In the Timeline, click the ⊕ button and choose Camera from the drop-down list. Right away the Camera appears in the Timeline with the default name: Camera.

> 4. With the Camera layer selected in the Timeline, now add a Peg using the  button.

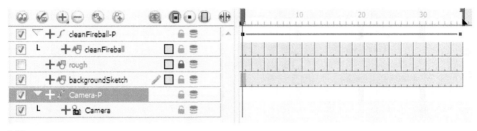

3.62

In the Camera View you may see nothing different, but a Camera does now exist in the scene and is attached to a Peg. As shown in Figure 3.62, the Timeline confirms this with a layer named Camera-P. It's ready to pan, zoom and rotate.

Rather than use the Transform tool for this, let's use the Advanced Animation tools. If you can't see them in your main toolbar above the Camera View, go to Windows → Toolbars → Advanced Animation and the tools will appear.

3.63

> 5. In the Tools toolbar, ensure Animate Mode is on.

> 6. In the Timeline, select frame 1 of the Camera's Peg layer, Camera-P.

> 7. From the Advanced Animation tools, select the Translate tool. Its shortcut is [Alt 2].

In the Camera View, a move handle appears, the cursor has a four-way move icon ✛ and the scene border is yellow.

> 8. Anywhere in the Camera View, click and drag to move the Camera Peg to a starting position, just as you did for the fireball Peg. As you drag, you can watch the scene panning. You could also use the Translate tool handles.

> 9. Select the last frame of the Camera Peg layer and then in the Camera View drag the Camera Peg to its end position.

As you might expect by now, the Timeline shows that the Camera Peg has two keyframes and the line between them indicates motion.

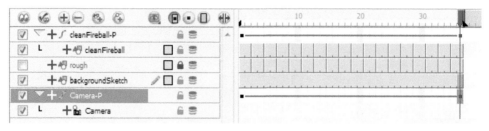

3.64

Experiment with the other Advanced Animation tools: Rotate [Alt 3], Scale [Alt 4] and Skew [Alt 5] and experiment with the pivot positions. Don't worry about Maintain Size and Spline Offset for now; we'll cover those later in this chapter.

COLOUR-CARD

The Colour-Card is just a plane of solid colour that sits behind all of your scene art, just like a theatre backdrop. It's useful as a background placeholder, or to simply replace the dull grey of the Camera View. Unlike Drawing layers, the Colour-Card cannot be drawn or painted on.

> COLOUR-CARD EXERCISE
  CHANGING THE COLOUR

> 1.   In the Timeline of the fireball scene, drop down the ⊞ menu and add a Colour-Card.

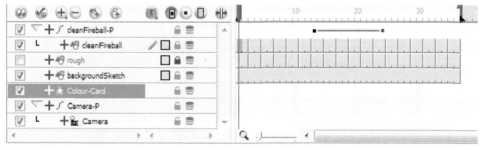

3.65

> 2. With the Colour-Card layer selected in the Timeline, go to the Layer Properties panel and down at the bottom, click the white colour swatch shown in Figure 3.66.

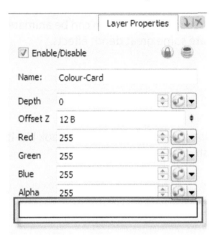

3.66

> 3. When the Colour Picker opens, change your Colour Card to any colour you like.

> 4. Close the Colour Picker window.

NOTE

When you make a test render of your scene, empty areas are rendered completely black. If your rough animation happens to be in black, and you don't have a background or Colour-Card, nothing will show up in the render.

This is how, particularly when creating quick, rough animation, Colour-Cards come in very handy. They're a quick solution to an otherwise empty backdrop.

QUADMAP

The Quadmap layer type is a super-cool feature for distorting layers. It also allows more realistic perspective distortion than the Perspective tool. The best thing is that the Quadmap distortion can be animated, so you can simulate and animate some great depth effects.

> QUADMAP EXERCISE 1
  DISTORTING A LAYER

In this exercise, you'll draw a flat chessboard, distort it to look like it's lying flat, then animate the distortion.

> 1. Create a new scene called quadmapTest with any resolution.

> 2. Rename the default layer 'chessboard' and select its first frame.

> 3. With the Shape tool in Line mode, draw an undistorted grid of eight squares high and eight squares wide as shown in Figure 3.67.

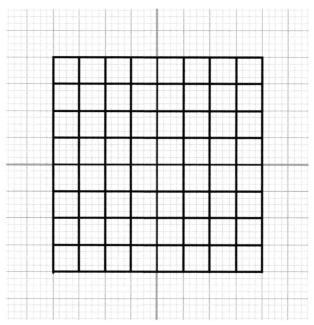

3.67

TIP
To help you draw your chessboard, turn on the grid using View → Grid → Show Grid and also View → Grid → Square Grid. Then activate *grid snapping* in the Shape Tool Properties.

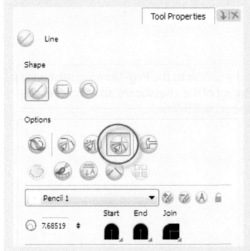

3.68

You may also need to add a Colour-Card to help you see the grid better. Don't forget to turn grid snapping off when you're finished, to avoid difficulty with other tools later.

> 4. If you'd like to paint the squares, go right ahead. Go nuts with detail and gradients if you really want to.

> 5. In the Timeline, choose Quadmap from the ⊕ drop-down menu.

NOTE
Harmony users: if you get an error when you try to add a Quadmap in the Timeline, change your display settings via Scene → Default Display → Display All.

> 6.   In the Timeline, drag the chessboard layer onto the Quadmap layer.

3.69

You've just created a hierarchy similar to the Peg–Drawing relationship. The Quadmap is now the *parent* of the chessboard art. Whatever you do to the Quadmap now, the art will follow.

> 7.   In the Timeline, select the Quadmap.

> 8.   Go to View → Show → Control to see the Quadmap manipulator handles. The shortcut to show controls is [Shift F11].

> 9.   In the toolbar, turn Animate Mode off. We're doing this so that no keyframes are created on the Timeline when we distort the chessboard.

The border surrounding the chessboard turns red. Once again, red borders indicate that Animate Mode is off. Note that you may need to zoom out a bit to see the Quadmap manipulator handles.

> 10.   Using the Translate tool [Alt 2] move the handles labelled 1, 2, 3, and 4 to distort the chessboard (Figure 3.70).

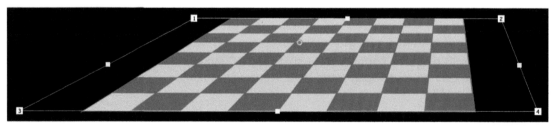

3.70

If you'd like to animate the distortion, feel free to turn on Animate Mode and create keyframes for the start and end frames.

USES OF THE QUADMAP

As you've just seen, the Quadmap can help give perspective effects and other types of distortion to a drawing.

One very common use for a Quadmap is character shadows, but you're only limited by how you think to use it. Why not try it out on helicopter rotors, or ripples on a pond? Animate those elements first without distortion, just as you did with the chessboard. Then apply the Quadmap to make them fit into perspective.

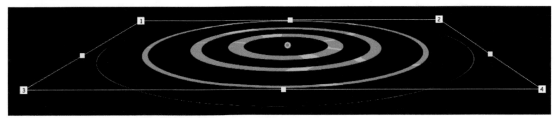

3.71

ANIMATE ONLY

The following two layer types, Masks and Effects, are available only in the Animate Timeline. Animate Pro and Harmony have their own versions of these (covered in the next chapter) but only in Animate can we access these via the Timeline.

MASK

Known also as a *cutter*, the Mask is a layer of art that hides or reveals parts of a Drawing layer. Creating a Mask effect requires two components: the *matte* and the art itself. The matte is the mask that will hide or reveal your art.

Because both matte and art are created on Drawing layers, Masks can be animated frame-by-frame or on pegs. They can also have transparency, blur and variable opacity effects for a huge range of possibilities.

MASK EXERCISE 1: ADDING A MASK

> 1.   Create a new scene called 'mask' and make two layers called 'window' and 'rain'.

> 2.   In the rain layer, with the drawing tool of your choice, draw a full screen of rain streaks.

> 3.   Now in the window layer, draw some filled shapes representing the glass in a window. It doesn't matter what colour you use here because the mask will be invisible.

3.72

> 4.   In the Timeline, use the ✛ button to add a Mask.

The Mask consists of a ready-made hierarchy waiting for your art. We need to drag the window and rain into this hierarchy. Inside the Mask is an empty *group* 🗗 also with the name Mask. Let's rename that group first, to avoid confusion.

> 5. Inside the Mask hierarchy, rename the Mask group to 'CutterArt'. This is the window pane art that will be used to cut or mask the rain.

> 6. Drag the rain layer onto the Mask layer name (Figure 3.73).

> 7. The window layer is your cut-out matte, so drag window onto the CutterArt group (Figure 3.73).

3.73

At this point the rain appears and the window matte, now invisible, is cutting out the rain art.

> 8. In the Mask Layer Properties panel, check the *Inverted* checkbox. Rather than cutting out the rain, the CutterArt is now revealing it.

> 9. In the Timeline, select the rain layer and add a Peg.

> 10. Animate the rain by creating start and finish keyframes on the rain Peg.

> 11. Test your rain animation by scrubbing the playhead, or using the toolbar's Play button.

This has been a simple demonstration of how masking works. As you might have guessed, the more obvious way to achieve this particular effect is to not use a Mask at all, but to simply make an upper layer – a wall with a window cut out of it – and have the rain on a layer underneath. However there may come a time when you're using a background that doesn't consist of layers, such as an illustration or painting done in another program.

Beyond just cutting out characters and backgrounds, there are many useful effects applications for a mask. Consider a sword glint. The sword could have a matte that reveals an entire scene reflection, or a simple band of light shimmering across its surface.

3.74

EFFECT

Effects are added by selecting a level and choosing the effect from the menu. For example, to add a glow to some animated lightning, simply choose Effect → Glow from the ➕ menu button. The Layer properties then allow you to control various aspects of the Glow, such as colour and blur values. The next chapter is on Effects but let's do a quick effect exercise now by applying glow to a lightning strike.

EFFECT EXERCISE 1: ADDING A GLOW EFFECT

> 1. Create a throwaway scene and in the Timeline, rename the default layer 'lightning'.

> 2. Select frame 1 of the new lightning layer.

> 3. Using the brush tool, draw a white lightning strike in the Camera View.

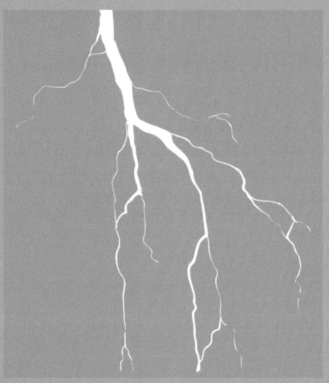

3.75

> 4. From the ➕ dropdown list, choose Effect → Glow.

> 5. In the Timeline, drag the lightning layer onto the Glow layer to create the glow hierarchy.

As the Glow is applied, the lightning art becomes semi-transparent. To see how this will look in the final render, let's check it in the Render View.

> 6. At the bottom of the Camera View, click the Render View button to show the render.

> 7. In the Timeline, select the Glow layer and open the Layer Properties panel.

> 8. Increase the blur's Radius value to 8.

> 9. At the bottom of the Glow properties, change the colour to a bright blue.

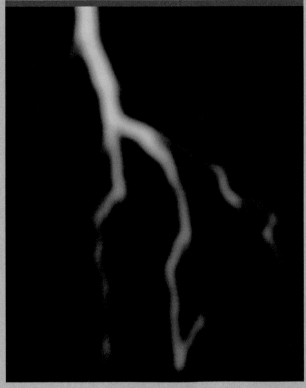

3.76

This isn't looking much like lightning. The bolt you drew has become the glow. We need to clone the lightning so we can use one for Glow and the other for the bolt itself.

> 10. In the bottom of the Render View, click the button to go back to the Camera View.

> 11. In the Timeline, select the lightning layer.

> 12. Above the Layers, click the Clone button (see Figure 3.77). Alternatively you can right-click the lightning layer and choose Clone Selected Layers.

3.77

> 13. Drag the original lightning layer to the bottom of the Timeline, so it's outside the Glow hierarchy.

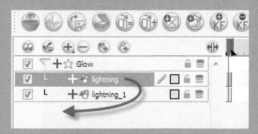

3.78

> 14. Now check the Render View again using the ⬤ Render View button. You should have a good solid lightning bolt, with a soft blue glow.

3.79

OTHER EFFECTS

In the Effects list, most of the other effects are added in the same way. To blur a drawing, for example, simply add a Blur Effect layer to the Timeline, then drag the Drawing layer onto it.

The next chapter is dedicated to effects so we'll go deeper into the technical controls for Effect layers. For now, you might like to explore the other Effects in the menu and experiment with their settings. Why not get a head start by applying the glow effect to your fireball animation? Just follow along with the previous exercise.

ANIMATE PRO & HARMONY ONLY

The layer types below can be found in the ⊕ menu in Animate Pro and Harmony only.

GROUP

A Group is a container for multiple layers of any type, even other Groups. This allows you to organise related elements. For example, sky, stars, moon and clouds might all go together into a *sky* Group. The *sky* Group may even then be placed with other background elements into a *background* Group.

3.80

GROUPING EXERCISE 1: GROUPING LAYERS

> 1. In a throwaway scene, use the ⊕ button in the Timeline to add an empty Group.

> 2. In the Timeline, drag any other layers onto the Group layer.

> 3. Just as you can with Pegs and any other hierarchy, you can collapse and expand the Group using the arrow button to the left of the Layer name.

SOUND

There is a full audio chapter later in the book, so the Sound layer is mentioned here merely to complete the list of layer types that can be added via the Timeline's Add Modules drop-down menu ⊕.

A specific audio file is best added through the top menu: File → Import → Sound…

ANIMATION TOOLS

The tools we covered in the previous chapter are dedicated to drawing and painting; the creation of art assets. Now that you've also seen frames and layers, let's revisit the toolbar and learn about the animation tools.

You've already seen a couple of them: the Reposition All Drawings tool and the Transform tool. As we look at some more, you'll put them into practice to see how they work and the situations to use them.

ADVANCED ANIMATION TOOLS

Advanced Animation tools are for transforming Drawing layers for animation keyframes and as such, they only work in the Camera View.

Even though they're called *Animation* tools, they're not exclusive to animation tasks. You may simply want to alter a layer as a whole without setting a keyframe, just as we did back on page 186 with the chessboard.

While the Transform tool encompasses the translate, rotate and scale functions, the Advanced Animation tools each take care of a specific type of transformation.

Before we look at the handles themselves, we should briefly cover some of their common attributes.

TOOL PROPERTIES

When you have one of the Advanced Animation tools selected, the properties panel shows just two options. We're interested in the second one, Peg Selection Mode (Figure 3.81).

3.81

When animating with Pegs, I always recommend selecting the Peg frames in the Timeline rather than the drawing in the Camera View, otherwise you mayl occasionally move the Drawing layer by accident, instead of the Peg.

Activating Peg Selection Mode ensures that if you move the object in the Camera View, it will ignore the Drawing layer and only let you move the Peg. As an extra safeguard against accidentally keyframing Drawing layers, you could lock them so they're impossible to alter.

If you're a beginner, this may not mean much to you right now, but it'll probably mean more after you have some experience with Pegs and the Advanced Animation tools.

HANDLE COLOURS

In Animate, objects can be manipulated in 2D (two dimensions: vertical and horizontal); in Animate Pro and Harmony, also in 3D (three dimensions: vertical, horizontal, depth).

- **Green**. The y axis is vertical. A green handle will move the object up and down, rotate it around the vertical axis, or scale it vertically.

- **Red**. The x axis is horizontal. A red handle will move the object left and right, rotate it toward or away from the viewer, or scale it horizontally across the scene.

- **Blue**. The z axis is also horizontal but runs toward and away from the viewer. A blue handle will move an object nearer or further away, rotate it around the z axis – think of a clock hand spinning around its pivot – or scale an object on that axis.

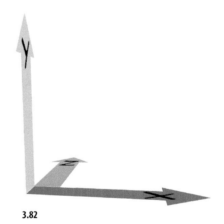

3.82

PIVOTS

As well as the manipulator handles, each of the Advanced Animation tools shows the pivot point of the selected Drawing or Peg. You can reposition Pivots by dragging them, but they cannot be animated.

Unlike the Select and Transform tool, the Advanced Animation tool Pivots remember where they were placed.

3D TRANSFORM TOOLS

Coming up on page 207, Animate Pro and Harmony users will see how to *enable 3D* on any Peg or Drawing layer and over the next couple of pages, you'll see the 3D manipulator handles for those tools.

TRANSLATE [ALT 2]

⊕ Not to be confused with Transform, *Translate* is for repositioning a Drawing or Peg layer. With this tool, there's no need to click-drag the object itself. With the four-way move cursor ✛ you can drag the object by click-dragging anywhere in the view.

3.83 There are also a couple of ways you can constrain the dragging to vertical or horizontal axes. The first way is to click the arrows. The arrowhead will turn pink when you're dragging on that particular axis. The second way is to hold [Shift] then click-drag either horizontally or vertically. The dragging will be constrained to whichever axis motion is detected first.

3D TRANSLATE

With 3D enabled (ahead on page 207), the Translate tool can move an object towards or away from the viewer. The blue manipulator arrow is for altering the layer *depth*, otherwise known as *Z-depth*. While Animate doesn't have 3D enabled layers (that is a Pro and Harmony feature only), you can still move your drawings forward and back in 3D space.

ROTATE [ALT 3]

⊙ Rotation happens around the Pivot, wherever that may be placed on the Drawing or Peg. A wheel or propeller rotates from a centre pivot, while a pendulum rotates from the end of a shaft.

3.84

3D ROTATE

Is it just me, or is rotating a 2D drawing in 3D the best thing ever? When you draw a flat door, for example, moving the Pivot point to the hinge location and rotating it open is something I never grow tired of.

While you can use 3D rotation for simple tasks like doors or the cover of a storybook, it can also be used to create 3D sets. Later in the book we'll set up a 3D environment by rotating and positioning walls, ceiling and floor in 3D.

If you're using Harmony, Appendix A has info on how to import 3D models that you manoeuvre into position using the 3D transform modes of the Advanced Animation tools.

SCALE [ALT 4]

There are a various ways to make objects grow or shrink, but it makes sense to use the Scale tool, in most cases. Like the Rotate tool, scaling happens around the Pivot point.

3D SCALE

Objects that have depth, particularly imported 3D models (see Appendix A), can be scaled on the z axis using the blue (z) scale handle of the Scale tool.

Z-scaling is only effective on 3D models. Ordinary Drawing and Peg layers are infinitely flat; their depth, or thickness, cannot be scaled.

3.85

SKEW [ALT 5]

Skewing distorts an object by sliding its opposite sides against one another, such as the top and bottom sides, or the left and right.

MAINTAIN SIZE [ALT 6]

While moving objects back or forward in z-space, they tend to shrink into the distance, or grow larger with proximity, as they should! The Maintain Size tool is for depth positioning (z-movement only) but it automatically scales the object so it appears to be the same size.

We'll use this incredibly useful tool later, when we start positioning scene layers at various depths, from extreme foreground bushes to distant mountains and skies.

VIEWS AND PREVIEWS

Toon Boom rendering is capable of the highest quality graphics and simulations suitable for feature films. However, the Camera and Drawing Views are optimised work spaces. The quality of graphics in these views is somewhat lower for real-time previewing, which is why you may see pixelated lines in those views. In the program, this preview quality is known as OpenGL mode, which is the name of the rendering technology and stands for Open Graphics Library.

OpenGL mode allows you to work without too much computer power spent rendering linework and effects. You can work in fast, low quality using ● OpenGL mode, then when you want to see how things look in final render quality, you switch to the Render View using the ● button.

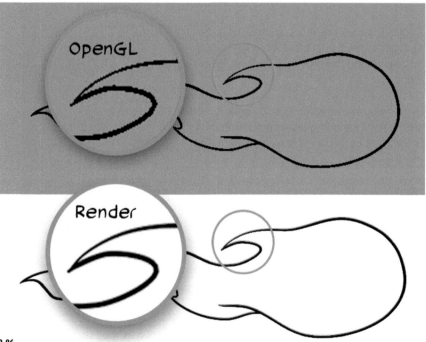

3.86

NOTE

If you have a fast computer, you may like to increase line smoothness in the Camera and Drawing workspaces. If so, go to Edit → Preferences → OpenGL tab. About halfway down, turn on Real-Time Antialiasing. With this enabled you can enter a value to increase the render factor, which relates directly to the smoothness of the line.

To test it out, in the OpenGL preferences activate Real-Time Antialiasing with a factor of 1. Click OK and the lines will appear smooth.

Go back into the OpenGL preferences and raise the Real-Time Antialiasing render factor to 2. When you close the preferences you should see your line quality is even higher now and you can zoom in further before the pixels start to show. Bear in mind that increasing this value increases the smoothness, but thereby increases the processing power required by the computer to draw lines and brush strokes.

3.87

Also remember that the OpenGL settings have no impact on your final render. It's only for the line quality in your Camera and Drawing working environment

Render View takes longer and is harder work for your computer, but it compiles all of your layers, levels and effects into a high quality rendered frame.

At the bottom left of the Camera View, there are a few additional options for the workspace. You've already seen the zoom menu and the render buttons. Click the Camera icon (Figure 3.88) to open a menu.

3.88

One at a time, in a scene with several layers, select each menu item here to see the result in the Camera View. Each of these options exists to make your work easier or more comfortable in one way or another. For example, in a complex crowd scene with many individual layers of characters, you can activate the Light Table or the Current Drawing on Top option so that a selected character is easier to work on, either by dimming the other distracting layers or bringing the selected one to the front.

3.89

DATA VIEW

You've seen the main parts of the Timeline, so let's now look at some of its underlying functionality. There is one particular view within the Timeline we haven't covered yet.

You can expand and collapse the Data View using the ◄▮► icon.

Expand a Drawing layer using its ➕ icon and you'll see all the various attributes listed in the Data View.

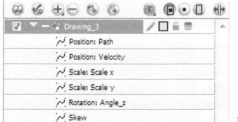

3.90

Earlier we touched briefly on how these layer parameters can be animated using Function Curves, such as Position, Velocity and Rotation. The Data View makes these accessible via the Timeline. For example, suppose you want to animate the Rotation attribute of a layer. Through the Data View, you can easily set keyframes by numerical input, such as 90° rotation on frame 1, to 30° rotation on frame 50.

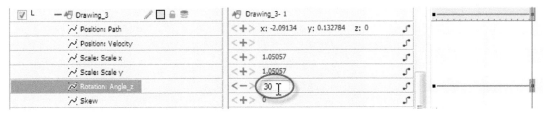

3.91

You can also add keyframes to any attribute on the Timeline simply by positioning the playhead where you want the keyframe, then click the + button on that attribute. Let's put this into practice right now.

> DATA VIEW EXERCISE 1
ANIMATING ROTATION

In this exercise we'll animate the arm of a metronome using only Data View inputs. If you need a starting file, open up 'metronome' from the chapter files.

If you're not musically inclined and were wondering what a metronome is: it's a kind of inverted pendulum that clicks as it sways from side-to-side. The regular, audible tick helps a musician keep to a beat.

> 1. In the Timeline add a new layer called 'metronome'.

> 2. Select frame 1 of the new metronome layer.

> 3. In the Camera View, with a drawing tool and colour of your choice, draw your metronome arm perfectly vertical, as shown over the page in Figure 3.92.

> 4. Extend the exposure of this drawing to frame 25.

> 5. From the Advanced Animation tools, choose the Rotation tool, or press [Alt 3].

> 6. In the Camera View, drag the pivot point to the bottom of the metronome arm.

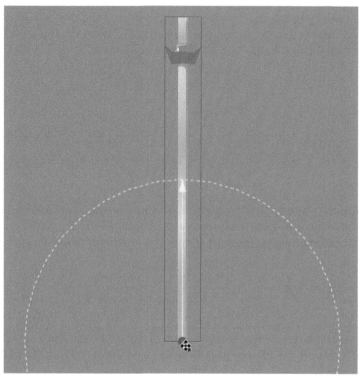

3.92

> 7. Expand the metronome layer's attributes using **+**.

> 8. If it's not already open, expand the Timeline's Data View using the ✛ icon.

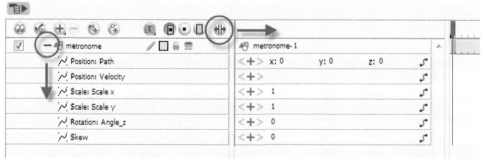

3.93

> 9. Making sure the playhead is on frame 1, click the Add Keyframe button ✚ in the metronome's Rotation attribute layer.

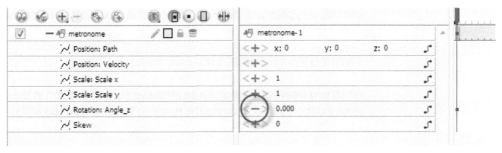

3.94

Even though you haven't actually input an initial value or rotated the arm, you've nonetheless created a keyframe with the value of 0° rotation.

> 10. Move the playhead to frame 12 and click the ✚ Add Keyframe button again to add the second keyframe of the swing.

Now you have two keyframes. Both have 0° rotation. Let's change them.

> 11. With the playhead on frame 1, type 45 in the Rotation value field.

> 12. Move the playhead to frame 12 and type -45; a negative value.

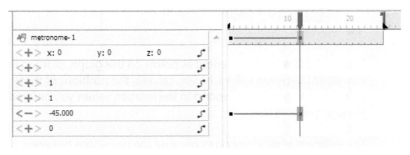

3.95

The arm swings from left over to the right. Now to make it swing back:

> 13. Move the playhead to frame 25 and again, for the Rotation value, type 45.

> 14. Save the scene with [Ctrl/⌘ S]

Over 25 frames, your metronome arm should now swing from left to right, then back to left. If you set your playback to loop and hit [Shift Enter], you'll see the arm going back and forth. The movement is linear and not very pleasant, but we'll address that next with some easing.

EASING WITH FUNCTION CURVES

When you create animation on an attribute, such as rotation in the previous exercise, you also create the function to which you can add easing.

> FUNCTION CURVES EXERCISE 1
  EASING

> 1. In the Timeline, double-click the metronome's Rotation Function
      Curve icon.

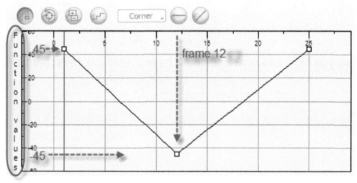

3.96

Your keyframes are represented as points on this graph, plotting linear movement between values. As you can see, the positions of these points on the graph correspond to the rotation values you entered in the previous exercise.

The jerkiness of motion occurs because the transitions between keyframes are absolutely linear. Moving from the first position, the metronome arm hits the second keyframe and jerks immediately back towards the first position. To soften this, we need to change these hard, straight lines into curves.

> 2. Click, or drag a selection around individual points, to reveal tangent
      handles; these are very much like those you've seen in the Polyline
      and Contour Editor tools.

> 3. Drag these handles around to slow down the movement on each side of the points, as shown in Figure 3.97.

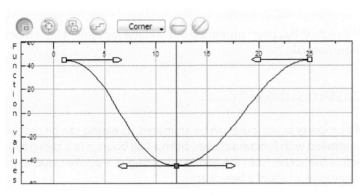

3.97

TIP

Generally you can just 'eyeball' the handle positions but if you'd like to be more precise, you can enter values for each handle's *length* and *angle*. Simply select a point and then enter values of 180° (left handles) and 0° (right handles) for perfectly flat handles, or 90° and 270° for perfect verticals. Equal values for handle lengths will ensure that the easing is identical on each keyframe, if that's what you want. Figure 3.98 shows how much fun you can have with timing movement in the Function Editor.

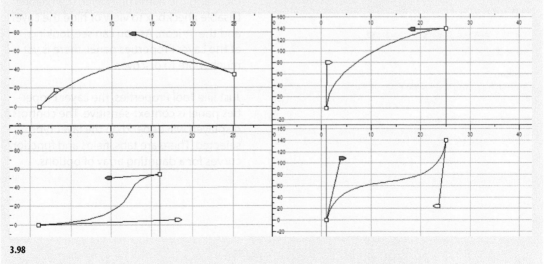

3.98

> 4. In the Playback toolbar, set the Stop marker to frame 24 (because frame 25 is exactly the same as frame 1, we no longer need it) and watch the playback.

The motion has been smoothed out and the movement feels much more natural.

EASING SUMMARY

If a property or attribute can be animated, its easing can be precisely controlled with function curves: from a ball bounce to a camera move across the scene; from the gentle morphing of a smoke cloud to the aggressive attack of a bee swarm.

LAYER PROPERTIES PANEL

Drawing and animation is obviously a huge part of what goes into creating a scene, but another crucial part is adjusting Layer Properties for fine-tuning the animation. You will need to visit the Layer Properties almost as much as the Tool Properties.

Each layer type has its own unique set of properties to modify. We've previously scratched the surface of Layer Properties, including the name of a Layer, the Enable/Disable checkbox to view or hide the Layer and the 🔒 icon. As you can see, looking at the Layer Properties panel, there is yet much more to discover.

Just like Tool Properties, the Layer Properties panel is context-sensitive. The controls displayed will depend on the layer type selected. There are tabs, fields and function curves for a daunting array of options.

3.99

As we go through the rest of this book, we'll frequently visit the Layer Properties panel for controlling the various Layer types, such as Drawing, Peg, Camera and Effect layers.

The big one here is in Animate Pro and Harmony only. It's the unassuming Enable 3D checkbox on Drawing and Peg layers (Figure 3.100), which allows you to use the 3D versions of the Advanced Animation tools.

Name:	Drawing		
Transformation		Drawing	Advanced
Enable 3D		☑	

3.100

PLAYBACK CONTROLS

As an animator, you'll frequently need to test the playback to ensure everything's moving well. Sometimes you'll want to flip back and forth between a couple of drawings to make sure things are looking right — other times you'll want to sit back and stretch while the whole scene plays on a loop. Traditional animators using pencil and paper learn a method of flipping paper between the fingers, known as 'rolling the drawings' for a mini playback.

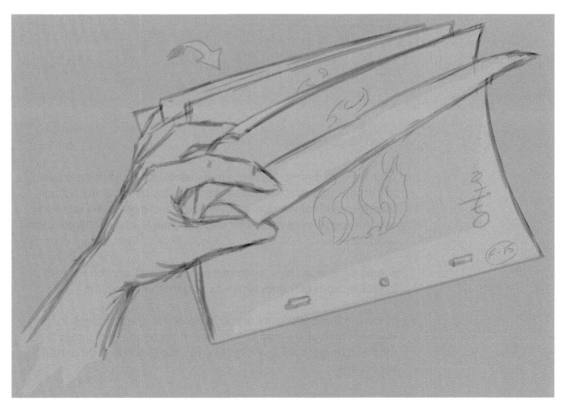

3.101

In those days no animator could get very far without this essential skill. Even today, digital animators frequently flip back and forth through the frames using shortcut keys to watch the movement and be sure everything is working well.

Apart from the Playback controls in the main toolbar (Window → Toolbars → Playback Controls), Toon Boom provides a number of helpful tools to support this useful technique.

STEPPING

If you cast your mind back to the frame-by-frame animation exercises, you'll recall stepping back and forth through single frames using the [,] and [.] keys.

This gets a little tedious if your drawings are timed on twos, fours or more, so you'll be pleased to learn that, rather than step individually through frames, you can step through *drawings* with the [F] and [G] keys, and through keyframes with [;] and ['].

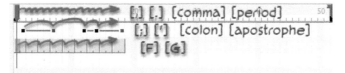

3.102

SCRUB AND JOG

Ordinary Timeline scrubbing is quite useful for short frame spans, but it's not very practical for long scenes. Try to scrub any further than the width of your program window and it gets a bit unwieldy and imprecise; even more so if your timeline is squeezed into a small window.

Scrubbing is aided by a *Jog frames* tool, which allows you to scrub longer sections of frames without using the Timeline at all.

In version 2 of both Animate and Animate Pro, the Jog tool is in the Playback toolbar. It's a small ⬤ button, right beside the Frames field. Click and drag it back and forth to scrub the Timeline without using the Playhead.

In Animate 3, Animate Pro 3 and Harmony, the Jog tool is much better. It's a spring-slider with variable speed scrubbing.

3.103

The further you drag the slider, the faster the scrubbing. When you release the slider, it springs back to the centre.

TIP
If you have playback looping enabled, Jogging will loop back to the start when it reaches the end.

LOOPING

The tiny triangular loop markers that you position on the Timeline define the start and end of a loop. By default, these are positioned at the start and end of your scene, but as you've already seen, you can position these in the following ways:

- By dragging them to the chosen start and stop frames.

- By entering values in the main toolbar.

- By positioning the playhead then clicking the Start or Stop frame buttons.

Once these markers are positioned, you can activate playback looping and hit Play to watch a looping playback.

EASY FLIPPING

While the [F] and [G] keys are definitely the easiest way to step through your drawings, there is a special tool provided for this. You may not see it in your toolbar, so go to Window → Toolbars → Easy Flipping to turn it on.

The Easy Flipping toolbar provides a handy slider that you can use in conjunction with your keyboard shortcuts for faster flipping. While using the [F] and [G] keys, the slider controls the flipping speed. Hold the slider slightly forward and use [G] to flip forward two or three drawings at a time. Hold it further forward, and the [G] key will leap over more drawings and reach the end of the scene very fast. The same goes for moving the slider backwards, then stepping back through the drawings with the [F] key.

3.104

The two buttons on the Easy Flipping toolbar do the same job as the [F] and [G] keys.

TIP
Two incidental Timeline shortcuts that you might find useful are [<] and [>] – i.e., [Shift ,] and [Shift .] – which send you to the Start and End frames, respectively. Note that these aren't necessarily the first and last frames of the scene, but the frames marked by your Start and End markers. Therefore, if you place the Start marker at frame 10 and the End marker on frame 33, these shortcut keys will take you to those frames.

At the time of this writing, the [<] and [>] shortcuts don't scroll the Timeline view for you. Suppose your scene has 500 frames – usually too many to fit in the Timeline view. Sitting on Frame 1, type [>] – that is, press [Shift .] – and the playhead will disappear from the start of the scene. The Frame field in the toolbar shows that you're on frame 500, but the Timeline view is still sitting on frame 1 and the playhead is nowhere in sight. Simply scroll along the Timeline and you'll find the playhead sitting silently, looking very guilty, on the final frame.

3D SPACE

I mentioned *z-depth* earlier with regards to moving Drawing layers toward or away from the viewer. While you may be familiar with y (height) and x (width), it's the third dimension, z (depth) that gives us a feeling of realistic space in the scene.

In Toon Boom there are some special views that give us a new perspective on the scene. These views show the scene layers as flat sheets existing in a 3D space. These are the Perspective, Top and Side Views.

PERSPECTIVE, TOP AND SIDE VIEWS

Consider traditional animation cels; clear sheets upon which characters are painted. When looking at them from the front, we can see them just fine. Look at them from the top though, and you can only see the top edge; little more than a thin, straight line. Here's an exercise to illustrate that point.

> 3D SPACE EXERCISE 1
   VIEWING LAYERS IN Z-SPACE

If you need a starting scene for this exercise, open up fireball_zSpace from the chapter files.

> 1.   In the fireball scene, click the panel menu ⬇ button and open the Perspective View. I suggest docking this view with the Camera and Drawing Views. If you'd like to add it to your workspace, remember to save it using the Save Workspace button.

3.105

> 2.   You should now be viewing the scene in 3D space, directly from the front with a reference grid beneath.

> 3. Hold [Ctrl Alt] to activate 3D space rotation. Drag left and right, up and down to tumble your view around the scene in 3D space.

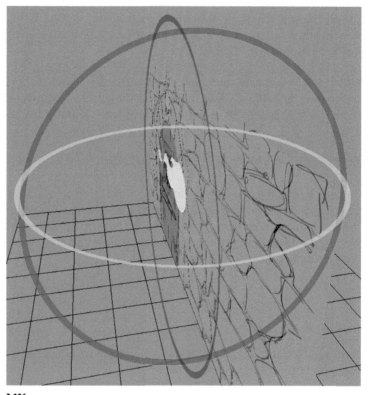

3.106

TIP
Use [1], [2] to zoom and [Spacebar] to pan. Press [Shift X] to reset the view if it starts getting away from you.

> 4. Manoeuvre the view so you're looking at the scene layers from directly above. Notice how, from that angle, the layers appear as thin lines.

> 5. Manoeuvre around now to see the layers directly from the side. Again, thin lines.

The Perspective View is a fantastic visualisation of your scene's depth. It's only for viewing the spatial relationships of the layers though; you can't draw or paint in here.

> 3D SPACE EXERCISE 2
THE TOP VIEW

> 1.   From the panel menu ⬇ button, choose Top to open the Top View. I suggest docking this view with other tall, thin panels, like the Colour panel or Tool Properties.

In the Top View, we're looking directly down on the scene. There's a list of layer thumbnails stacked in order on the left, shown in Figure 3.107 (A). Showing as a solid black line (B), the scene layers are stacked at the scene centre. The triangular shape (C) represents the field of the Camera View.

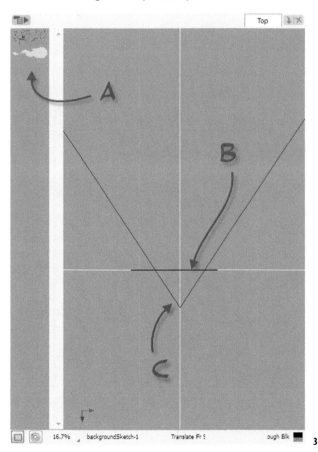

16.7%   backgroundSketch-1   Translate Fr 5   ough Blk   3.107

> 2. Ensure the Top View has focus, then, on your keyboard, press [2] to zoom out and [1] to zoom in. Just like other views, you can also pan around the view using [Spacebar].

> 3. In the Timeline, select the background Peg layer.

> 4. Choose the Translate tool [Alt 2] from the Advanced Animation toolbar.

See in the Top View how, with the layer selected and the Translate tool armed, there are the Translate handles. Be sure to have the Camera View open so you can watch the result as you move it around.

> 5. In the Top View, drag the blue handle (z) up and down. Remembering that this is a top-down view of your scene, the blue handle is actually moving your layer forward and back in z-space.

> 6. When you're happy with the z-depth of this layer, return to the Perspective View and orbit around the scene to see how all this is corresponds to the Top View.

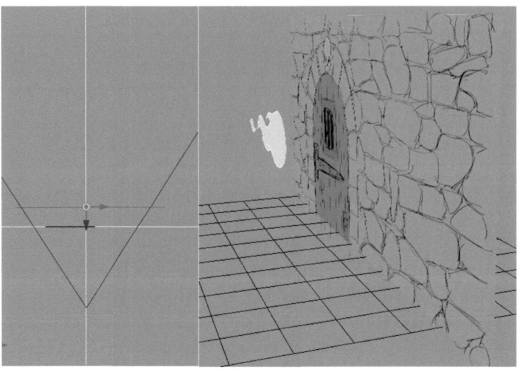

3.108

USING MAINTAIN SIZE TOOL

Something you may have noticed, and will no doubt understand, is
that when moving a layer back in z-space, it shrinks into the distance.
Likewise, bring it toward camera and it appears to grow.

This may be the desired effect. However, there are times when you
might want to move your layer back into space without it shrinking. In
the previous exercise, moving the background away has made it shrink
and it's now too small for the scene (Figure 3.109).

3.109

Usually the solution is to simply use the scale tool [Alt 4] to resize the
layer after moving it. But there is a better way.

The Maintain Size tool is a *z-only translate* tool. It allows you to move a
layer forward and back, but it also resizes the layer automatically so it
appears unchanged in the scene.

> 3D SPACE EXERCISE 3
  MAINTAIN SIZE

> 1. In the Timeline, disconnect the background Peg from the back-
     ground, and then delete it using the  button.

> 2. Select the background layer and add a brand new Peg using the
     button.

> 3. Make sure Animate mode is off, then select the Maintain Size tool
     [Alt 6] from the Advanced Animation tools.

> 4. In the Timeline, select the background's new Peg layer. In the Top
     View, provided you have Animate mode off, the Peg will be high-
     lighted red.

> 5. With the Maintain Size tool, anywhere in the Top View, click and
     drag upwards to move the background a short distance behind the
     fireball.

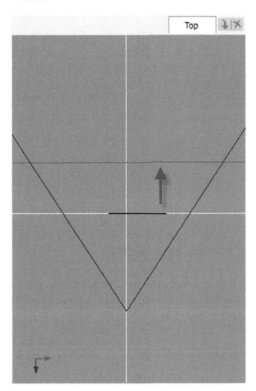

3.110

> 6. Open the Perspective view and orbit around using [Ctrl Alt].
>   Depending on how far back you moved it, you'll see how the back-
>   ground has been scaled larger to compensate for the distance.

Now that the depth of the scene has changed, scrub the Timeline to
see that the Camera move isn't quite the same. You may like to rework
the Camera Peg start and end positions, so that it travels the full length
of the background. In turn, you may also need to rework the fireball
Peg's keyframes so they work with the new Camera move.

3D SPACE SUMMARY

Why would anyone bother with all this z-space arrangement? Hopefully the answer to that question was mind-meltingly obvious when
you saw the Camera move in the previous exercise. In any 2D scene,
the combination of camera motion and layers arranged in z-depth
never fails to impress.

TYPES OF ANIMATION

Toon Boom software caters to several different schools of 2D animation. In this final part of the chapter we'll look at each of these in turn,
starting with the various traditional frame-by-frame methods, before
moving on to the modern, digital methods.

FRAME-BY-FRAME

Frame-by-frame animation means the animator has hand-drawn every frame of a movement.
Instead of making a four-drawing bird cycle and
sliding it across the scene on a Peg, the bird is fully
animated, frame by frame, over the entire length
of the scene with few, or no reused drawings.
Figure 3.111 shows 13 drawings of bird animation
which is only possible with frame-by-frame.

3.111

It's very common for frame-by-frame animation to be timed on double frames (twos) which, depending on frame rate, equates to 12–15 drawings per second. Sometimes, however, for a particularly fast or smooth motion, we need to work on singles (ones), which means doing the full 24–30 drawings per second. For this reason, frame-by-frame animation, also known as 'full animation' has the most line mileage of all.

3.112

Despite its complexity and high skill prerequisite, the big advantage of frame-by-frame is that in experienced hands, there's no type of motion that cannot be animated. If you can draw it, you can animate it: full character turnarounds, tumbling props, realistic elemental effects, fluid lip-sync and natural expressions – each of these falls short if not done frame by frame.

3.113

Traditional frame-by-frame animation has always been expensive not only in terms of time and money but also in terms of equipment and physical space – after all, those scene folders containing tens of thousands of individual drawings and paintings need storing somewhere. Generally speaking, only big budget studios (if any at all) embark on full, traditionally animated frame-by-frame feature films nowadays.

Beneath the umbrella called frame-by-frame – which I'll abbreviate hereafter as FxF – there are a couple of sub-categories. They are 'Straight Ahead' animation and 'Pose to Pose' animation. Let's look at them both.

STRAIGHT AHEAD

In the 'Straight Ahead' method, the animator starts with the first drawing, then moves on to drawing number 2. When drawing 2 is complete, the animator starts on drawing 3 – and so on until the animation is complete, with many individual hand-drawn frames.

You'll recall at the beginning of this chapter when you animated the ant wandering across the scene using this method.

Straight Ahead is ideal for special effects animation such as explosions, fire, water splashes or electricity. By their nature, these animation tasks are best animated linearly, from the beginning of the effect to the end.

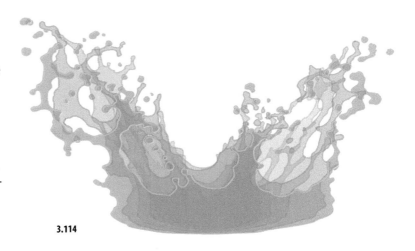

3.114

Straight Ahead is ideally suited to chaotic action or unpredictable things, like explosions, fire, electricity and water splashes. For more predictable movements – i.e., actions that, once started, have a predictable end, like a falling object – the Pose to Pose method would be more suitable and we'll talk about that next. For now, try out this challenge.

STRAIGHT AHEAD CHALLENGE

Try out the Straight Ahead method by animating an exploding fireworks projectile; starting with the initial rocket drawings, then upward into the explosion. When you're done, play it back using [Shift Enter]. If you notice any animation problems, stop the playback and address those, then replay and refine some more. If you need to add or reduce exposure to drawings, simply select them in the Timeline and use the [-] and [+] shortcut keys.

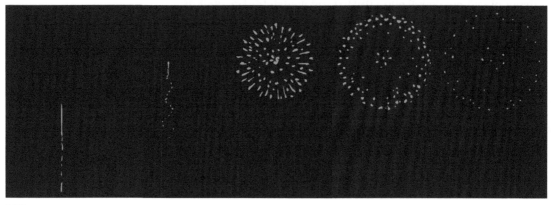

3.115

POSE TO POSE

As the name suggests, this style of animation is roughly sketched as a sequence of key poses. To animate a character dancing or fighting, for example, you'd first draw the key poses of the moves and then work on the exposure timing for each key.

3.116

When the timing is working, you may need to smooth out the movement with one or two extra drawings between the keys. These extra drawings are known as *breakdowns* because they break down the movement.

Pose to Pose is good for predictable actions. With a character movement that you have planned in your head, you can often predict the character's pose before you draw it.

To go back to the much simpler example of a falling object, once the fall is in motion, the object has a predictable end position.

> POSE TO POSE EXERCISE 1
KEY POSING

Let's suppose we have a closed book falling open. In the first key pose the book is lying on its spine, and in the final key pose it's lying open on the table.

> 1. Start a new throwaway scene called 'bookOpen'.

> 2. Rename the default layer 'rough'.

> 3. Grab the Brush from the toolbar, and a sketching colour from the Colour panel.

> 4. On three single keyframes, sketch the poses of the book:

- standing on its end;

- open on the desk with some pages yet to fall;

- lying open on the table, all pages settled.

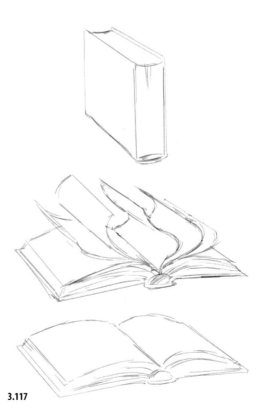

3.117

EXPOSURE TIMING

Once the key drawings are done, you're ready for the process of timing: adding exposure to each pose in the Timeline. Three singles will be way too fast for this movement. Realistically, the front and back covers will start falling slowly and speed up slightly until they hit the desk.

In your mind, visualise and play back the natural motion. Use your mind's stopwatch to guess how long you think it should take. Half a second? A whole second? Maybe a gigantic wizard's book takes more than a second to open, while a smaller book might only take a few frames. You could even grab a camera and record your own reference to study the real life motion and count the frames.

>POSE TO POSE EXERCISE 2
TIMING

In this exercise, we'll work on the timing for the book poses you did in the previous exercise. If you'd like to use my key poses, you can open up the bookOpen scene from this chapter's download files and follow along.

> 1. In the Timeline, right-click the book's first key pose and choose Exposure → Set Exposure…

> 2. Enter your desired exposure value and click 'OK' (I set mine to 10). Your first key now has its new exposure, and the other drawings have been shifted along to make room.

> 3. Add exposure to the two remaining keys. Try to guess how long each key will need before the next comes in. Using your intuition then testing it with a playback helps you develop your sense of timing.

As shown in Figure 3.120 I've added exposure to each keyframe for what I think might be natural falling, impact and settle speeds for this large book. For traditional animators, I've started the timing charts with circled keyframe numbers.

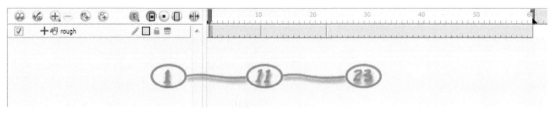

3.120

TIP

Circled in Figure 3.118 is a handy Timeline button you should add if you like to use this method of timing. Rather than right-clicking a frame to change its exposure, you can select a frame and hit this button.

3.118

To add it to the Timeline toolbar, do the following:

1.   Right-click the Timeline toolbar and choose Customize…

2.   In the left-hand pane, scroll down to find Set Exposure.

3.   Click the right-facing triangle to add it to the toolbar and click 'OK'.

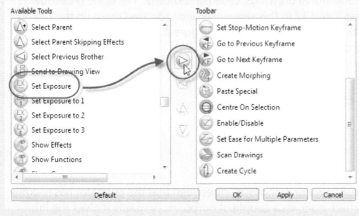

3.119

Now, whenever you want to add a specific exposure value, simply select the drawing in the Timeline and click this button.

Drawing 1 is the first keyframe and is exposed for ten frames. The second drawing sits on frame 11, so it's numbered 11 and is exposed for a further 12 frames. Finally, the last drawing is on frame 23, so it's numbered 23 and is exposed until the end of the scene.

TIMING CHARTS

In the days of traditional animation, we needed to draw the *timing charts*, or *inbetween scales* on each key (illustrated in Figure 3.120). This important step is so the inbetweener knows in what order to create the inbetween drawings. If you're not familiar with these processes, we'll talk more about inbetweening in just a bit.

NOTE

If you were to play back the book scene now, it wouldn't appear natural because there are no inbetween drawings to smooth out the action. Even so, if you watch it a few times, it's easy to mentally fill in the motion as it plays. As you work on a scene, it's a good habit to watch it play as often as possible so you can visualise and refine as you go.

At this point, the animator decides where to break down the motion with additional drawings, called *breakdowns*. I've done breakdowns for frames 7 and 17 in this sequence, and indicated them on the timing charts with a transversal stroke (Figure 3.121). These are numbered accordingly, but not circled.

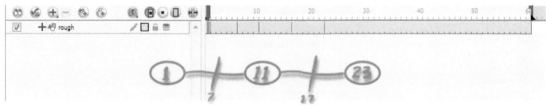

3.121

A breakdown drawing is an inbetween that the animator has roughly sketched. It serves a couple of purposes: primarily it gives the inbetweener a helping hand and clarifies the animator's intentions. It also smooths out the play test for a better glimpse of how the motion looks.

The heavy covers of the book will fall open faster, but a few pages will open a bit slower because they're light and floaty. Later in this section we'll talk about smoothing out the motion with some inbetweening. Figure 3.122 shows the remaining strokes on the timing chart each representing a drawing with its frame number.

3.122

The length of the strokes indicates which inbetweens are drawn first. For example, in the first set (frames 1–11), breakdown 7 is done first, followed by 5 and then 3 and 9. This order of inbetweens determines the easing and is decided by the animator in the timing process.

CLEANUP

At some point you need your rough sketches turned into clean line drawings. Typically, in a collaborative studio environment with special-ised artistic departments, the animator's rough drawings are turned into clean line drawings by an assistant animator, sometimes called a cleanup artist.

In Toon Boom, as you saw with your fireball scene, rough animation can be done on its own layer, then cleaned up and inbetweened on a separate layer. This is the suggested workflow for Animate users.

In Animate Pro and Harmony, while you could do it in the same way, you also have the sub-layer options. The rough animation can be done on the Underlay sub-layer, while the cleanup is done on the Line sub-layer. Any notes or timing charts may be done on the Overlay.

> CLEANUP EXERCISE 1
  CLEANUP WITH THE LIGHT TABLE

A cleanup artist only cleans the key poses and – depending on the studio or the animator – may clean up the breakdowns too.

> 1.   If you animated your own book in the previous exercises, you can use that here. Otherwise, you can use bookOpen_cleanup provided in the chapter files.

> 2.   Create a new layer called 'clean' and, in the Timeline, make sure it's above the 'rough' layer. Select the first frame of this layer, ready to clean up

> 3.   With the drawing tool of your choice, start tracing the first rough key drawing onto your clean layer.

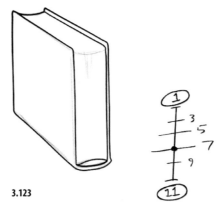

3.123

NOTE

If you're finding it difficult to see your rough layer, it could be that you have the Light Table on and it's faded. You could give your sketch colours a higher Alpha value so they're not so transparent, or if the Light Table is on, you can disable it. Both will help.

To turn the Light Table off: use the ▦ icon at the bottom of the Camera View and uncheck Light Table in the menu.

> 4. Continue your cleanup of the keys. Be ever mindful of closing gaps, as this linework will need filling with paint, eventually. Show strokes with [K] to see where you have gaps in the linework.

> 5. Draw the timing charts on each key too (see Figure 3.123); the inbetweener will need those. Draw them outside the movie border so they don't show up in the final render.

> 6. When cleanup is complete, hide the original rough sketches layer so they don't cause visual interference when inbetweening.

ANIMATE PRO & HARMONY ONLY
If you've used the Overlay and/or Underlay sub-layer for your rough keys and timing charts, you can now hide these sub-layers as follows:

> 1. In the Timeline, select the layer of your book animation.

> 2. In the Layer Properties panel, go to the Drawing tab.

> 3. Uncheck the Underlay and Overlay layers to hide them from the scene.

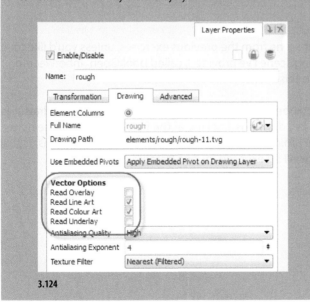

3.124

Now that all the rough animation is hidden, the scene only has clean linework and timing charts for when the inbetweener takes the reins.

INBETWEENING

If you want to be an animator and you're lucky enough to land a trainee position in an animation studio, chances are you'll be trained in inbetweening first. It's the starting point from which you learn about every other department and the entire process of animation.

Many inbetweeners aspire to become animators, while some are happy to settle into a career of inbetweening. To maintain high quality for the long term takes a special kind of inbetweener.

The inbetweener is the heavy lifter of animation. The line mileage must be high in both quality and quantity. It involves doing all the drawings between the key poses, so the movement is smooth and natural.

Let's continue the opening book scene by inbetweening it.

> ### POSE TO POSE EXERCISE 3
> INBETWEENING

Open up your scene from the previous exercises, unless you'd like to use the starting scene I've provided, called bookOpen_inbetweening. You'll find it in this chapter's file downloads.

To prepare for inbetweening, the first step is to create empty drawings between the key drawings. Looking at the first key drawing, the numbering on the timing chart is in two-frame increments. This tells us that each drawing will be exposed for two frames.

> 1. In the Timeline, select frame 7 of the clean book layer and click the Create Empty Drawing button (Figure 3.125). The shortcut key is [Alt Shift R].

3.125

> 2. Do the same for frames 3, 5 and 9.

Once this is done, the first inbetween set of your clean book layer should have a bunch of blank drawings – like blank pieces of paper – ready for inbetweens.

> 3. Move the Playhead to frame 1 (Figure 3.126) and look at the timing chart.

3.126

According to the timing chart, the first inbetween to be done here is the drawing on frame 7 because it has the longest line.

> 4. Select frame 7 of the clean layer and clean up the drawing. If you're using the provided scene file, you should use the Pencil tool with the settings shown in Figure 3.127.

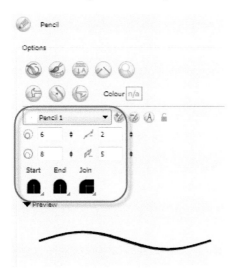

3.127

> 5. Once again, go back to look at the timing chart on drawing 1. The next inbetween is frame 5, which is a halfway drawing between 1 and 7.

> 6. In the Timeline, select frame 5 and drag the Onion Skin handles to cover frames 1 to 7 (Figure 3.128).

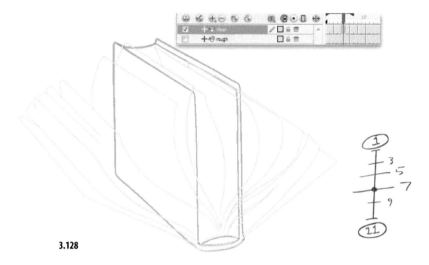

3.128

> 7. Draw the frame 5 inbetween. Sometimes if the inbetween isn't an easy one, it helps to do a rough sketch first.

> 8. Yet again, revisit frame 1 to look at the timing chart. Now that frame 5 is done, frame 3 is the next inbetween to be done.

> 9. Select frame 3 and adjust the Onion Skin handles so they only cover frames 1 to 5.

> 10. Repeat the steps for the frame 3 inbetween.

> 11. Finally, select frame 9 in the Timeline.

> 12. This drawing is an inbetween of 7 and 11, so adjust the onionskin handles to only cover drawings 7–11.

> 13. Complete the inbetween for frame 9.

> 14. Scrub the Timeline back and forth, step through the keys with [F] and [G], or use the jog wheel to watch the animation.

If you'd like to go ahead and do the next set of inbetweens from 11–23, just follow the same steps. The first inbetween, frame 17, has a break-down sketch. Wasn't it nice of the animator to provide that?

Once all the inbetweening is done, providing all the linework is closed, the scene is ready to paint. Feel free to go ahead with that using what you learned in the previous chapter.

FRAME-BY-FRAME SUMMARY

Because we don't have unlimited pages in this book, take a look at Appendix A in which I introduce you to some really awesome specialised tools for advanced inbetweening and traditional animation workflows.

One of these is the X-sheet view. It's a fundamental part of traditional animation but because it's so vast and specialised, I only mention it briefly throughout this book where necessary.

The other is called Shift and Trace, which is a handy interface designed to make complex inbetweens much easier.

PEG ANIMATION

Earlier you learned that the Peg is a *movement layer* to which you attach drawing layers. A fireball cycle was animated in place and then attached to a Peg layer. The Peg was then keyframed across the scene taking the fireball cycle with it.

Pegs are also suitable for transforming non-animated art, like a rising moon, a spinning wheel or an entire background. In fact, when it comes to animating cutout characters in the puppet style, you could have every limb segment controlled by its own Peg.

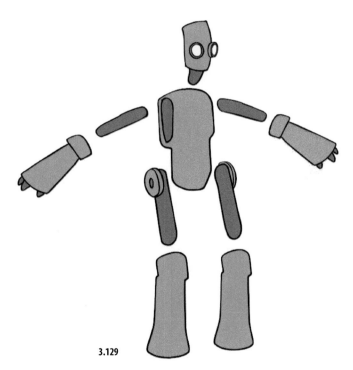

3.129

KEYFRAMES AND INTERPOLATION

When animated, Pegs take numerical values from one keyframe and transition them into values on another keyframe. When two keyframes are set, the position value of the first keyframe will gradually transition into the position value of the next. In the Timeline, the gradual interpolation between them is marked by a horizontal line (Figure 3.130).

3.130

EASING

Any motion you add between keyframes is completely linear at first, and you may need to add your own custom easing. Just like the Drawing layers, you can expand the transform values of a Peg layer to see the parameters that you can animate. Once values have been keyframed and values entered, double-clicking any of these parameters will bring up the easing graph for the layer.

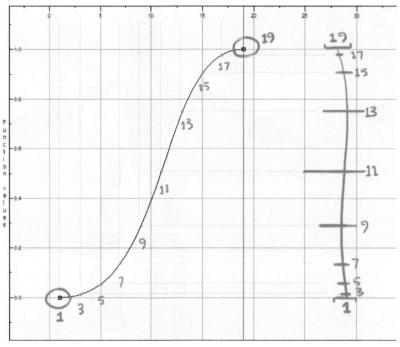

3.131

For traditional animators still coming to grips with the software, you may initially find a line graph confusing. There is another way to look at it though. In this figure you can see exactly how a graph translates to a traditional hand-drawn timing chart. The only real difference is that the first key is on the bottom and the next key is at the top. Hopefully this image also explains to digital animators exactly what a timing chart means.

SET EASE FOR MULTIPLE PARAMETERS

There is a simplified easing graph, accessible from the Timeline, which allows you to set ease on several parameters at once. You'll find it by right-clicking any layer and choosing Set Ease for Multiple Parameters.

There's also a button you can add to the Timeline toolbar. If you can't see the 'Set Ease for Multiple Parameters' button, open the Timeline's toolbar manager (right-click the Timeline toolbar and choose Customise…) find the button in the left-hand list and add it to the toolbar using the right-facing triangle button (Figure 3.132).

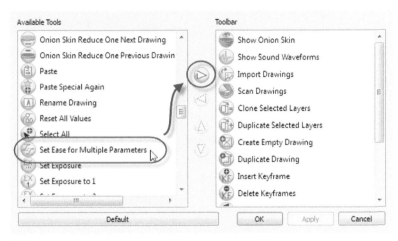

3.132

If you can't find the Timeline toolbar, you can also turn it on via Windows → Toolbars → Timeline View (Figure 3.133).

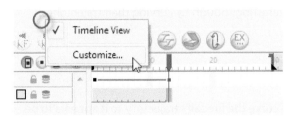

3.133

With this fairly self-explanatory easing interface, the parameters you selected in the Timeline are shown. If you selected the whole Peg, or Drawing layer, then this window displays all of the parameters for transforming. You can apply easing to multiple parameters at once, or

isolate any of them using the checkboxes. Click Apply/Next to advance
through the keys, or Apply/Previous to go back.

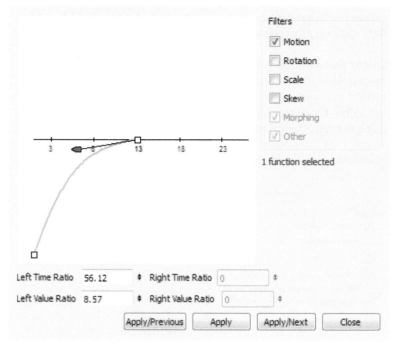

3.134

TRAJECTORIES

When we first talked about Pegs back on page 177, the fireball exercise
stepped you through creating a straight-line path. We can make these
paths much more interesting though by curving their trajectories.

> PEG ANIMATION EXERCISE 1
  TRAJECTORIES

In this exercise you'll curve the fireball's trajectory so it appears to be
thrown in an arc. If you'd like to use my fireball scene file, you'll find it in
this chapter's download files. It's called fireball_trajec.

As we work on the fireball trajectory, the background and camera
movement may be a little distracting, so let's turn those off first.

> 1.   In the Timeline, uncheck the background and the Camera to turn off those layers.

> 2.   In the Timeline, select frame 1 of the Fireball-P layer (the Peg).

> 3.   Grab the Translate tool [Alt 2]. The Translate handles appear on the fireball.

WARNING
Is the fireball – or the box around it – pink? If so, you have the colourFireball layer selected! You don't want that for this exercise. You need to select the Peg layer. When the Peg layer is selected in Animate Mode, the fireball or box around it should have a yellow tint, or yellow bounding box as shown in Figure 3.135.

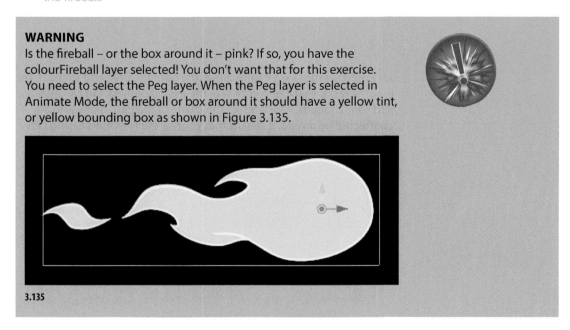

3.135

Now let's Show Control so we can see the Peg's trajectory.

> 4.   With the fireball's Peg selected in the Timeline, press [Shift F11], or go to View → Show → Control.

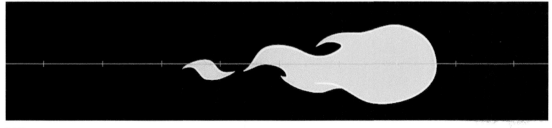

3.136

The Peg trajectory appears, complete with strokes representing frames. If you haven't added any easing to the fireball, the strokes are evenly spaced along the perfectly straight line, making a very consistent movement. Choose the Select tool from the toolbar so the translate handles disappear. Now, as you scrub the Playhead back and forth, you will see that the current frame is highlighted on the trajectory with a tiny bright green marker (Figure 3.136).

TRAJECTORY CONTROL POINTS

We could set more keyframes along the path to curve and shape it, but in some tasks, that can complicate the easing process. We can instead add *control points*, which affect the shape of the path alone and are unaffected by timing. It means that your carefully crafted easing can be independent of the trajectory!

> PEG ANIMATION EXERCISE 2
  CONTROL POINTS

> 1. In the Timeline, select the fireball's Peg layer.

> 2. Make sure you can see the trajectory. If not, press [Shift F11].

> 3. Select the Transform tool, or any of the Advanced Animation tools.

> 4. With one of these tools, hover the cursor over the trajectory and press [P] on your keyboard to add a control point. Simple as that!

3.137

> 5. Using the Transform or one of the Advanced Animation tools, move the control point around to watch the trajectory changing.

A fireball thrown by a wizard may have a natural arc, just like a javelin or baseball. However, feel free to experiment by adding more control points for a more complex path.

> 6. Delete any unwanted control points simply by selecting them and hitting your keyboard's [Delete] key.

3.138

If you now expand and double-click the Peg's velocity parameter in the Timeline, the easing graph will show you this movement has only two keyframes. You can now apply independent easing to this trajectory and even add extra keyframes for more interesting timing.

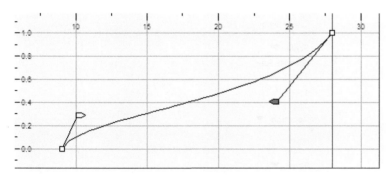

3.139

CONVERTING CONTROL POINTS TO KEYFRAMES

There may be times when you want to convert one or more of your control points into keyframes so that you can apply specific easing at that part of the trajectory. The Locked in Time feature was made for this purpose.

> PEG ANIMATION EXERCISE 3
  CONTROL POINTS LOCKED IN TIME

Locked in Time is really just another way of saying 'convert control point to keyframe'. Once you grow comfortable working with control points you might like to keep the Coordinates and Control Points panel (Figure 3.140) within reach. As always, you'll find this in the panel menu ⬇.

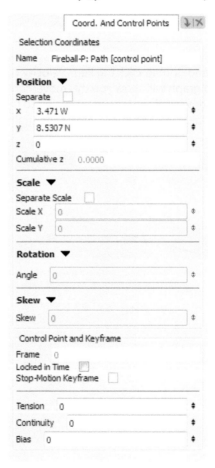

3.140

NOTE

If you find yourself doing a lot of work with control points, there is a condensed version of the Coordinates and Control Points panel in the form of two small toolbars. You can access them via Windows → Toolbars → Coordinate, and Windows → Toolbars → Control Points (Figure 3.141). Once added, these will appear at the top of the program window along with your other toolbars, and they can be positioned and docked to your liking.

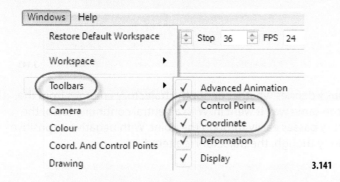

3.141

The Coordinates and Control Points panel gives you ultra-fine control over your points. The one we're looking for here is the Locked in Time checkbox (Figure 3.142). This converts the selected Control Point to a keyframe which then appears on the Timeline and has its own tangent handles in the easing graph.

3.142

Also worth noting is that the selected control point's coordinates are listed in the Position section of the panel.

TENSION, CONTINUITY, BIAS

Unlike vector points and function keyframes, control points don't have handles to help you alter the trajectory. However, there are three parameters you can adjust, should you need that fine level of control. The T, C and B fields can be found in the control points toolbar and at the bottom of the Coordinate and Control Point panel. All three parameters have a default value of zero and take inputs between -1 and +1.

Tension controls how tight the angle is. At the maximum tension of +1, the trajectory is pinched to a tight corner. At -1, it's a nice easy curve.

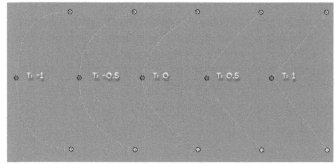

3.143

Continuity defines whether or not the trajectory emerges from the point the same way it went in. With a neutral continuity (zero) the trajectory passes easily through the point. With negative or positive continuity though, the trajectory is altered.

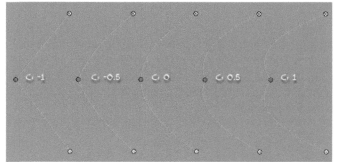

3.144

Bias is the side that the curve favours. With a negative value, the bias favours the left side of the point, while a positive favours the right.

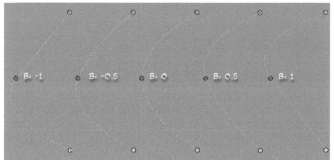

3.145

OFFSETTING THE TRAJECTORY

With the fireball's Peg trajectory visible, you may find it gets in the way. You could always hide the control altogether using [Shift C] but if you still want it to be onscreen, you can move it aside using the Spline Offset tool. This is the last of the Advanced Animation tools.

3.146

It's a tool dedicated to moving trajectories around. With any trajectory visible, simply select that layer in the Timeline, then with the Spline Offset tool, drag anywhere in the Camera View to move the trajectory around.

Crucially you'll notice that the Peg's pivot point remains where you left it.

TRAJECTORIES IN Z-SPACE

A final point about trajectories is that they can have depth. In the Top View, you can manipulate control points and keyframes on a trajectory so that the object travels along a 3D path. This is ideal not just for novelties like a helical trajectory (Figure 3.147), which you might create for rising bubbles, or a character being whipped up into a tornado, but any object or character that moves away or toward camera.

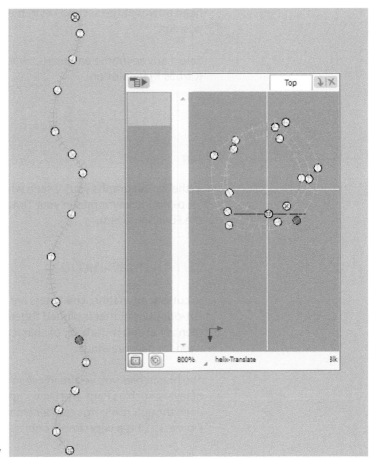

3.147

MOTION AND STOP-MOTION KEYFRAMES

In the Timeline, you know that the line drawn between keyframes indicates motion, or a gradual transitioning, or interpolation, from one parameter value to another.

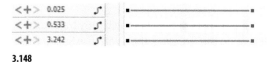

3.148

We love our Motion keyframes dearly but from time to time you'll want two keyframes without motion between them. For example, if you want a sorceress to magically 'pop' from one side of the scene to the other with no inbetween motion, you can set the first keyframe to be Stop-Motion. This will keep her in place and then when the Play-head arrives at the second keyframe, she instantly appears at the new position.

Select any keyframe and use [Ctrl/⌘ L] to set it to Stop-Motion or [Ctrl/⌘ K] for Motion.

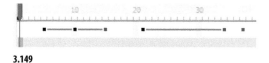

3.149

In the easing graphs you've seen what motion looks like. Create some Stop-Motion keyframes in your Timeline and then check them out in the Function editor.

CUT-OUT ANIMATION

In cut-out animation, characters are drawn in segments, like a paper cut-out puppet that is pinned together at the joints. Maximising segmentation and reusability of character parts, this style minimises the need for new drawings.

The hierarchies you've already seen are the parent–child relationship of layers, such as Pegs and Drawings. Cut-out hierarchies are the same, even though some rigs can become very complex. The hierarchy in Figure 3.151 is a very simple one!

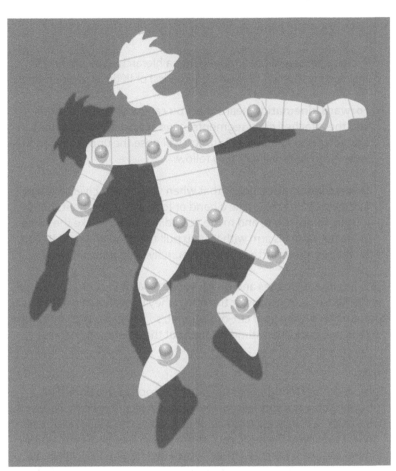

3.150

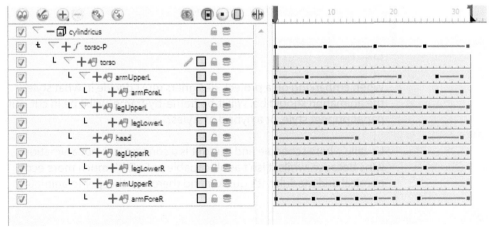

3.151

WHAT ARE FK AND IK?

With character segments arranged into a hierarchy, you are fully set up to animate in either FK (forward kinematics) or IK (inverse kinematics).

- **Forward kinematics** means that you can move a *parent* segment, and the attached child segments move accordingly. To animate a character raising his arm then, you will pose the upper arm, and the lower segments will naturally follow.

- **Inverse kinematics** means that when you move a *child* segment at the *end of the chain*, like a hand or foot, all the segments above it (shin, thigh) rotate and move accordingly. So to make the same character raise his arm with IK, you pull the hand and raise it high. All the segments further up the hierarchy will rotate naturally.

Each has its advantages and disadvantages. Most importantly, you're not locked in to using one or the other; they're really just two different methods for posing your cut-out puppet, so you can switch from using FK to IK and back at any time throughout the animation process.

NOTE
Complex character rigging is beyond the scope of this book. Full cut-out rigging is a specialised, technical subject. This book would be twice as thick if we were to cover all of it. What you'll learn in this section will show you the basics of cut-out hierarchies and some simple rigging exercises. There is a more substantial rigging project ahead starting on page 273 and you can study the nitty-gritty in the Toon Boom documentation [F1] → User Guide → Cut-Out Animation.

DESIGN

When embarking on a project, designers must decide in what style the animation should be. Will it be frame-by-frame, will it be in cut-out paper puppet style, or a hybrid of styles?

Usually where schedule and budget is a concern, cut-out animation wins because, while it isn't as all-capable as F×F, it's much more economical and modular. It's quicker and therefore cheaper to animate.

The majority of the hard work in cut-out animation is in the setup. Much like 3D animation, the characters are designed, modelled, rigged and fully prepped for trouble-free animation, so the animator can concentrate on the puppetry.

The whole idea of the cut-out style is to eliminate drawing from the job of animation. Just like 3D, once the character is rigged, it's all just puppetry.

SEGMENTS

Segmentation is at the heart of the cut-out style. In the following exercise you'll draw an arm in segments and then arrange them in a hierarchy.

>CUT-OUT EXERCISE 1
LIMB SEGMENTS

It's always easier to start animating a character from a boring, neutral pose, rather than from some cool, dynamic pose that may not always be suited to the scene you're animating. If you plan on rigging characters or objects, it's generally good practice to create them in a neutral pose. In 3D, this is called the T-pose or bind pose.

I'll be drawing this arm in a horizontal position. Vertical would also be suitable.

> 1.   Start a new scene called 'hierarchy'.

> 2.   Rename the default layer 'rough' and sketch the arm from shoulder to hand. You might also like to plan the segmentation in your sketch as I've done in Figure 3.152.

3.152

> 3. Add three new layers. This will be a right arm, so I've named the layers arm Upper_R, armFore_R and hand_R.

> 4. In the Timeline, select the first frame of the armUpper_R layer, and do a clean drawing of the upper arm.

NOTE
Good, clear layer naming becomes crucial in character rigging and building hierarchies. A full rig can have dozens within dozens of individual parts and it's important that you're able to easily find any particular segment in the Timeline.

> 5. On the armFore_R Layer, draw the forearm, then draw the hand_R on the hand layer.

> 6. Extend the exposures of all three layers to the end of the scene.

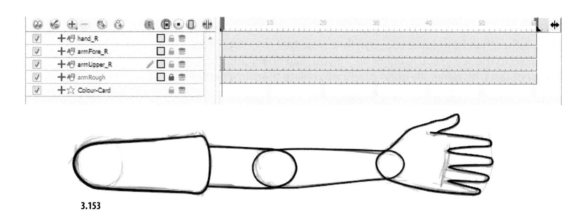

3.153

> 7. Finally, fill each segment with colours of your choice. Don't worry that the parts may appear in the wrong order for now. We'll fix that next.

> CUT-OUT EXERCISE 2
  HIERARCHY

If you'd like a starting file for this exercise, open up hierarchy_arm from the chapter files.

> 1.   In the Timeline, drag the hand_R layer onto the armFore_R layer (Figure 3.154). The hand is now 'parented' to the forearm.

3.154

> 2.   Complete the hierarchy by dragging the armFore_R layer onto armUpper_R.

DEPTH ORDERING

You may notice that once your hierarchy is created, there could be a layer ordering problem. For example, the hand is appearing behind the forearm, but what if the character is wearing a glove? In that case you may want the hand in front of the forearm.

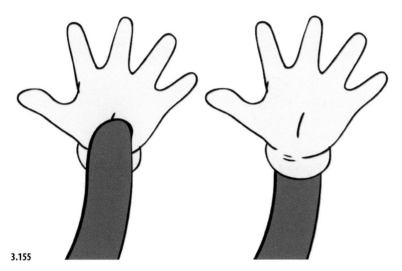

3.155

Animate Pro and Harmony have advanced layer ordering as you'll see in the next chapter. If you're using Animate though, you'll often need to 'nudge' layers backwards and forwards, depending on the segment ordering that your scene requires.

This depth nudging can be keyframed too, so a character can place his hands behind his head, and then in the same scene place them over his mouth, achieved without swapping layers in the Timeline but simply by keyframing the depth order.

> CUT-OUT EXERCISE 3
DEPTH NUDGING

While this method is necessarily used in Animate, it's a handy technique for Animate Pro and Harmony users as well.

> 1. In the Timeline, select the hand_R layer

> 2. In the Coordinate toolbar or panel, set the z (depth) Position value very slightly forward by entering a number greater than zero. Larger numbers will mean a more noticeable distance, so very small numbers are usually best.

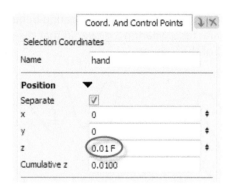

3.156

As shown in Figure 3.156, I've nudged the hand forward 0.01 F. The F here stands simply for 'forward'. You can also nudge elements *back* which are denoted with B.

Entering values into fields will set keyframes on the Timeline, regardless of Animate Mode being on or off.

Once placed correctly into their hierarchies, each of these segments can move and behave in accordance with its connections.

NOTE

Something staring us in the face right now is the fact that no matter what the ordering, the segment outlines are showing. There are a few ways of getting around this, but perhaps the most obvious solution is to simply not have outlines – a lineless style is quite popular in cut-out animation.

If you do have outlines in your work, one particular solution involves 'patching' or covering the lines with a small patch of skin colour on another layer. You can learn about this and other cut-out techniques in the documentation [F1] → User Guide → Character Building.

PIVOT POINTS

In order to have segments rotating properly, it's necessary to place pivots for each of them. If you grab the Rotate tool [Alt 3] and rotate any of the segments, you'll find that they're rotating around a point at the centre of the scene. In this exercise you'll place that rotation point for each segment.

> CUT-OUT EXERCISE 4
  PIVOTS

In the toolbar, there's a dedicated Drawing Pivot tool that looks like a crosshair. This is for precise placement of drawing pivots.

> 1.   From the Tools toolbar, choose the Drawing Pivot tool [Shift P].

> 2.   In the Timeline, select the armUpper_R layer.

> 3.   In the Camera View, click where the shoulder joint would be to place the pivot.

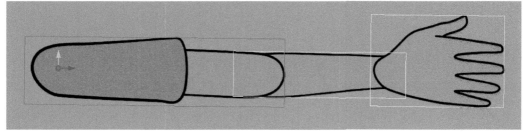

3.157

> 4. Next, select the armFore_R layer and place the Pivot on the elbow.

> 5. Finally on the hand_R layer, place the Pivot at the wrist.

ANIMATION KEYFRAMING

You have just rigged a character limb and the most time-consuming part of this simple rig is complete. In this exercise, we'll start moving it around and take a look at the IK tool's modes and options.

> CUT-OUT EXERCISE 5
INVERSE KINEMATICS

> 1. In the toolbar, make sure Animate Mode is on and then select the IK (inverse kinematics) tool [Shift I].

The bones and joints appear in the Camera View as red kite-shaped wireframes and white circles.

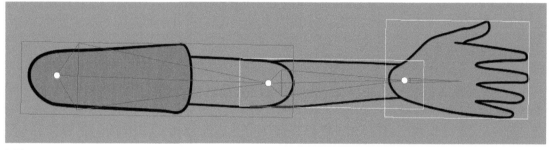

3.158

> 2. Ensure the Playhead is sitting on frame 1.

> 3. Using the IK tool in the Camera View, drag the hand bone around to see the arm bending.

> 4. Hold [Alt] to rotate any bone from its joint without moving its parent.

> 5. [Shift]-click a joint or bone to lock it in place. This activates the 'Nail' constraint (see the IK Tool Properties). [Shift]-click the joint again to unlock it.

> 6. Place the limb in various poses by dragging the other bones and joints.

When you finish dragging, take a look at the Timeline. Because Animate Mode is active, it has automatically set keyframes on each layer.

> 7. In the Timeline, move the Playhead to frame 10.

> 8. In the Camera View, drag the hand to another position. Keyframes will be set on frame 10 for all three layers.

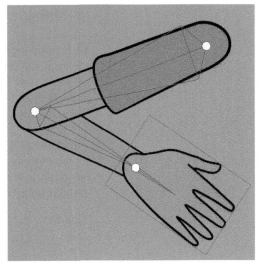

3.159

Go ahead and experiment with some more poses and animation. Why not animate the arm waving? You have already learned how to add easing to layer motion, so you could apply some natural easing on various parts of this arm. Revisit page 204 if you need a refresher on easing.

Finally let's look at some of the IK tool's settings and what they mean.

A. **IK Manipulation** – could possibly be called 'Pose Mode', as it's the main mode you'll use when moving bones and joints for posing.

B. **Apply IK Constraints** – applies selected constraint options (E) for the active bone.

C. **Edit Min/Max Angle** – (Animate Pro and Harmony only) limits how far joints can bend so they don't fold up too far, or bend the wrong way, e.g., knees and elbows.

D. **Bone Editing** – lets you change the angle and size of a bone so it suits the art. Useful for extremities like feet and hand bones.

E. **Constraints** – each of these will constrain the selected bone or joint in some way.

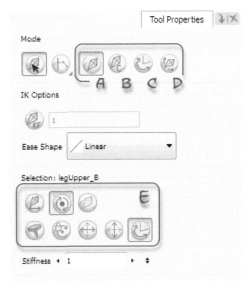

3.160

Coming up on page 273 is a rigging project to which you can apply all that you've learned here.

DRAWING SUBSTITUTION

Each static segment of the arm is on its own Drawing layer, which means it can also contain several frames within it. The hand layer, for example, may contain a number of different hand shapes. This allows you to switch hands during the animation, depending on what the scene requires.

If a character is standing idle, with hands hanging loosely by his sides, then suddenly points at something, you can't very well leave the relaxed hand on the end of his arm. Here you'd want to swap to a hand with finger pointing, so it actually looks natural.

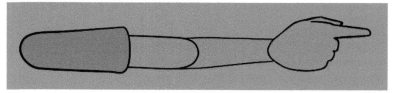

3.161

In limited animation, Drawing substitution is also used for lip-sync. Mouth drawings are swapped in and out to match the dialogue. When the character is making the 'CH' sound, the CH mouth shape is inserted at that frame.

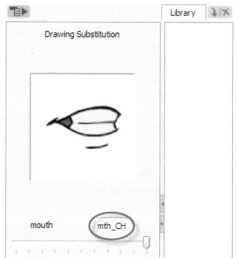

3.162

At the end of this chapter there is an animation project that will have you animating lip sync using Drawing substitution.

MORPHING

As the name implies, the Morphing tool is designed for transitioning one shape into another. It works by animating the *vertices* of the art itself.

Long, slow sequences of very gradual movement are particularly well-suited to morphing. In traditional animation, it's very difficult to create a smooth sequence with perfectly consistent volumes and line widths. Morphing makes this process easier and helps to ensure every drawing in the sequence is consistent.

MORPHING TOOL [F3]

Finally we get to the last tool in the toolbar. The Morphing tool isn't required to create morphing, but you'll need it if you want to control the morphing.

Almost like some kind of robot inbetweener, a morph creates all the drawings between two key poses. A simple ribbon of smoke rising from a dying fire may have several key poses, each morphed into the next. Rather than give this scene to a human inbetweener, it might be quicker and easier to give it to the robot.

Morphing doesn't have a creative mind. It makes purely mathematical decisions on which vertices should move where. For this reason, it often needs your guidance with the Morphing tool.

With the Morphing tool selected in the toolbar, take a look at the options in the Tool Properties panel.

3.163

3.164

Most Morphing options are available only with a morph selected in the Timeline, so let's get started on creating a morph.

RULES OF CONSISTENCY

There are a few rules of consistency to bear in mind for morphing. Most of these will become fairly obvious once you've used the Morphing tool successfully a few times.

- Same colour – you can only morph shapes or lines if they use the same colour swatch. You cannot morph a green shape into a red one, for example. If you want to create colour transitions, you'd use Effects, which we'll cover in the next chapter.

- Shapes and lines – a key pose drawn with line tools (Pencil, Shape, Polyline) can only be morphed with other line drawings. Likewise, drawings created with the Brush tool only morph into other Brush strokes, or other paint shapes.

- Sub-layers – make sure your keys are on the same sub-layer. A morph will not work if one drawing is on the Line sub-layer and the next is on the Colour sub-layer.

- Disappearing and appearing – if the morph doesn't find a corresponding shape in both key drawings, parts of it will either appear or disappear throughout the morph. You can use this to your advantage in some scenes.

- Same layer – morphing only works between drawings on the same layer. You cannot morph a drawing from Layer A into a drawing on Layer B.

- Symbols and drawings –if you have symbols in your layer, you cannot morph them with ordinary drawings. You can however create morphing inside symbols.

SIMPLICITY IS KEY

Morphing almost always works when used on simple art; the fewer vertices, the better. You can still create complex morphs but these generally require more guidance. The more you need to guide it, the more time-consuming and less practical it all becomes.

While morphing the fire drawings in Figure 3.165 is certainly possible, it's definitely much quicker just to draw the inbetween by hand.

3.165

If you plan on using a morph, you should deliberately design your key poses to suit the morph. The first lesson is to keep it simple! The tangled mess in Figure 3.166 is the result of morphing those ill-considered fire drawings.

3.166

> MORPHING EXERCISE 1
  MORPHING SIMPLICITY

For the following exercise I've provided a scene file called morphing_ simple in the chapter files. The steps below are written specifically for this file, but feel free to create your own similar scene and follow along.

> 1.   In the Timeline, select a frame of the first drawing.

> 2.   Right-click the selected frame and choose Morphing → Create Morphing [Alt M]. In Animate Pro and Harmony there's also a handy Create Morphing button in the Timeline toolbar (Figure 3.167).

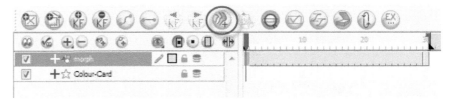

3.167

In the Timeline, the morph appears as a series of arrows between the two drawings (Figure 3.168).

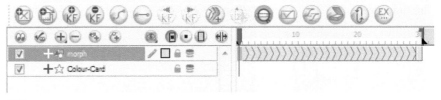

3.168

> 3.   Scrub the Timeline back and forth to watch the morph.

> 4.   Save this scene ready to use in the next exercise.

Really, there's not much that could have gone wrong here. As you can see, we've morphed a very simple shape into another and it has worked perfectly well. The interesting thing here is that before we applied the morph, we weren't really sure how it would turn out. We merely hoped that the robot would do a good job and the result was a mild surprise. 'Oh look, the points rotate slightly. That's nice.'

What if you didn't want this though? Suppose that instead of pulling slightly anti-clockwise into the circle, you wanted each point of the star to roll *clockwise*? Or do something entirely different?

The Morphing tool provides you this type of creative control so let's now look at how that works.

MORPHING HINTS

When the software guesses how and where to move vertices throughout a morphing sequence, it will sometimes get it right and sometimes get it wrong. The Morphing tool is essentially a guidance system to help you guide the morph whenever it guesses wrong.

In the parts where a morph isn't quite working, you can place a hint in the first drawing on the problem area. Then, in the second drawing, you place a corresponding hint where you want it to be at the end of the morph.

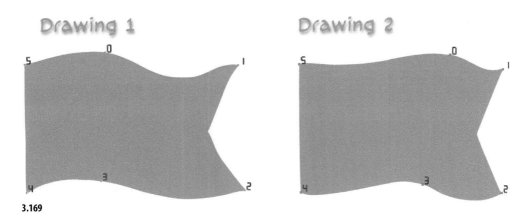

3.169

In Figure 3.169, the first drawing has hints placed at key points on the flag. The second drawing has corresponding hints guiding the morph so the flag moves as the animator intended.

> MORPHING EXERCISE 2
  HINTS

In the morphing_simple scene file, let's make those star arms move in a different way using hints.

3.170

> 1. Scrub the Timeline back and forth to remind yourself of how the morph looks without any guidance.

> 2. Select the Morphing tool from the toolbar. Cast your eye over the Morphing tool properties in the Properties panel.

> 3. In the Timeline, select frame 1. This is the first key drawing.

> 4. In the Camera View with the Morphing tool, click to place your first hint.

> 5. You can now drag it and it will snap to the art. Position it on the top point of the star.

This places your first hint, labelled 0 (zero). It's green, indicating that this is a starting hint.

3.171

> 6. In the Timeline select your second drawing at the end of the scene.

At this point, the hint you're seeing in the Camera View is red, indicating that it's a *destination* hint.

> 7. Now position the destination hint where you'd like that star point to move to.

Scrub the Timeline once again to watch the morph doing something completely different.

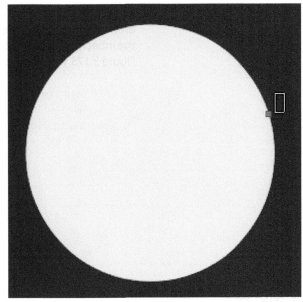

3.172

TIP
When working with morphing hints, you can select the morph in the Timeline, then use the [F4] key to toggle back and forth between your key drawings..

> MORPHING EXERCISE 3
MORPHING MULTIPLE KEYS

Morphing a star into a circle isn't really that impressive, so let's do something a little more interesting. In this exercise you'll create a number of key poses and then apply morphing between each of them.

If you'd like a starting file with key poses already done, open up morphing_smoke from the morphing_simple folder.

> 1. In the Timeline, add a new layer called 'smoke'.

> 2. If you're not using the provided file, use the Brush tool and a colour of your choice to animate several key poses of a rising smoke ribbon.

Just as you would for a human inbetweener, consider carefully each drawing and how it relates to the previous pose and the next. Make sure the inbetweener can easily understand how the smoke should move. In Figure 3.173 you can see how there's a certain flow in the key drawings.

> 3. On each key drawing, fill the smoke with paint so that each pose is a flat, solid area of colour. For now, resist the temptation to add more colours or any detail to the smoke.

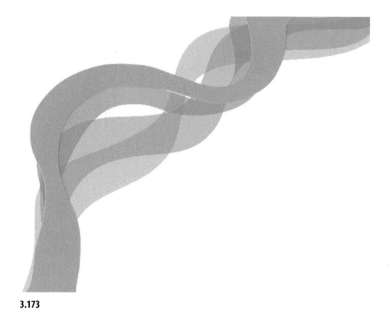

3.173

> 4. Extend the exposures so that, together, the drawings span the length of the scene.

> 5. In the same way you applied the morph in the first exercise, do so between each key pose of the smoke. That is, select the exposure of each drawing, then hit the Create Morphing button, or [Alt M].

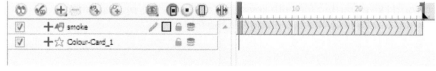

3.175

> 6. Scrub the Timeline or hit [Shift Enter] to watch the results.

TIP

It's a good idea to flatten your drawings before you use morphing. It's not always necessary but it reduces the number of strokes and vertices, thereby reducing the chance of tangled morphs.

3.174

You could work with Auto-Flatten turned on in the Brush properties. To flatten a finished drawing, first drag a selection around it in the Camera or Drawing View using the Select tool. Then choose Drawing → Optimize → Flatten [Alt Shift F], or simply hit the Flatten button in the Select tool properties under Operations (see Figure 3.174).

If you're incredibly lucky or you've just been very careful with your key drawings, maybe everything moves perfectly. Chances are that there are some tangles here and there, or bits that don't move quite the way you'd like.

> 7. For each problem area, identify which part could benefit from a hint or two, apply them and scrub again.

The process of guiding a morph to perfection takes some time, but it's nowhere near the amount of time it would take to draw those inbetweens by hand.

HINT TYPES

The hints you've used so far are contour hints, placed on the perimeter of the shapes. In the properties panel you can see this option, and the other hint types behind it.

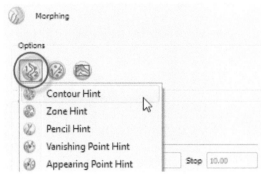

3.176

- Contour hints – these are placed on paint edges, including inner edges and colour borders within a drawing.

- Zone hints – place zone hints in areas to influence the surrounding area, rather than edges.

- Pencil hints – these are specifically for use with lines drawn with the Pencil, Shape and Polyline tools.

- Vanishing point hints –in the case of something that exists in pose 1, but is gone in pose 2, these Hints tell pieces of the drawing where to vanish.

- Appearing point hints – converse to the vanishing point hint; define the point where art missing from pose 1 will appear in pose 2.

MORPH EASING

There are a couple of ways to ease your morphing. The first is found within easy reach at the bottom of the Morphing tool properties. Knowing what you already know about easing graphs, there's not much to say about this one; only that it's very limited and as you adjust the values, there's a small line representation of the easing as a visual aid.

The second, more powerful way is via the Velocity editor's easing graph.

> MORPHING EXERCISE 4
  MORPHING VELOCITY

> 1. In the Timeline, select any frame of a morph.

> 2. In the Layer Properties panel, go to the Drawing tab and scroll all
      the way to the bottom. If you're using Animate, you'll find this at the
      bottom of the Advanced tab.

3.177

> 3. Click the function curve button shown in Figure 3.177 to create a
      function curve for the Morphing Velocity.

> 4. Click the button a second time to open the graph.

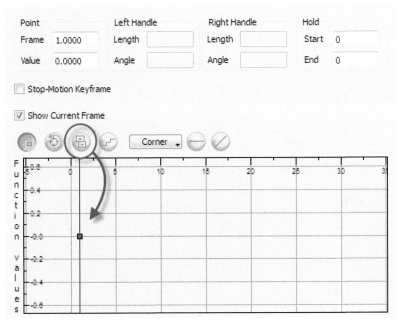

3.178

> 5. Move the playhead to frame 1 and, in the Velocity editor, add a
      keyframe with the add/remove keyframe button (see Figure 3.178).

> 6. In the Timeline, move the playhead to the end of the scene, then once again click the add/remove keyframe button to add that second keyframe.

> 7. Enter 1 into the Value field and the diagonal line appears with handles, ready for easing (Figure 3.179). You can pan and zoom in the graph view using [1], [2] and [Spacebar].

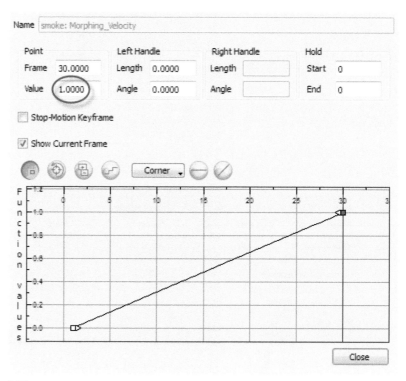

3.179

NOTE
This has applied a single curve over the entire length of the scene. Using the add/remove keyframe button (see Figure 3.178), you can add more keyframes on the line for easing individual morphing sequences between particular drawings.

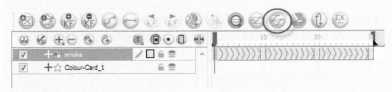

3.180

Also worth noting is that by creating a function curve, you can now use Set Ease for Multiple Parameters, which you saw earlier in the Peg layers section.

A WORD ON MORPHING LAYERS

The middle section of the Morphing tool properties is dedicated to Morphing Layers. This gives you the ability to separate layers of motion within a single drawing; kind of like a timeline within a timeline. All of this is controlled from within the Morphing tool properties panel.

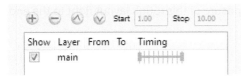

3.181

However, for most users, especially if you're just getting comfortable with the main Timeline, it's quite painful to try to learn a new visually and functionally different Timeline.

For this reason, we'll skip this section. If you'd like to read up and learn to use Morphing Layers, you'll find it in the Toon Boom documentation [F1] → User Guide → Morphing Chapter →Morphing → Morphing Layers.

ANIMATION PROJECTS

We've almost reached the end of the animation chapter, so now's the time to practise what you've learned by completing a few simple projects. Each of these will have you calling upon what you learned in this chapter and the previous one.

Every step in these projects has been covered so far in the book and there are page references throughout, in case you need to revisit topics covered previously.

ANIMATION PROJECT 1: FRAME-BY-FRAME ANIMATION

In this animation project you'll use drawing tools, frame-by-frame animation, Peg animation, trajectories and a mask layer. You'll create a scene in which a balloon rises and bumps against the angled ceiling a few times before escaping through an open skylight. When you think about it, this gentle upward bump-bump motion is merely a slow-motion, upside-down ball bounce.

> PROJECT 1 – STEP 1
  SCENE SETUP

Start a new scene file and increase the scene length to 200 frames. Rename the default layer 'bg_layout' and draw a rough layout of your background. Extend the exposure of this rough layout right to the end of the scene.

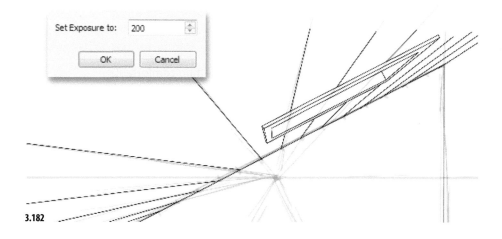

3.182

> PROJECT 1 – STEP 2
  ANIMATION LAYOUT

Add a new Layer called 'anim_layout' and draw rough layout poses for the balloon and string positions throughout the scene.

The layout artist is not an animator! So there's no need to add timing at the layout stage. You're just putting in the rough balloon positions for the scene with just a few key poses, as shown in Figure 3.183. It's very common for the animator to deviate from layout poses, as they're merely a guide for scene composition.

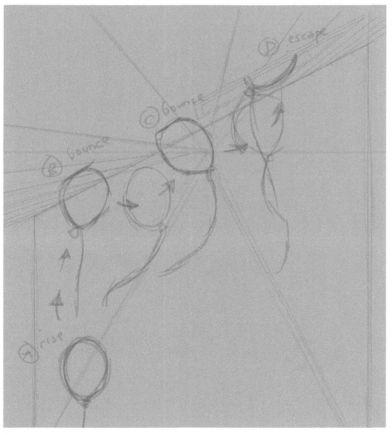

3.183

> PROJECT 1 – STEP 3
  BALLOON SETUP

On a new layer called 'balloon', draw and fully colour your balloon. I've used the Ellipse shape tool, and then manipulated the vertices with the Contour Editor [Alt Q] before adding the knot with the Pencil tool.

In the Timeline, extend the balloon's exposure to the end of the scene. Select the balloon layer and then click the ⚙ Add Peg button. In the Timeline, select the new balloon Peg, then in the Camera View use the Translate tool [Alt 2] to drag the pivot to the centre of the balloon. Revisit page 79 to revise pivots.

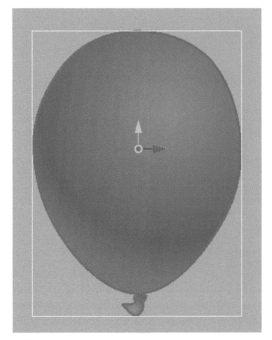

3.184

> PROJECT 1 – STEP 4
  BALLOON ANIMATION

In the Timeline, select frame 1 of the balloon's Peg. Turn on Animate Mode and, in the Camera View, use the Translate tool [Alt 2] to set the balloon's first key position. Position the Playhead to where you'd like the next keyframe and move the balloon into its second pose.

Add keyframes for the bounces, show the trajectory (Shift F11) and bend the path with Control Points. Remember you can set the Tension values on those Control Points for sharp corners in the trajectory (see page 241). Finally, expand the Peg layer and add a function curve to the Velocity so you can apply easing for each bounce.

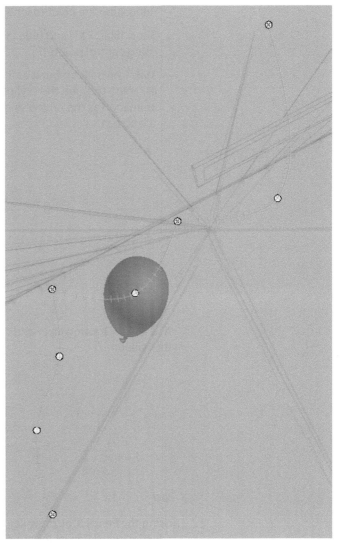

3.185

TIP

Where necessary, you should feel free to:

- Use other Advanced Animation tools, or just use the Transform tool.

- Either use [F6] in the Timeline to create keyframes on the Peg layer, or just let Animate Mode set keyframes automatically as you move the balloon.

- Reposition the pivot to wherever you think it works best.

- Show [Shift F11] and hide [Shift C] the trajectory and practise using control points [P].

- Make the balloon burst as it touches a nail or splinter, instead of escaping through the skylight. This will require frame-by-frame animation as the rubber and string (see next step) fall down off the screen.

3.186

> PROJECT 1 – STEP 5
  STRING ANIMATION

Add a new Drawing layer and call it 'string'. Parent the string layer to the balloon.

3.187

Using the Pencil tool, draw key poses of the string on fours or eights, taking care to keep its length consistent. Apply a morph between the key poses, adding Pencil hints, easing and timing adjustments where necessary (see page 253).

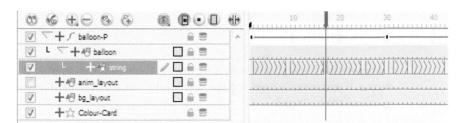

3.188

You'll note in Figure 3.188 that I've got extra drawings in the morph, right where the bounces take place. This is where I've animated the string reacting to the bounce. To convert a morph to drawings so you can hand-tweak and manipulate them, just right-click the morph in the Timeline and choose → Morphing → Convert Morphing to Drawings.

> PROJECT 1 - STEP 6
MASK

If you're using Animate Pro or Harmony feel free to skip this step, as you'll be using Cutters in the next chapter. As suggested back in step 4, you may instead like to animate the balloon bursting as it touches a nail or splinter.

If you're using Animate, add a Mask to the Timeline and then create artwork for the skylight that cuts off the balloon as it escapes (reference masking on page 188).

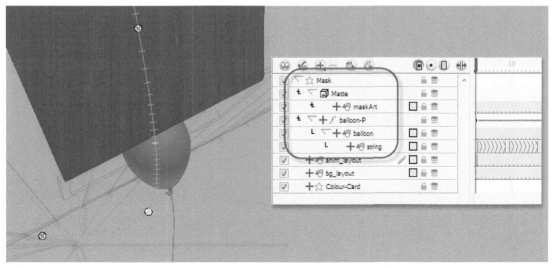

3.189

> PROJECT 1 – STEP 7
  BACKGROUND

Complete the background with the drawing tools and colours of your choice. If you're really enjoying the scene, why not add a camera move to follow the balloon?

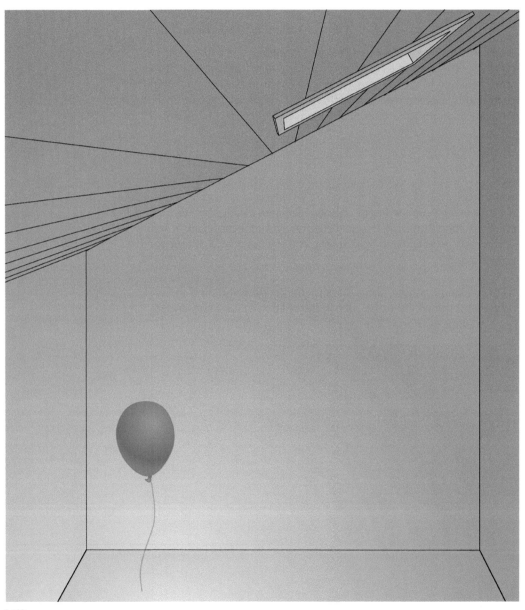

3.190

ANIMATION PROJECT 2: SIMPLE RIGGING

In this project you'll practise what you learned about hierarchies to build a partial character rig. As mentioned earlier, rigging is a huge subject that we can't completely cover in this book. This project won't have you fully rigging a character, but it'll get you started with just a couple of limbs.

>PROJECT 2 – STEP 1
SCENE SETUP

Create a new scene file called 'eyebot' with the resolution of your choice. In the Timeline, rename the default Timeline layer 'rough'. For now, set the scene length to one frame via Scene → Scene Length… Later when you start animating the rig, you'll lengthen the scene.

>PROJECT 2 – STEP 2
ROUGH SKETCH

In the rough layer, sketch a walking pose of a two-legged robot as shown in Figure 3.191. As you can see, this simple machine is a spherical body on two legs … probably piloted by a tiny supervillain.

>PROJECT 2 – STEP 3
LAYERS AND SEGMENTS

In the Timeline, add new Drawing layers for the body and the leg segments for one leg only – later we'll duplicate one leg to make the other. I've named the leg segments with '_F' because it's the front (nearest) leg.

3.191

3.192

>PROJECT 2 – STEP 4
ART

For each of the layers, create the art. You might like to start with the body so you have a reference point for the legs.

A reminder that whatever your character, the limbs are best created in a neutral pose. For the eyebot, I've created its leg segments vertical and will pose them more naturally once the hierarchy is set up.

3.193

>PROJECT 2 – STEP 5
HIERARCHY

Now to arrange the layers into a hierarchy: in the Timeline, drag the foot onto the lower leg, then drag the lower leg onto the upper leg and finally, drag the upper leg onto the body.

Looking at the bot now, it's obvious that there are some depth issues. In order to layer the segments at the proper depth, they'll require moving forward or backward in z-depth. In my eyebot example, the body is at zero z-depth, and I've nudged the segments 0.01 F (forward).

3.194

Do this via the Timeline's Data View, as shown in Figure 3.195, for each leg segment.

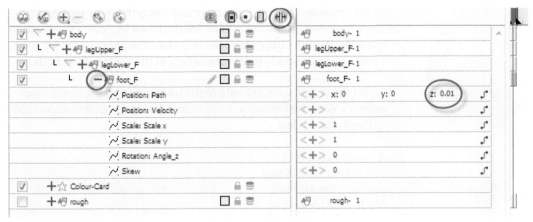

3.195

> **TIP**
> You won't need to arrange them at 0.01, 0.02, 0.03, etc. Once placed into a hierarchy, each segment inherits the transform values of its parent. So you only need to bring each individual segment forward 0.01.

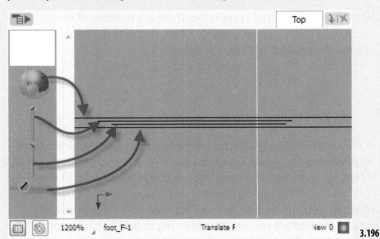

3.196

In the Top View, zoom in to see the spaces between the layers.

> PROJECT 2 – STEP 6
> PIVOTS

In the Timeline, select the foot layer and using the Pivot tool [Shift P], place the pivot on the ankle joint. For the lower leg, place the pivot on the knee. With the upper leg selected, place the pivot on the hip joint. Finally, place the body pivot somewhere at the centre of the body.

Select the IK tool with Animate Mode turned on and the bone chain appears. With the hierarchy, z-depth and pivots complete, you're ready to duplicate this leg.

If you drag the foot around with the IK tool now (ensure Animate Mode is on to see the bones), the body will be pulled around. I suggest 'nailing' the body's bone and joint in place by [Shift]-clicking them both. They'll change colour to indicate that they're locked.

3.197

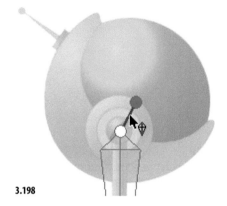

3.198

Note that in the IK tool's properties there is a number of options for controlling joints, one of which is a Nail. This pins the joint to the spot so it can be rotated, but not translated.

> PROJECT 2 – STEP 7
> DUPLICATE THE LEG CHAIN

In the Timeline, [Shift]-select all three leg layers and duplicate them (Right-click → Duplicate Selected Layers…). A brand new leg with all its hierarchy, pivot and keyframe information is now a child of the body.

The final step is to nudge the new leg back into z-depth so it sits behind the body. If you set the upper leg to 0.03 B (back), you shouldn't need to touch the values on the other segments.

This simple rig is now complete and ready for animation!

>PROJECT 2 – STEP 8
ANIMATE THE RIG

Just a reminder that you must have Animate Mode enabled if you want to see the bones. If you'd like to use IK, choose the IK tool [Shift I] and take a look at the tool properties, shown in Figure 3.199. For a refresher, revisit the cut-out animation section starting on page 242.

3.199

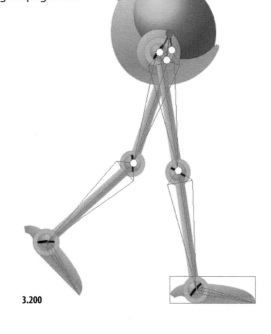

Once the rig is all set, extend your scene length to 60-80 frames, and then start animating the eye-bot's walk animation. With Animate mode turned on, pose the animation keys using IK and FK.

3.200

RIGGING SUMMARY

This project and the introduction starting back on page 277 have been a simple introduction to rigging. If you'd like to go deeper into this technical subject, I recommend getting comfortable with simple rigging tasks like the one in this project, and gradually iterate on rig complexity. When you're ready to go further, I recommend studying the rigging chapter in the Toon Boom documentation [F1] → User Guide → Cut-Out Animation.

ANIMATE PRO & HARMONY ONLY
In Appendix A, you can read a bit about *deformation*, which is in many ways superior to simple segment rigging. You'll also find a video called "Introduction to Deformation" on this book's companion website.

ANIMATION PROJECT 3: DRAWING SUBSTITUTION

In this project, you'll create a layer of mouth shapes and animate them in sequence using Drawing Substitution.

>PROJECT 3 – STEP 1
SCENE SETUP

Create a new scene file with a resolution and frame rate of your choice. Rename your default Timeline layer 'rough'.

>PROJECT 3 – STEP 2
ROUGH SKETCH

On frame 1 of your rough layer, loosely sketch out a character head with the standard face parts: eyes, eyebrows, nose and mouth. For the sake of simplicity, make it a front-on pose.

From this sketch, think about the parts that you need separated for animation. For this project, you need only separate the mouth, but in future, you may need to separate eyebrows, eyes and maybe even hair.

3.201

> PROJECT 3 – STEP 3
  MOUTH SHAPES

Create a Drawing layer called 'mouth' (Figure 3.202). On this layer, with
clean linework, draw a number of different mouth shapes, each on
their own frame.

3.202

Figure 3.203 is a set of nine essential mouth shapes you'll see in limited
animation, for example in television and web cartoons.

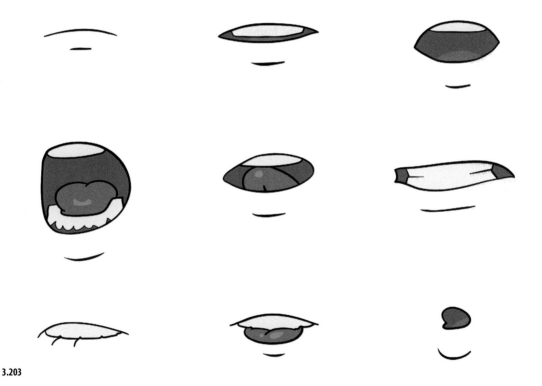

3.203

There's nothing stopping you from adding more than nine mouth
shapes. It's not uncommon to have dozens of them in one Drawing layer. The mouths in Figure 3.203 should suffice for most simple

dialogue scenes but it's a *neutral* set. If a character is smiling while talking, it will need a separate set of smiley mouths. Likewise, if the character is raging angry, a set of angry mouth shapes will be required for those scenes. This is not to mention mouth shapes for different head angles, such as three quarter and profile sets.

>PROJECT 3 – STEP 4
ANIMATING LIP-SYNC

Later in the book we'll be learning how to use audio on the Timeline to synchronise mouth shapes with dialogue. There's no audio on this Timeline, but it's not necessary for this project.

In the mouth layer, delete all but the first drawing from the Timeline, and then extend the exposure of the first drawing to the end of the scene. Now you'll use Drawing Substitution to put your chosen mouth shapes on specific frames.

In the mouth layer, select frame 10. Then in the Library move the Drawing Substitution slider along to choose another mouth shape (Figure 3.204). The chosen mouth shape appears in the Camera View and the Timeline shows a separation mark between your drawings.

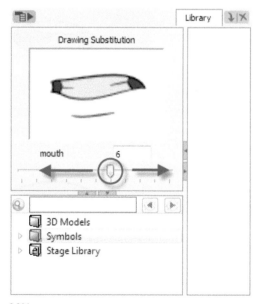

3.204

Repeat the above steps for any mouth shape you want to use; simply select the frame of the mouth layer and then use the Drawing Substitution slider to choose the mouth shape you want at that frame.

If you place the wrong mouth shape, simply select it in the Timeline and change it using the Library slider. By the end of this step, your mouth layer should have a bunch of drawings.

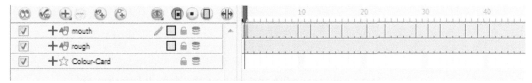

3.205

>PROJECT 3 – STEP 5
EYES AND EYEBROWS

With the same method you used for mouth shapes, you can make eye blinks and eyebrow shapes. Simply draw your different states on the respective layers, and then use the Substitution slider to place a blink or a frown anywhere in the scene.

>PROJECT 3 – STEP 6
PEGS AND DRAWING KEYFRAMES

It's a great idea to add a Peg to a mouth or eyebrows layer, because sometimes you just want to move them up and down, or side to side without changing their shape. Of course, you can do this without a Peg if you prefer; simply keyframing the Drawing layer will have the same effect.

3.206

ANIMATION PROJECT 4:
DEPTH AND MORPHING

In this project you'll create a campfire scene. You'll add z-depth to the background layers and morphing smoke for the dying campfire. At the end, you'll create a camera move to zoom slowly in on the ashes and coals.

> PROJECT 4 – STEP 1
  SCENE SETUP

Start a new scene file and rename the default layer 'rough'.

> PROJECT 4 – STEP 2
  ROUGH LAYOUT

Roughly sketch the layout of the scene elements. The fireplace will be the main focus in the middle of the scene. Other campsite ideas might be a tent, some bushes, a pile of firewood, folding chair and so on.

3.207

> PROJECT 4 – STEP 3
> LAYERS

Add new layers for each major element of the scene. You'll need a ground and sky layer on the bottom, then bushes, firewood, tent and fireplace all on their own layers. In the Timeline create as many layers as you like and then arrange them into their proper order.

At this stage you may like to fully colour and finish the background elements, or you could just add some basic, temporary colour for now. Either way, don't forget to extend the exposure of each layer to the end of the scene.

3.208

Using the Maintain Size tool [Alt 6] (see page 215), position each layer in 3D space. Using the Top and Perspective views, think about the proportional distances that might realistically separate each element; for example, the tent's distance from the background bushes, or the space between the firewood pile and the fireplace. Putting some thought into these distances will make your Camera moves work much better.

> PROJECT 4 – STEP 4
> KEY ANIMATION

In the smoke layer, use the Brush [Alt B] and a dark, temporary colour to draw key smoke poses as it rises skyward. As you'll be morphing the smoke, take care to make the key poses suitable for morphing; that is, don't make them too complex. Try to make each drawing flow as smoothly as possible from the previous and into the next.

You might consider making the smoke lineless, as this reduces the complexity of the artwork to make it more morph-friendly. The lineless style also happens to suit realistic smoke effects very well.

3.209

> PROJECT 4 – STEP 5
  MORPHING AND HINTS

If you didn't use Auto-Flatten when cleaning up and painting, it's a good idea to select each smoke drawing and flatten it [Alt Shift F] before applying a morph. Once again, this isn't always necessary, but simplifying the art increases the chance of trouble-free morphing.

In the Timeline, whether you have just two keys or many, extend the exposure of each smoke key so they go to the end of the scene. Still in the Timeline, select each drawing of the smoke layer one by one and click the Create Morphing button, or press [Alt M].

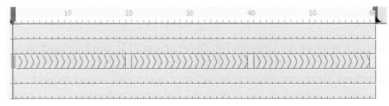

3.210

Scrub or play back the morph to see if there is any tangling or oddness. If so, use the Morphing tool to smooth out those problems with hints (see page 257).

TIP
With ribbon-style smoke, if you've been very careful designing your key poses, I've found that one or two hints at the base will fix most problems by locking the smoke at its source, as shown in Figure 3.211.

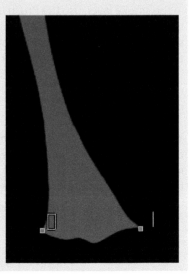

3.211

> PROJECT 4 – STEP 6
EASING

If the morph is jerky or the timing isn't quite what you'd like, you can add some easing via the Layer Properties panel.

- In Animate, the morphing velocity field is at the bottom of the Advanced tab.

- In Animate Pro and Harmony, you'll find it at the bottom of the Drawing tab.

3.212

Click the function curve icon to first create the function curve, and then click it again to open the Veolcity Editor. From there, it's a matter of adding keyframes and using the tangent handles to control the easing (see page 262).

> PROJECT 4 – STEP 7
CAMERA

Back in step 3, the reason we separated the scene elements with z-depth is for the benefit of a Camera move. If you're not using a Camera move in any given scene, z-depth between your layers may not be necessary.

Add a Camera to the scene via the Timeline's ⊕ button. With the Camera layer selected in the Timeline, click the ⊕ button to add a Peg for the Camera.

In the Timeline, select the first frame of the Peg layer. Then in the Camera View, using the Translate tool [Alt 2] with Animate Mode on, drag to move the Camera around the scene.

Note that a keyframe is created on the Timeline in the Peg layer. If, at any time, you're not happy with the Camera position, you can always reset the move by deleting that keyframe from the Peg. Simply select it in the Timeline and press [F7].

3.213

SUMMARY

This enormous chapter has given you a mere glimpse into what you can do with Toon Boom and there's a lot we were unable to cover due to page count restrictions.

Once again, if your experience is in traditional animation and you'd like to use the X-sheet, there's nothing really to stop you opening it from the panel menu and using it, much like you would have in the old days, except with an infinite number of levels (layers) and crazy modern enhancements.

On the other hand, if you're an animator with mostly digital experience, but would like to learn about the X-sheet all the same, I recommend learning it from the Toon Boom documentation [F1]. It's just another Timeline, after all.

The same goes for learning IK and rigging. As I mentioned earlier, rigging is a massive topic that is best taken in small steps. The documentation is more than enough to get you started and keep you going!

In the next chapter you'll learn about effects and how to polish your scenes to a professional level.

CHAPTER 4

Effects

EFFECTS ANIMATION AND EFFECTS FILTERS

In *traditional* animation, the term 'effects' covers elemental phenomena such as dust, water, smoke, lightning and fire. You often see these written as 'FX' (effects), 'VFX' (visual effects) or 'SFX' (special effects). Throughout this chapter we'll refer to these as 'effects animation'.

In *digital* animation, 'effects' is a generic term referring to digital *treatments* and *filters* such as blur, glow, refraction, lens flares and so on. So when we talk about these in Toon Boom and this chapter, we'll use the term effects 'filters' or 'treatments'.

4.1
Elemental hand-drawn effects animation

4.2
A digital refraction treatment

HOW TO APPLY EFFECTS

Depending on which Toon Boom program you're using, effects are either layer-based, or node-based. This means that you'll apply effects in one of two ways: via the Timeline or via the Network view. The Network view is a feature of Animate Pro and Harmony, so if you're using Animate, you'll be working in the Timeline.

ANIMATE ONLY
In Animate, effects are added via the Timeline menu.

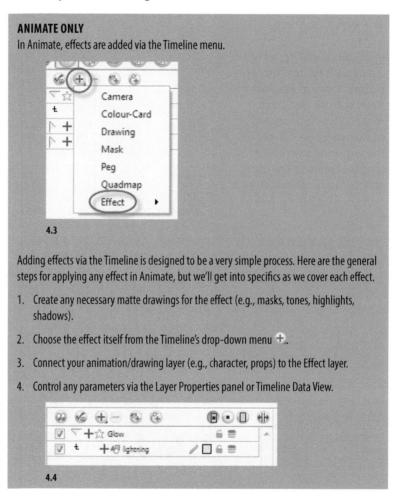

4.3

Adding effects via the Timeline is designed to be a very simple process. Here are the general steps for applying any effect in Animate, but we'll get into specifics as we cover each effect.

1. Create any necessary matte drawings for the effect (e.g., masks, tones, highlights, shadows).

2. Choose the effect itself from the Timeline's drop-down menu ⊕.

3. Connect your animation/drawing layer (e.g., character, props) to the Effect layer.

4. Control any parameters via the Layer Properties panel or Timeline Data View.

4.4

The next 15 pages are for Animate Pro and Harmony only. So if you have Animate, you should now skip forward to page 306.

ANIMATE PRO AND HARMONY ONLY

NODE-BASED EFFECTS

In Animate Pro and Harmony, Effects are found in the Module Library and then dragged into the Network View. Like any other panel, you can open the Module Library panel using the button.

Effects are generally added as follows, but we'll go into specifics as we cover each effect.

1. Create any necessary art for the effects.

2. Drag the effect from the Module Library into the Network.

3. Connect the effect to the appropriate art layers.

4. Control the effect's parameters in the Layer Properties panel.

THE NETWORK VIEW – ANIMATE PRO AND HARMONY ONLY

OK, time to come clean: I could have introduced you to the Network View much earlier. Indeed many layering and organisational tasks, like hierarchies and layer ordering, are much easier via the Network View. However, for most beginners (especially those with little software experience) it's a very daunting view, so to keep your mind from cluttering too early, I reckoned it best saved for later. Well here we are!

> **NOTE**
> The Network View is not a drawing or animation view; you can't control any timing or frame-by-frame aspects of the scene. It's a scene-structuring view by which you organise layers and create connections between them, such as connecting effect filters to a character.

When it comes to layer ordering, the Timeline is limited to simple top-down stacking. Unless reordered in z-space, layers are always displayed in their Timeline stacking order, with lower layers appearing behind higher layers. In Figure 4.5, the eyes will appear behind the head layer, because they're at the bottom of the hierarchy, so you'd need to nudge them forward.

4.5

The Network View, on the other hand, allows you to have something at the bottom of a hierarchy, yet appear on top of the other layers, with no nudging required. The eye layers, while at the bottom of the hierarchy in the Timeline, can appear in front of all other elements.

In Figure 4.6, the head layer is the top of the hierarchy, yet is 'plugged in' at the far right, underneath all the other layers.

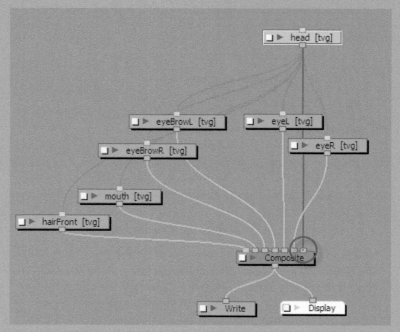

4.6

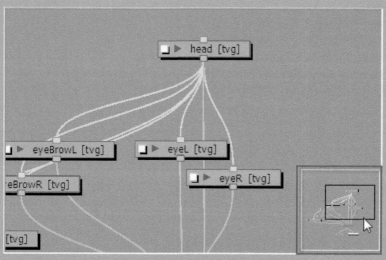

4.7

NAVIGATION

Moving around in the Network View is similar to the Drawing and Camera Views, except there is no rotation. Hold down [Spacebar] to pan around the view.

Those of us who have played RTS (real-time strategy) games are familiar with the kind of panning navigator that you see in the Network View. Much like a mini-map, it allows you to move quickly around large networks by simply dragging the square. Notice that the size of the square adjusts according to your zoom level.

If you'd like to hide the navigator, or position it in any other corner, you can do so via Edit →
Preferences [Ctrl/⌘ U] and then go to the Network tab.

4.8

WHAT ARE MODULES?

Your scene layers are represented as rectangular nodes called *modules*, all plugged into the
main scene 'Composite'. These can be dragged around to your liking. It's the plugging order that
matters, otherwise there's no right or wrong position for these; you are free to organise them
however you see fit. When you have a large network containing dozens upon dozens of modules,
you'll need to move things around so everything is laid out in a readable fashion.

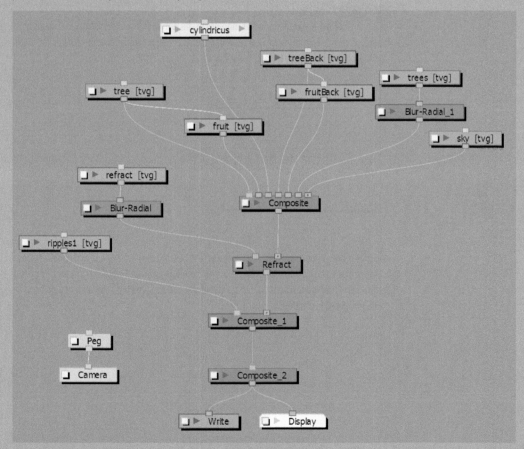

4.9

Without knowing what the cables and modules do, you may be daunted by Figure 4.9. Let's start off simple by going over the default modules in a new scene. When you create a new scene file, the default Timeline layer is called Drawing. Opening up the Network View reveals Drawing as a module, connected to a couple of other modules.

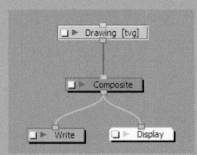

4.10

THE DRAWING MODULE

Layers in the Timeline are reflected as modules in the Network. The [tvg] suffix on a Drawing module is the file format of the layer, saved in the elements folder of your scene. If you were to import any other image format, the suffix would appear on the module.

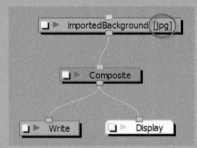

4.11

Click the yellow box on any module to bring up the Layer Properties in a floating panel. Previously you've accessed this information by selecting Timeline layers and opening the Layer Properties panel. Either method can be used, because modules and Timeline layers are essentially the same thing, visualised in different ways.

4.12

THE COMPOSITE MODULE

You might compare Composite modules to rainwater tanks. Art and Effect layers flow down the pipes into the tanks and all the tanks ultimately feed into a main reservoir.

4.13

The Composite is a meeting point where all of the layers in your scene come together. There is a bit more to it than that though; it not only brings everything together but, via the Properties panel, it also decides *how* your scene layers are brought together – or *composited*.

Everything that goes into a Composite module is flattened into a single image for output. A Composite that you might name 'headComposite' for example, with *head*, *eyes* and *mouth* all plugged in, will be flattened into one complete head image.

4.14

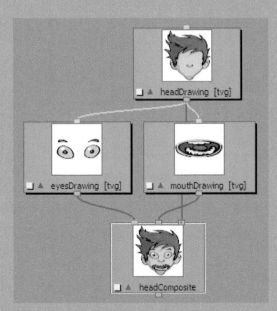

4.15

In turn, you could plug the headComposite and body into another Composite called 'characterComposite'. Finally, plug the characterComposite along with a sky layer into the main scene Composite.

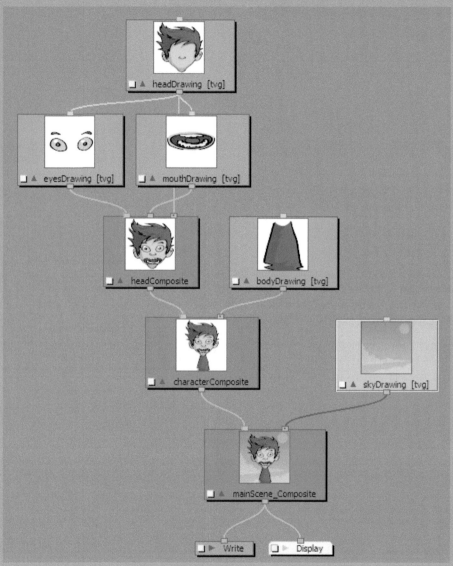

4.16

NOTE
Besides the water tank comparison, another way to illustrate how the network works is by using it to represent a typical studio workflow. Each department flows down into the others, resulting in a finished product ready for publishing.

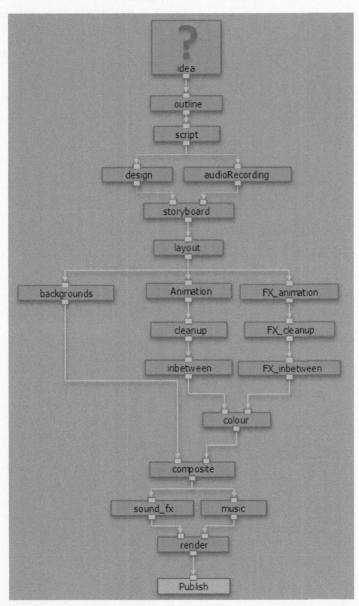

4.17

THE DISPLAY MODULE

A Display module is responsible for displaying your scene. Without it you wouldn't see anything at all, which is why it's one of the default modules in a new network.

You can plug most layers into a Display module. This is particularly useful when you want to render only part of a scene. By default, the Display module is plugged in at the bottom of the network, which means it'll render everything above it.

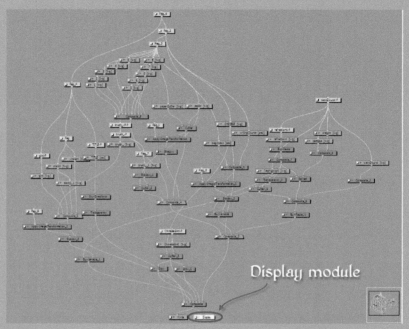

Display module

4.18

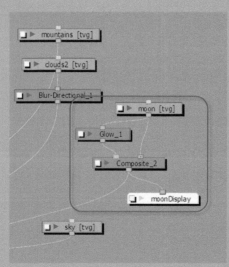

4.19

Right at the bottom of the network isn't the only place for a Display module. Suppose you have this monstrous, technical nightmare of a scene with dozens of layers and tons of effects. Rendering the entire scene may take some time but maybe you're working on a small part, like a simple moonlight glow. Simply plug the moon and its glow into a Display module and you can now render these alone, without the need to render the entire scene.

Your scene can contain multiple Displays and ahead on page 302 you'll learn how to add other modules to the Network. Any particular one can be rendered via the Display drop-down in the main program toolbar. If you don't see it anywhere, you can bring it up with Window → Toolbar → Display. When you render a scene or a single frame, your chosen Display module determines what will be rendered.

4.20

THE WRITE MODULE

When your scene is composited and you're ready to export it, you'll want to 'write' it as a movie or sequence of images. The Write module is where you control this output. In the Layer Properties panel you will specify the resolution, number of frames, output directory and format, whether video or images. Later in the Rendering chapter, we'll export some of each.

4.21

NODES, CABLES AND PORTS

Almost every module has one or more 'ports' or input/output sockets by which you connect it to others.

- Input – top ports are 'in' ports.

- Output – bottom ports are 'out' ports.

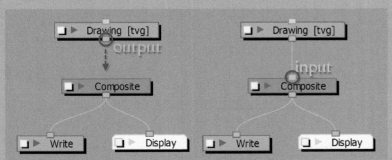

4.22

Click and drag any of these ports to make or break a connection. Try it out by unplugging all of the modules, drag them around and reconnect them in different ways. There are some rules and you'll find that not all connections are possible; for example, you can't plug an input into another input. To unplug a module, you remove its plug from whatever it's plugged into, exactly like the plug of a household electrical appliance.

TIP
You can drag several output cables from a single module. This enables multiple inputs from a single layer. For example, a sun drawing can be plugged in twice, and a Glow attached to one of them. In turn, that Glow can be plugged in multiple times for a stronger effect.

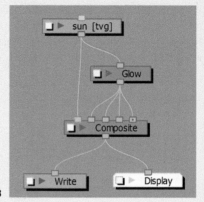

4.23

Once you've experimented with plugs and cables, you'll need to reconnect everything properly if the scene is to be displayed. You should be able to refer back to any of the screenshots all the way back to Figure 4.10 if you need guidance.

LAYER ORDER
When you have multiple layers in your scene, such as with a character hierarchy or a multilayered background, they will all be connected to your main scene Composite, which automatically lengthens to accommodate more connections.

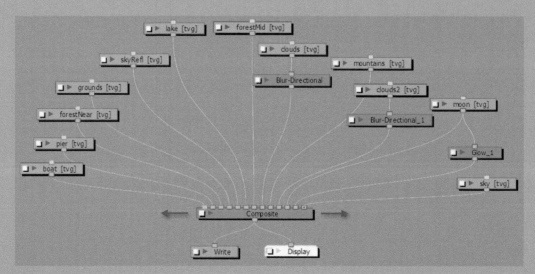

4.24

The right-most connections correspond to the lowest layers of your Timeline. Therefore, in a typical scene, the background elements will be plugged in on the right, while foreground elements are plugged in further to the left.

This method of layer ordering, by simply adjusting the order of connections, is a very fast and easy way to organise your scene. Believe me, once you've done this a few times, shuffling Timeline layers feels so very clunky!

And now we return to what I said about advanced layering. Mouth, nose and eyes layers may be at the bottom of a 'head' hierarchy, but in the Network View you can simply plug the head in *behind* (to the right of) all the face parts. There's no need to nudge anything forward or back in z-space.

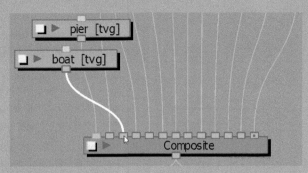

4.25

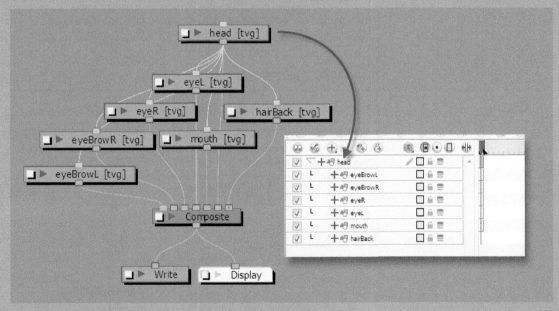

4.26

NOTE
Don't worry; your z-space nudging skills aren't obsolete. Just like layers in the Timeline, the order of these connections cannot be animated. A time will come when you want a layer to initially appear in front and then move behind. For example, a character running around a boulder: he runs in front, runs behind and then comes around in front again. In a scene like this, you'll nudge that character, or boulder, forward and back in z-space.

MODULE BUTTONS

You may have already found them by clicking around, but each module has two or more clickable buttons. Each of these is listed below.

4.27

A. **Module/Layer Properties** – as you've already seen, the yellow box (A in Figure 4.27) opens the Layer Properties in a separate window. This is the same window that opens when you double-click a Timeline layer. If you have your Layer Properties panel docked and open in your workspace though, you may never need to click the yellow box.

B. **Preview** – the dark triangular arrow on the left side of a module (B in Figure 4.27) expands a thumbnail preview of the art on that layer. As shown in the face hierarchy screenshots, you can expand a module preview for Drawing, Group and Composite layers. If you expand a Group or Composite module, the thumbnail preview will display everything contained within. But be warned that a large network with all thumbnails displayed may slow down your computer.

C. **Enter Group** – Group modules have a second triangular arrow button (C in Figure 4.27) that, when clicked, takes you inside that Group.

ADDING AND DELETING MODULES

When you add Timeline layers, they automatically appear as modules in the Network. Another way to add modules is via the Module Library, which we'll talk about in just a moment.

To delete any module, you only need to select it and use your keyboard's [Delete] key. For certain modules there will be no confirmation, but for others, such as Drawing layers containing drawings and animation, you'll get a popup warning (Figure 4.28) that you're about to delete them, along with a choice to keep or delete them from the scene file directories.

> Selected module(s) and column(s) are about to be deleted
> Please Confirm.
>
> ☑ Delete Drawing Files and Element Folders.
>
> [OK]   [Cancel]

4.28

4.29

THE MODULE LIBRARY

While Animate users access effects through a Timeline menu, you'll be using the Module Library. This panel is designed to work hand-in-hand with the Network View; therefore, they should be in separate panels so you can drag effects from the Module Library into your Network.

What is immediately obvious is that the Module Library is conveniently organised into several tabbed categories. You can even create your own tab by choosing New Category from the panel menu.

FAVOURITES

For effects that you use a lot, you'll want to add them to your Favourites tab for quick access. The Favourites tab is already populated with a few frequently used modules. You can remove any of these using the [Delete] key, if you don't think you need them. Don't worry; you can always add them back later. In the following exercise we'll add some others.

MODULE LIBRARY EXERCISE 1: FAVOURITES

On the various Module Library tabs, modules are listed in alphabetical order. Your most frequently used effects may be far down the list, like Tone and Transparency, which are way down at the bottom of the Filters tab..

> 1.   In the Module Library, go to the All Modules tab.

> 2.   Scroll all the way down to find the Tone module.

> 3.   Drag and drop the icon onto the Favourites tab (Figure 4.30).

4.30

NOTE

Depending on how narrow your Module Library panel is, you may not be able to see the Favourites tab. In this case you can shuffle along the tabs using the horizontal arrows (Figure 4.31).

4.31

I always have my Module Library docked with the Timeline (Figure 4.32), because you rarely need both open at the same time, and I find it's much easier to find things in a wide Module Library.

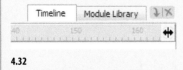

4.32

> 4.   Add the following modules to your Favourites tab:

  •   From the Filters tab – Blur Directional, Blur Variable, Brightness Contrast, Gradient, Highlight, Matte Blur, Refract, Shadow.

  •   From the Move tab – Apply Image Transform.

Browsing the other tabs, you may see modules that you recognise. For example, on the Move tab, you have your Camera, Quadmap and Peg modules. Dragging these into your network and connecting them up is quick and easy as you'll see next.

MODULE LIBRARY EXERCISE 2: ADDING MODULES TO THE NETWORK

Make sure your Module Library and Network View are both open.

> 1. In the Module Library, go to your Favourites tab.

> 2. Drag a Camera and a Peg into your Network and position the Peg above the Camera.

> 3. From the bottom (output) port of the Peg module, drag the cable and plug it into the top (input) port of the Camera (Figure 4.33).

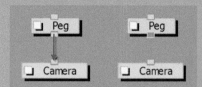

4.33

> 4. Click the yellow properties box of the Peg layer and rename it 'Camera-Peg'.

> 5. Close the Layer Properties window.

In the Timeline now, you'll see those layers have been added.

After adding effects to your Favourites tab, there's no need to save them. They're automatically saved to your preferences and are available for use in other scenes.

ORGANISING THE NETWORK

The easiest way to add Drawing layers is with the Add Drawing ✤ Timeline button, or to press [Ctrl/⌘ R] in the Timeline or Network. As you do this, those new modules are automatically added to the Network. However, they're added at the centre of the Network View. Quite often, after adding many layers in the Timeline, you may switch over to the Network View to find a multitude of layer modules all clustered at the centre.

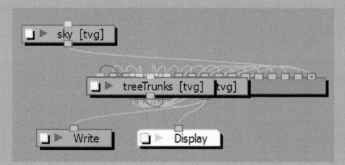

4.34

It's a tangled nightmare. You could spend time dragging and positioning all of your modules so the network is readable, but there's an automatic process that can do it for you with the click of a button. In fact, there are two buttons!

The first button (marked A in Figure 4.35) orders your Network *upwards*. You select a module at the bottom of the Network (the main Composite, Write or Display module will do) and then click this button.

You have a few spacing values to play with, but generally you can simply click 'OK' and everything above the selected module is shuffled and spaced out nice and evenly.

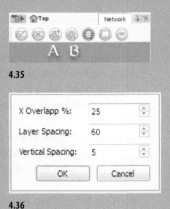

4.35

4.36

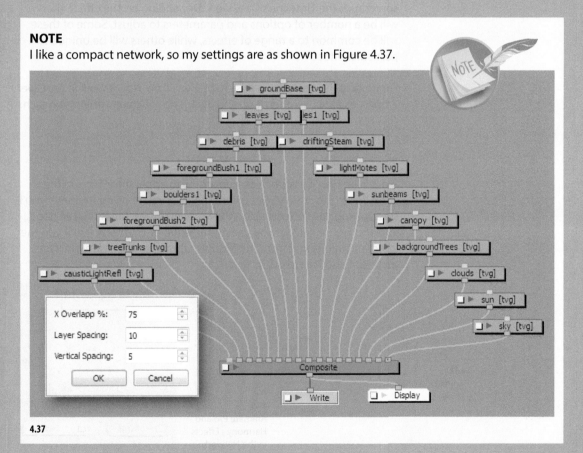

NOTE

I like a compact network, so my settings are as shown in Figure 4.37.

4.37

The second button, marked B in Figure 4.35, orders the Network *downwards*. Select a module at the top, click this button, then after OK on the popup window, everything below it is ordered.

Whether you use upward, downward or specific spacing values will depend on how you use it and how neat you like to keep your networks. It's a huge time-saver if you're working on files from colleagues who don't keep their networks tidy.

EFFECTS

Between now and the end of the chapter, we'll cover many effects. In Animate Pro there are more than 50 effects; in Harmony, more than 100. We don't have the page space to cover them all in this chapter, so we'll be looking at a number of the most common and useful.

First up, we'll look at the Glow effect in depth to get a feel for how effects are generally applied and controlled. Thereafter, we'll be relatively brief with the other effects, unless specifics are necessary.

We'll be controlling these effects via the Layer Properties panel and sometimes the Timeline's Data View. Depending on the effect, there will be a number of options and parameters to adjust. Some of these will be common to a range of effects, while others will be unique to a particular effect.

For most of the exercises in this chapter you'll do a lot of work in the Layer Properties panel, so open it up and dock it somewhere within easy reach.

APPLYING THE EFFECTS

From here on, I'll assume you know how to apply the effects in the Toon Boom program you're using. That is, if you're using Animate, you'll be applying your effects using the ⊕ menu in the Timeline (see page 290 and Figure 4.38). If you use Animate Pro or Harmony you'll add the effect by dragging it from the Module Library into the Network (see page 304 and Figure 4.39).

4.38
Animate - Effects in the
Timeline

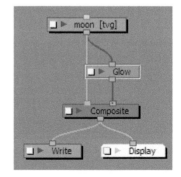

4.39
Animate Pro and
Harmony - Effects
in the Network

In Animate Pro and Harmony, there may be additional steps listed for any effect that might have special connecting instructions, but we'll cover those as we come to them.

MATTE EFFECTS

4.40

A number of effects require additional art to act as a matte, so let's look at them first. For some of these you can duplicate your animation and use it as the matte, while others may need a separate layer of art or animation created especially.

GLOW

Let's start with the Glow effect. We've already seen it in action back in the previous chapter on the lightning example. The steps for this effect will be very similar to most other effects covered in the coming pages.

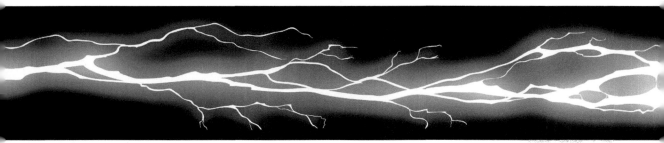

4.41

> EFFECTS EXERCISE 1
  GLOW

> 1.   In the download files for this chapter, open the effects_glow scene.
        If you prefer, you might like to use your fireball scene.

A Glow needs a shape or matte. You could create a new layer and draw
a dedicated Glow matte, but as we've already seen, it's often easier
and quicker to reuse existing art, especially with animated things like
lightning or, in this case, fire. We'll use the fireball and all its flame animation as the glow matte.

4.42

> 2.   Prepare the glow matte:

  Animate – in the Timeline, clone the fireball layer (Right-click
→ Clone Selected Layers) and rename it 'fireballClone' (Figure
4.43).

4.43

  Animate Pro and Harmony – in the Network, drag a second cable
from the fireball module and plug it into the main Composite
(Figure 4.44).

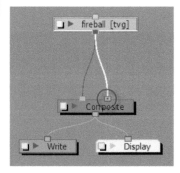

4.44

> 3. Using what you now know about applying effects, add a Glow effect to your fireball clone.

 Animate – select the Glow from the Timeline's ⊕ → Effect menu and then drag the *fireballClone* layer onto the Glow layer (Figure 4.45).

4.45

 Animate Pro and Harmony – drag the Glow module from the Module Library into the Network (Figure 4.46). Once it's in the Network View, hold down [Alt] and drag it onto the cable to connect it under the fireball module.

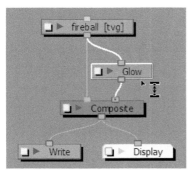

4.46

Now that your glow is applied, you can control its values to get the look you want. The following steps are the same for Animate, Animate Pro and Harmony.

> 4. Ensuring the Glow layer (in the Timeline) or Glow module (in the Network) is selected, open the Layer Properties panel to see its parameters.

> 5. Enter a blur **Radius** value of about 25 and give it a suitable colour. I've used the values shown in Figure 4.47.

> 6. At the bottom left of the Camera View, activate the Render View by clicking the ✹ button.

4.47

> 7. To make the Render automatically update when you change these values, ensure Auto-Render is turned on at the bottom-left of the Camera View.

4.48

NOTE

In the future, when you're working in complex scenes with lots of effects, the program may slow down significantly. One reason may be that you still have Auto-Render turned on and it's rerendering in the background each time you make changes, even small ones. You can always turn it off via this little menu (see Figure 4.48) and only turn it on when you need it.

> 8. Play with more settings and values to get a glow you're happy with. Be sure to try out the 'Directional' blur (as opposed to the default Radial), which is useful for giving the fireball an interesting motion effect.

> 9. Switch out of the Render View and back to the Camera View by clicking the OpenGL ⚫ button at the bottom-left of the Camera View.

4.49

If your fireball layer is underneath the Glow, any internal fireball detail may be obscured. This may not be such a big deal for certain things, like a moon, electricity or a magical effect. For a glowing character, though, you may need to put the glow layers behind so as not to obscure features and other linework. As you can see in Figure 4.49, when this particular glow is in front of the character, it flares brightly, obscuring his features. It works much better behind.

> 10. To move the Glow behind or in front of the fireball:

 Animate – in the Timeline, move the fireball layer above, or below the Glow layers.

 Animate Pro and Harmony – in the Network view, drag the Glow connection to the left or right of the fireball connection.

Finally, you may find that the glow is weak, even at full alpha settings. Higher blur values will also soften it considerably. To strengthen a glow:

 Animate – double the strength by simply duplicating the entire Glow hierarchy (Figure 4.50).

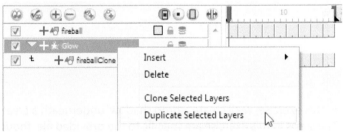

4.50

 Animate Pro and Harmony – drag a second connection from the Glow module into the Composite module (Figure 4.51). You can go crazy with this and drag many connections as you like, if you want a really intense glow.

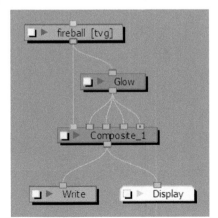

4.51

SHADOW

To make a shadow, you first create a shadow matte. This matte can take any shape you like. It can be a fully animated silhouette, or a shapeless blob of darkness at the character's feet. The latter is the simplest, so that's what we'll do in this exercise.

4.52

> EFFECTS EXERCISE 2
  SHADOW

In this exercise, we'll create a 'drop shadow' underneath a creature. The steps in this exercise are specific to the provided file, though you should be able to follow along with your own, if you prefer.

> 1. Open effects_shadow scene from the chapter files.

> 2. Create a new layer, rename it 'dropShad' and ensure it is below the creature layer (Figure 4.53).

4.53

> 3. On the new dropShad layer, using bright green paint, draw the creature's shadow (Figure 4.54).

You're right: bright green *is* an odd colour for a shadow. In fact, you can use any colour you like. Green is just for the purpose of demonstration and I'll clear that up just ahead in step 5.

4.54

> 4. Add and connect the Shadow effect to your dropShad art:

Animate – with the ⊕ → Effect menu, add a Shadow layer, and then drag the dropShad layer onto the Shadow layer (Figure 4.55).

4.55

Animate Pro and Harmony – Drag a Shadow module from the Module Library into the Network view. Hold [Alt] and drag the Shadow module to connect underneath the dropShad layer (Figure 4.56).

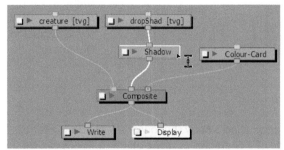

4.56

Immediately you'll notice that the shadow has turned light grey. This is the default colour for a Shadow effect and it ignores whatever colour you used for the artwork.

> 5. In the Layer Properties panel, adjust the Shadow parameters to your liking, including the Shadow colour. Experiment with different alpha and Radial blur values.

4.57

Remember to switch to Render View ⚇ so you can see the changes update as you make them.

> 6. Save your scene if you wish to keep it for later.

TIP

In the Shadow layer properties, you could try out the Directional blur. This may be useful if you find an ordinary Radial blur isn't matching the ground plane, or otherwise doesn't look natural.

ANIMATE PRO & HARMONY ONLY

Generally you would apply a Peg to offset a clone's position. However, there is a module ahead that was designed specifically for offsetting a layer.

Just as you cloned the fireball to use as a Glow matte, you could clone the creature to use as a Shadow matte. The creature and its shadow would occupy the same space though, so the shadow would need repositioning as well as some distortion with a Quadmap.

TONE

Sometimes also called a *body shadow* or *self-shadow*, a tone is the dark, shadowy side of a character or scene element. Tones can be simple, complex or anywhere in between.

The simplest tones may be little more than a few broad stripes of shadow across the face, torso and limbs; while complex tones may be much finer, with hair, eyebrow and nose shadows on the face and wrinkle shadows on clothing.

4.58

Just like the glow and shadow, a tone requires a matte input. A hand-drawn matte layer has the best results in terms of precision and quality but is usually time-consuming. Even so, for the sake of using the Tone module for its intended purpose, let's learn the hand-drawn matte method.

> EFFECTS EXERCISE 3
  TONE

> 1. Open the effects_tone scene from the chapter files.

> 2. In the Timeline, use the ⊕ button to create a new ordinary Drawing layer and name it 'toneMatte'.

> 3. On this new layer, using a solid colour for the matte artwork, draw the line of shadow (see A in Figure 4.59).

Before they can be filled with colour, the shadow areas need to be closed. You can do this by looping outside the character silhouette, because the tone only affects the character. Everything outside the silhouette will be cut off automatically.

> 4. Close off the shadow areas (B in Figure 4.59) and fill them with colour (C).

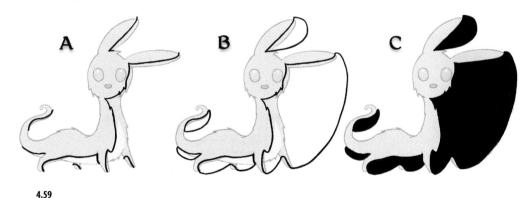

4.59

> 5.   Add a tone to the scene:

Animate – in the Timeline's ... → Effect menu, select Tone.

Animate Pro and Harmony – from the Module Library → Favourites tab, find the Tone module and drag it into the Network. You'll also find it on the Filters tab, in case you didn't add it to your Favourites back on page 303.

> 6.   Apply the Tone to the creature:

Animate – In the Timeline, drag the creature layer onto the Tone layer, and then drag your new toneMatte layer into the Mask group (Figure 4.60).

4.60

Animate Pro and Harmony – Connect the creature module into the tone's **top-right** input port, and your toneMatte module into the tone's **top-left** input port.

Finally plug the tone's output port into the Composite. Unplug the existing creature connections to the Composite so the creature is only connected to the Composite through the Tone module as shown below.

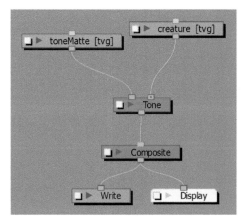

4.61

Once connected, your tone artwork affects the character.

> 7. Switch to the Render view to see how the tone looks

> 8. Adjust the various parameters in the Tone's Layer Properties, such as blur Radius, colour and alpha settings.

In the next exercise we'll create the tone in a different way that requires no matte drawing.

> EFFECTS EXERCISE 4
OFFSET TONE

In the previous exercise you saw how to create a tone effect using a dedicated hand-drawn matte. This time we'll use a clone of the creature layer. This is called an *offset tone* because we offset the position of the clone. It's a great time-saver and quite effective, though it may not be suitable in all instances.

> 1. Open effects_offsetTone from the chapter files.

> 2. Create a clone of the creature layer and rename it 'creatureClone'.

> 3. Add a tone effect to the Timeline (Animate) or Network (Animate Pro and Harmony).

> 4. Apply the tone to the clone:

Animate – in the Timeline, drag the creature into the Tone group, and the clone into the Mask group (Figure 4.63).

4.63

Layer Properties panel:

☑ Enable/Disable	
Name:	Tone
Truck Factor	☑
Blur Type	Radial
Radius	0.2
Directional Angle	0
Directional Falloff Rate	1
Invert Matte	☐
Use Matte Colour	☐
Multiplicative	☐

Colour

Red	-228
Green	-234
Blue	-171
Alpha	120

Close

4.62

Animate Pro and Harmony — Connect the clone to the Tone's top-left input port (Figure 4.64).

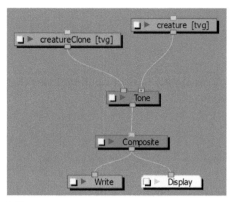

4.64

> 5. In the Timeline or the Network view, select the creatureClone layer. We'll now offset it from the creature.

> 6. Using the Translate tool [Alt 2] in the Camera View, move the tone slightly up and to the left.

4.65

Right now we have the tone taking up most of the character, with a thin edge of light on the bottom right. This looks pretty cool and would suit the scene if the light was behind and below the creature. However, for more of a daylight feel, we need to invert this effect.

4.66

> 7. Select the Tone layer or module, and open its Layer Properties and check the Invert Matte option (Figure 4.66).

That's all there is to the offset tone effect. While it's quite limited, it can often quickly and cheaply add quality to almost any scene.

HIGHLIGHT

There will be no step-by-step exercise for the highlight because the process is identical to the tone. Rather than an area of shadow, however, a highlight creates a light area.

To try this one out, follow the steps in both tone exercises, substituting a highlight in place of the tone effect.

Some useful examples of this effect are: a low, flickering highlight for a fireside scene; a bright, white highlight on a character lit by a flash of lightning; or perhaps some soft, blue under-lighting in an underwater cavern. Figure 4.67 shows two uses of the highlight: the hand-drawn matte (left) and the offset effect (right).

4.67

CUTTER

You could think of a Cutter as an invisibility cloak. It's a mask of artwork that hides (or reveals) a layer. If you use Animate, you saw how to apply masking in the previous chapter with a rainy window scene and the balloon through the window project. In both scenes, you created matte art especially for the purpose of cutting other layers.

> EFFECTS EXERCISE 5
  CUTTER

In this exercise we'll use the Cutter to create an old traditional effects animation trick called the 'scribble cel'. This clever technique added life to a water surface with a glistening effect, using just two drawings.

> 1. Create a new scene file called scribbleCel with a resolution of your choice.

> 2. In the Timeline, rename the default Drawing layer 'scribble' and using white paint in the Camera View, draw some random scribble with the Brush tool (Figure 4.68).

4.68

> 3. Add a new drawing layer and call it 'moonlight'.

> 4. On the moonlight layer, in any colour, paint a bunch of small dots and strokes representing glints on a water surface, as shown in Figure 4.69.

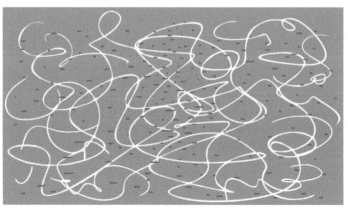

4.69

We now have two layers of art, ready for the Cutter.

> 5.   Add a Mask/Cutter to the scene:

Animate – from the Timeline's ⊕ → Effects menu, choose Mask. Inside the Mask hierarchy, rename the Mask group 'Matte' to avoid confusion with the following steps.

Animate Pro and Harmony –in the Module Library, from the Filter tab, drag a Cutter into the Network.

> 6.   Set up the Mask/Cutter hierarchy:

Animate – drag the moonlight layer into the Matte group, and then drag the scribble layer onto the Mask effect layer (Figure 4.70).

4.70

Animate Pro and Harmony – connect the modules as shown in Figure 4.71.

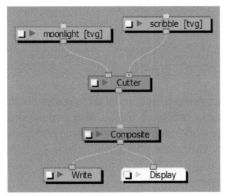

4.71

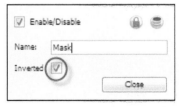

4.72
above: Animate;
below: Animate Pro, Harmony

So now the scribble is being cut by the moonlight, but for this partic-ular effect we actually want it *revealed* by the moonlight; we want the scribble visible only through the glints. To do that, we need to *invert* the effect.

> 7.   Go into the Mask/Cutter's Layer Properties and turn Invert *on* with the checkbox (Figure 4.72). The scribble should mostly disappear from the Camera View, visible only where the moon-light glints are.

> 8. Extend the exposure of both your scribble and moonlight layers to the end of the scene.

> 9. In the Timeline, select the scribble layer and then equip yourself with the Translate tool [Alt 2]

> 10. Ensure Animate mode is *on*, and in the Camera View, drag the scribble cel upward slightly.

Even before it is keyframed, you may already see this remarkable effect in action. It's easy to see how it works just moving the scribble around in the Camera View. The scribble is only revealed through the moonlight glints and when panned very slowly, adds this subtle glistening surface effect with just two drawings.

> 11. Move the playhead to the end of the scene, then using the Translate tool, drag the scribble downward slightly (Figure 4.73).

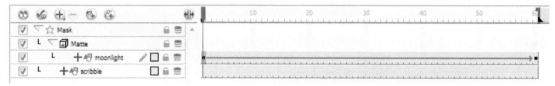

4.73

> 12. Finally, play the scene with [Shift Enter] to watch the scribble cel in action.

I've found that this effect works best when the movement is slow and subtle, but how it moves is entirely up to you. Also, experiment with different designs and animation for both the scribble and glint mattes. Here are some things for your experiment list:

• A morphing matte layer.

• A rotating scribble cel.

• A mask/cutter painted with alpha gradients instead of solid colours.

• A slightly blurred scribble layer for a more subtle glint effect.

Cutters have innumerable applications, from obvious cutter effects, to some cool, not-so-obvious tricks, like the scribble cel.

The following matte effects are found in Animate Pro and Harmony only. If you have Animate, this marks the end of the matte effects section and you should skip to the filter effects section starting on page 329.

ANIMATE PRO & HARMONY ONLY

REFRACT

A Refract module lets you create interesting warp effects, such as 'heat haze' and water reflections. Even though a heat haze is invisible, it bends light so the background appears to warp and shimmer. You've probably seen this for yourself on a highway in summer where distant objects appear fragmented at ground level.

4.74

EFFECTS EXERCISE 6: REFRACT

In this exercise you'll make a simple heat haze effect using the Refract module. Just like the other matte effects, this effect module requires two inputs:

- a layer to be warped;

- an art layer to do the warping.

> 1. Open up effects_refract from the chapter files.

> 2. In the Timeline, above the background layer Group, create a new layer called 'warp' (Figure 4.75).

4.75

> 3. Select the Brush tool [Alt B] and choose white paint from the colour panel.

> 4. On your new warp layer, paint some strokes to act as the heat haze matte. I've gone with some swirly lines to loosely illustrate clouds of heat (Figure 4.76).

4.76

> 5.   From the Module Library's Filters tab, drag a Refract module into the Network and plug it into the main Composite.

> 6.   Disconnect your warp module from the Composite and plug it into the **top-left** input port of the Refract module.

We want this effect to warp the entire background. I've grouped all the background layers so we can run a single cable into the Refract input. You could have done the same thing by adding a Composite module for all the background layers. You'll learn more about Groups up ahead, starting on page 343.

> 7.   Disconnect the background Group from the Composite and plug it into the **top-right** input port of the Refract module (Figure 4.77).

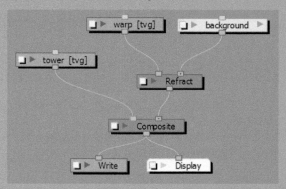

4.77

If connected as shown, the warp art has vanished from the scene. Don't worry, it's still there; it's just an invisible matte now. We're now ready to work on the Refract settings.

> 8.   With the Refract module selected in the Network, or Timeline, open the Layer Properties panel to see the settings (Figure 4.78).

4.78

Intensity and *Height* are the two values that control a Refract effect, using your warp matte. Note also that these values can be animated using function curves. Let's switch to Render Mode so we can watch the effect updating as these parameters are adjusted.

> 9.   Switch to Render mode using the  button at the bottom left of the Camera View.

With its default settings, you may already be able to see the Refract working in the scene. It's pretty hard-edged at the moment but we'll soften it in the next steps.

> 10. In the Refract layer properties, set *both* the intensity and height to 10.

Because you have Auto-Render activated, the frame should rerender each time you update the values. Remember that Auto-Render is turned on in the bottom left of the Camera and Render views.

NOTE

There's a good reason that the provided scene file is at *half HD* resolution (960 × 540). Refract is a heavy effect. It takes significantly more processing power to calculate and render than simpler ones like Shadow and Glow. For this reason, frames will take longer to render; the render time of each frame depends on the resolution of the movie, the complexity of your scene and the power of your computer.

Once the frame rerenders and the new values have taken effect, it's still looking hard-edged. The solution is to soften the warp layer by blurring it.

> 11. From the Module Library, drag a Blur module into the Network.

> 12. Holding down [Alt], connect it underneath your warp module.

> 13. In the Blur properties, enter a Radius value of 5 (Figure 4.79).

4.79

Your heat haze has been softened by blurring the warp art. Let's take a quick look at how that's working before we move on to rendering the scene.

> 14. In the Network view, drag a *second* output cable from the Blur module and plug it into the Composite above everything else (far left). The blurred warp art should now be showing in the Render view.

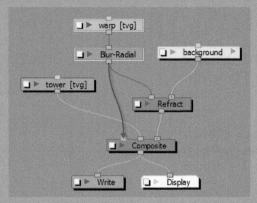

4.80

4.81

If you look carefully at the rendered image, you may see where the background is being distorted by the warp art. This illustrates how blur makes the warp transition gradual, rather than hard-edged.

> 15. Disconnect the second cable from the Blur module. The blurred warp art should disappear from the scene leaving just the warp through a single cable connection.

> 16. Switching back to the Camera View, go ahead and animate a few frames of the warp clouds. You might consider using morphing, Peg or frame-by-frame animation on the warp layer.

> 17. In the Playback toolbar, select Render and Play.

4.82

NOTE
Rendering may take a minute or two, depending on the speed of your computer. Refraction is one of the heavier effects, so don't be alarmed if it does take a few minutes even for a simple scene like this, especially if you have animated those Blur and Refract values and even more so if your scene resolution is high.

4.83

When rendering is complete, **Toon Boom Play** opens. Once the frames are loaded, you can play the preview using the playback controls at the bottom of the Play window.

If you're not quite satisfied with the heat haze effect, close the Play window and tweak those values before rerendering.

4.84

NOTE

With a render preview, Toon Boom Play generates the frames, storing them in the scene's frames directory. Each time you run a new render preview, you'll receive a warning that your previous preview will be overwritten (Figure 4.85).

> **?** Some frames have already been rendered. Do you want to render these frames again?
>
> Yes   No   Cancel

4.85

In most cases like this, it's safe to click 'Yes'. There will be some more on this subject in the Rendering chapter.

VARIABLE BLUR

This filter effect uses white and black values from a matte layer. Here, transparency = black. Either can be used, because both are essentially an absence of white.

4.86

With a white and black/transparent matte layer, you can input values into the layer properties, as well as animate those over time.

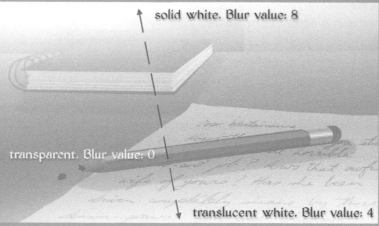

solid white. Blur value: 8

transparent. Blur value: 0

translucent white. Blur value: 4

4.87

4.88

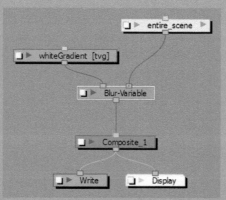

4.89

The scene in Figure 4.87 has a matte that uses white and transparency values to blur the scene. As shown in the Variable-Blur properties (Figure 4.86), the white part of the matte will apply a blur of 8. Then as the gradient becomes more transparent, it applies less blur until finally it arrives at 0. Because of the way the matte drawing was created for Figure 4.88, it gives field depth, with the foreground and background blurred, while the pencil is in sharp focus.

The Network for a Variable Blur is similar to the Refract network (see previous exercise). Into the Variable-Blur's top-left port, the white gradient matte is connected. In the top-right port, the rest of the scene is connected.

As well as this kind of field depth effect, variable blurs are useful in many other ways, particularly in the area of animated effects, like light, smoke, water and so on.

FILTER EFFECTS

Blur-Directional   Blur-Radial   Brightness Cont... Colour-Override   Colour-Scale   Motion-Blur   Transparency

4.90

The filter effects in this section are quick and easy to apply because they require no matte to control the effect. A filter merely affects the layer with the values it is given. For example, a Blur filter will simply apply blur to the entirety of a layer. No fuss.

There isn't room to cover all filter effects, so those covered here are the seven most common. Let's take care of these in order of how frequently you might use them.

TRANSPARENCY

In any situation where you need something to fade on or off you'd animate the Transparency effect. As shown in Figure 4.91, it's not only useful for animated fades. A 'local' (static) transparency value comes in handy for things like reflections, shadows and much more.

4.91

4.92

With a Transparency layer or module selected, the Layer Properties panel has a Transparency input field for a value between 0 and 100 (Figure 4.92). A low value (e.g., 20) is slightly transparent, while a higher value (e.g., 80) is mostly transparent. 100 therefore is completely transparent.

This value can also be animated for fading effects, like titles and credits or a dissipating dust cloud (Figure 4.93).

4.93

BLURS

Blurring is often used for depth effects, like blurring a foreground element to make it appear closer. Directional blur in particular is very useful for showing motion, for example, a fast-moving character or object.

Let's not forget how vital blurs are for animated effects too. Dust and smoke, for example, are given realism with some animated blur; starting the scene with a sharp-edged, dense cloud and gradually blurring more and more as the cloud expands, thins and dissipates.

4.94

If you're using Animate Pro or Harmony, you've already seen the Variable blur back on page 328. The remaining blurs, available in all three programs, are *Radial*, *Directional* and *Motion*. Harmony users also have a number of new blurs that were added in Harmony 10.3. They are *Box*, *Gaussian*, *Zoom* and *Spin*. Let's look at all of these now.

RADIAL BLUR (LEGACY)

Radial blur is the basic depth blur that you would use in everyday focal effects. For example, darkened foreground foliage framing the scene always looks nice with a bit of Radial blur.

4.95
Image by A. Phillips for Clear Vision 3, courtesy of
Dan Erhard Olsson.

In Animate, this effect is simply called Blur, but in Animate Pro and Harmony, you'll find it in the Module Library with the name Blur-Radial.

In Harmony 10.3 powerful new radial blurs were introduced (starting on page 337), so this one is considered obsolete. In the Harmony 10.3 module library it's called Blur-Radial-Legacy.

In the Layer Properties, you simply increase the Radius value for more blur, or decrease it for less. Watch the blur update in the Render View as you experiment with different values.

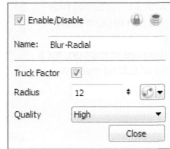

4.96

> EFFECTS EXERCISE 7
> RADIAL BLUR (LEGACY)

> 1.   To apply a Radial blur to any drawing layer:

 Animate – from the Timeline's ⊕ menu, choose Effect → Blur. In the Timeline, drag your drawing layer onto the Blur layer. Animate the values using the Timeline's Data view.

4.97

 Animate Pro and Harmony – from the Module Library's Filter tab, drag the Radial Blur into the Network. Then, holding down the [Alt] key, drag it onto your drawing's cable to connect it just underneath. Adjust the values either in the Timeline Data view, or in the Blur module's Layer Properties.

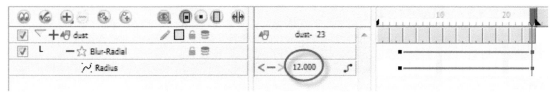

4.98

DIRECTIONAL BLUR

When you use blur to show movement, you can only get so far with the standard fuzzy radial blur. With ordinary radial blur, an object flying through the air looks very much like... well, a blurry object flying through the air!

With a Directional blur you can make a drawing appear smeared or streaked in motion, for a bit of added realism.

4.99

> EFFECTS EXERCISE 8
DIRECTIONAL BLUR

In this exercise we'll drop a rock through the scene and you'll apply a directional blur. Incidentally, this needn't necessarily be a rock; anything with some weight will do. It can be a ball, a briefcase or a whole person, if you like.

> 1. On a new layer with drawing tools of your choice, draw a rock and attach it to a Peg.

> 2. Apply the Directional Blur to the rock:

Animate – select Directional Blur from the Timeline's Effect menu and drag the rock layer onto it.

Animate Pro and Harmony – from the Module Library's Filter tab, drag a Directional Blur into the Network. Connect it to the rock layer's cable, just underneath (Figure 4.100).

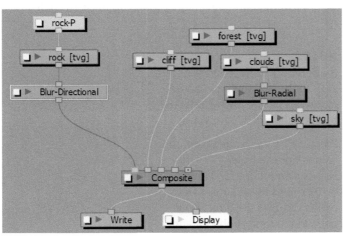

4.100

> 3. In the Timeline or the Network View, select the Directional Blur and open the Layer Properties panel.

> 4. In the Radius field, type in 25. Note the Angle field shows 0 by default.

> 5. Switch to the Render View and see how your rock looks with a blur value of 25.

4.101

The default angle is 0° which makes a horizontal blur. The right edge is not blurred which can be useful in some effects (e.g., fire), but in this case we want to blur both edges, as well as make the blur angle vertical.

NOTE

In Toon Boom effects, angles start at 0° to the left, then go counter-clockwise to 90° downwards, 180° to the right and 270° upwards.

You may also enter negative values. For example -45° is the same as entering 315°. Figure 4.102 shows these angle values, which includes the directional blurs in the tone, highlight and glow effects.

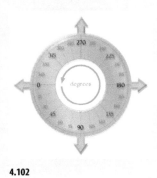

4.102

> 6. Using Figure 4.102 as reference, you can see that an upward blur is 270°, so enter that into the Directional blur's Angle field.

The hard bottom edge may work for this particular scene and other motion, but in live action film, objects are realistically blurred both ways, in line with the direction of travel.

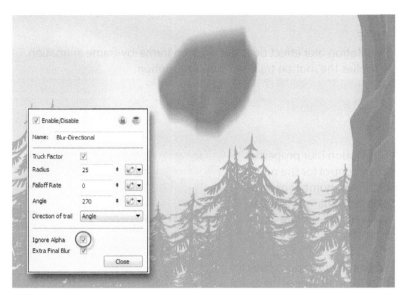

4.103

> 7.   Turn on Ignore Alpha by checking its checkbox (Figure 4.103).

In the Angle field you can enter negative or positive values between 0 and 359, depending on what your scene requires. This value can also be animated, if you need it to change direction over time. For example: an object thrown in an arc might initially have a 45° directional blur that flattens to 0° at the top of the arc and, as it falls, rolls around to a value of -45°.

MOTION BLUR

This module simulates a motion blur by creating a trail of faded images. Suppose you have a superhero flying over the city skyline. The superhero is attached to a Peg and zooms across the scene.

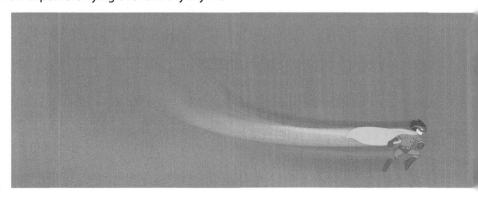

4.104

NOTE
The Motion blur effect does not work on frame-by-frame animation.
It applies the motion trail based on Peg motion.

The Motion blur properties allow control for the number of frames, number of samples (how many images in the trail), fall-off rate and intensity.

While the effect does have a port for matte input (in case you'd like to use a custom shape for the trail) no matte is necessary for a simple trail effect.

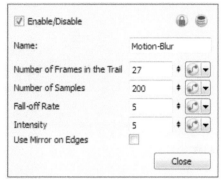

4.105

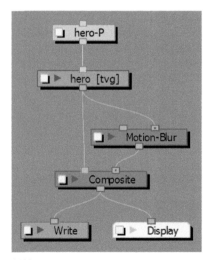

4.106

HARMONY ONLY

NEW BLURS IN HARMONY 10.3

The new blurs introduced in Harmony 10.3 open up a world of new effects possibilities and supersede the standard Radial and Directional blurs. Each of these outlined below also has a matte input (left port) if you want to confine or mask the blur effect, just as you would with a cutter module.

4.107

BOX BLUR

This works by separately blurring horizontally (X) and vertically (Y), creating a boxy blur effect. The X and Y parameters are locked to take a single value, but, using the Directional checkbox, may be unlocked to take separate values. For example, Length:0 and Width:12 creates a horizontal blur. Additionally, you can input an angle value to suit the blur direction you need, and check the Bi-directional checkbox to make the blur go both ways.

GAUSSIAN BLUR

This is a smoother, stronger and all round more attractive blur. Just like the Box blur, you can use the Directional checkbox to separate the horizontal and vertical parameters, add an angle value for directional blur effects, and make the effect bi-directional.

RADIAL

The amazing new type of Radial blur has two main modes: zoom and spin, but also has halfway modes for a twist blur effect. These are selected as preset buttons, or a custom field that you can animate with a function curve!

4.108

- Zoom blur works by blurring towards, or away from, a point.

- Spin blur works by blurring around a point.

- Twist blur is a combination of zoom and spin.

By default the blur is at the centre of the scene, but chances are you'll need to centre it at the pivot of your spinning object; for example, the middle of a wheel (Figure 4.109).

The centre point is revealed by first selecting the Radial blur module, then in the Camera View pressing [Shift F11] or via the menu Show → Control. It appears as a small red dot that you can drag into position.

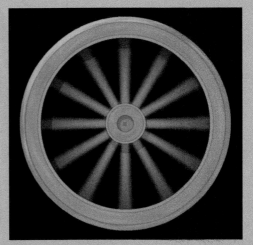

4.109

BRIGHTNESS CONTRAST

With this effect you can make a drawing layer bright, dark, dull or vivid. In Animate Pro and Harmony, you'll find Brightness Contrast on the Module Library's Filter tab, as well as the Plugins tab.

For both Brightness and Contrast, the value of zero means the colours are unchanged. The Brightness value can be raised to a maximum of 255 and a minimum of -255. The Contrast however requires values between 100 and -100. Anything outside that range may result in weird colours.

4.110

While the Brightness value makes the difference between lightness and darkness, the Contrast value exaggerates (positive values) or reduces (negative values) that difference.

4.111

COLOUR OVERRIDE

This effect lets you alter the colours of drawing layers without repainting them. It means you can take a character painted in ordinary day palette and apply a Colour Override with, say, an underwater palette.

4.112

Just like all other effects, you attach a drawing layer to the Colour Override in the following ways:

Animate — Drag your drawing layer onto the effect layer (Figure 4.113).

4.113

Animate Pro and Harmony — the Colour Override module has three input ports. Plug the drawing layer into the top right port. For a standard colour override, the other ports need no input (Figure 4.114).

4.114

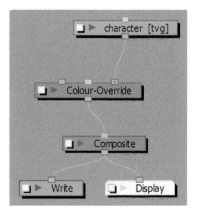

339

At first, the Colour Override interface in the Layer Properties panel may seem a little overwhelming, but we can start by minimising the palette sections leaving just the colour sections.

For the colours you want to override, drag them into the Colour Overrides pane.

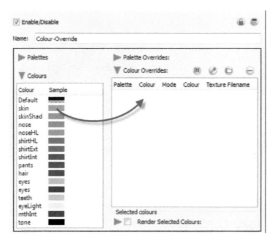

4.115

In the Colour Overrides pane, double-click a colour swatch (A in Figure 4.116) and then use the Colour Picker to change it. Repeat this for each colour you want to override.

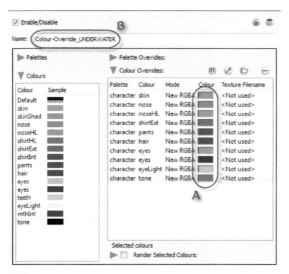

4.116

If you'd like to use the same override for this character in other scenes, it might be worth renaming the module (B in Figure 4.116) so you can find it later and import it into other scenes. Saving and importing templates will be covered in Appendix A.

NOTE
The Colour Override only works on .tvg layers (the native format for drawings created and painted in Toon Boom). This means you cannot use Colour Override on an imported image; say, a .jpg or .png.

COLOUR SCALE

Suppose your project has a nightmare sequence where the scene starts in normal colours but gradually becomes blood red. To animate this transition, you can use the Colour Scale module to increase the Red channel, or animate the Hue value.

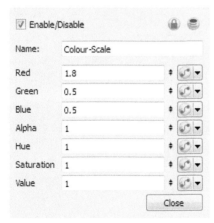

4.117

In the RGBA-HSV fields of the Colour Scale properties, the channel fields each have a default value of 1 which indicates that the colour is unchanged.

Generally you'll work with numbers between 0 and 2. For example, a Red value of 0.1 is an extremely small amount of red, while a value of 1.8 is approaching maximum red.

There are a couple of quirks worth mentioning here.

- An Alpha of 1 is 100% opaque, so anything over 1 is pointless; you can't get more opaque than that.

- Hue is a looping value. It starts at 0 and as you increase it, you eventually return to the same hue as the 0 value. It works on the principle that a colour wheel starts at red, goes through the spectrum and returns to red. That said, Hue takes your artwork colour and applies the value to its current position. So for example if you have a blue sky and apply a 0.5 hue, it will likely result in the orange-yellow range. Again, think in terms of a colour wheel.

You can always set each of these fields back to 1 if your experiment starts getting away from you.

4.118
Image by A. Phillips for
Clear Vision 3, courtesy
of Dan Erhard Olsson.

In Appendix A, you'll see ways to alter an entire colour palette in just a few clicks and slides, but using Colour Scale you can very easily disable, or delete the module to return to normal scene colours. Additionally, you can save a Colour Scale module and its settings and import it into any scene. Again, that's covered in Appendix A.

ANIMATE PRO & HARMONY ONLY

OTHER USEFUL MODULES

Not all effects and modules in the library can be classified as matte effects and filters. Now let's look at some really important modules that you'll find useful across a wide range of tasks.

THE GROUP MODULE

A Group is a module containing other modules; a network within the Network. You place modules into a Group in order to organise the Network and keep things tidy. For example, in a background hierarchy, you might have a sky Group that contains sky, stars, clouds, and moon.

First, it's best to organise these layers into sets, each with their own Composite (see Figure 4.119), to help you organise the scene better.

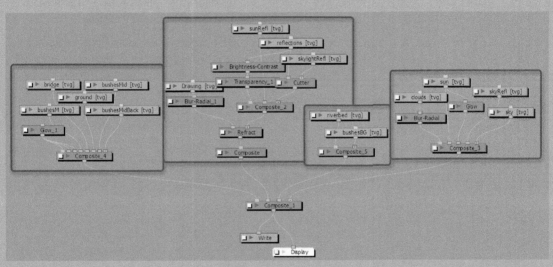

4.119

The easiest way to group modules is to select each set, including their Composite module (to multiple-select, drag a selection around modules, or [Ctrl]-click them one-by-one) and then press [Ctrl/⌘ G]. In Figure 4.120, each set of layers has been grouped and renamed. You can enter a Group by [Shift]-clicking it, or simply clicking the module's right-most triangular button.

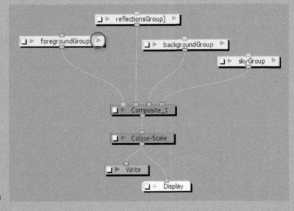

4.120

NOTE

There's a handy keyboard shortcut for grouping a set of modules that also automatically inserts a Composite module. Multi-select all the layers you want to group and then press [Ctrl/⌘ Shift G]. In the Network you'll find the layers have been grouped and inside each group, you'll find them all plugged into a Composite module – often it's somewhat untidy in there, so you may need to shuffle things around a bit, or use the Order Network buttons (see page 305).

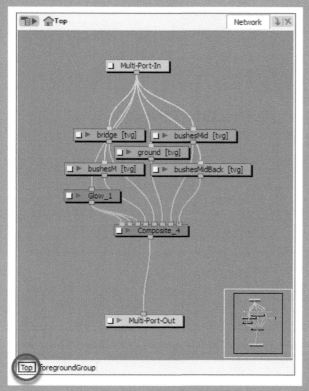

To leave a Group, click the word 'Top' in the bottom left of the Network view to go back to the top Network. New in Harmony 10.3, when inside a Group, a prominent, blue triangular button appears at the top of the Network. You also can click this to leave the Group.

In the Timeline, all layers within a group will appear nested under the Group layer. Like any hierarchy, the Group itself can be expanded and collapsed with the triangular button and the expand + and collapse — icons on the Group layer.

4.121   4.122

The best thing about all of this is that you can attach your Group to a Peg, or plug effects in underneath it, so the Group can be controlled as a single element.

APPLY IMAGE TRANSFORM

This is a special 'offset' module particularly useful for matte effects because it makes cloning layers unnecessary. It's called Apply-Image-Transformation, and you'll find it in the Module Library on the Move tab.

4.123

The name doesn't exactly roll off the tongue but the Apply-Image-Transform module is exceptionally useful, especially in complex scenes where many duplicates or clones could get heavy and messy.

IMAGE TRANSFORM EXERCISE 1: OFFSET AND SHADOW

Follow along with a scene of your choice. In the following steps, I'm reusing the creature shadow exercise scene file from back on page 312.

To use the Apply Image Transformation module with your animation (see Figure 4.124):

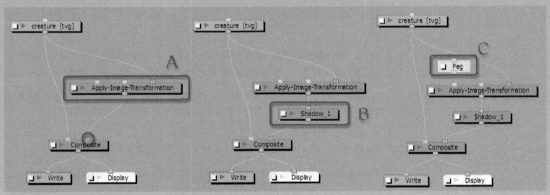

4.124

> 1. Drag a second cable from the animation into the input port of the Apply-Image-Transform module. Then connect it to the Composite (A).

> 2. Run the Apply-Image-Transform output cable through a Shadow module (B).

Excellent! There are now two creature inputs; one of which is a shadow that needs offsetting.

> 3. Connect a Peg to the top-left input port of the Apply-Image-Transform module (C). Don't worry about the middle input port at all here.

> 4. Finally, select the Peg you just added, go to the Camera View and, using the Translate tool [Alt 2], move the Shadow into place.

This same process can be used for tones or highlights; any matte effect where you might otherwise use a clone or duplicate. Figure 4.125 shows the Apply Image Transform setup for an offset tone effect.

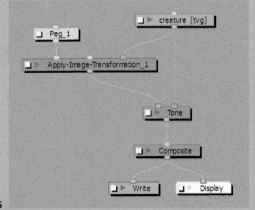

4.125

HARMONY ONLY

PARTICLE EFFECTS

4.126

A completely separate book could be written on all there is to learn about Particles. In this section we'll just cover some basics by creating a simple Particle system that generates snowflakes.

If you'd like to go beyond what's written here, I recommend turning to the [F1] Help files for Particle reference. This will help you understand the purpose of each module and its controls.

There are endless applications for Particle effects in any given project. From a snowy blizzard, a smashing pane of glass, a swarm of insects or feathers in a pillow fight.

Traditionally, hand-drawn Particle effects are among the most time-consuming of all animated effects in 2D. Before advances in technology made particle simulations possible, all of these had been meticulously hand-drawn by skilled effects animators.

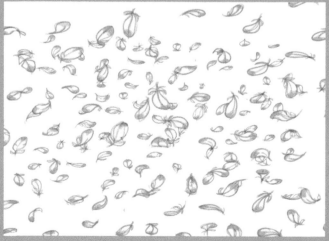

4.127

Because particles generally have individual movement and behaviour, though they may be part of a larger cloud or swarm, each one needs individual attention in animation. Imagine a 2D marble; essentially it's just a circle. Ten marbles bouncing on a hard surface will each require careful timing and trajectories, ensuring it moves realistically. Now imagine a scene with a bucket full of marbles spilled onto the floor and you can begin to see why these tasks are nowadays usually handled with sprites and particle emitters. In the past, due to the sheer number of manual animation hours required, it would have been madness to put such a scene into production.

4.128

Toon Boom's particle systems make a wide range of effects possible that would otherwise take many hours, days, even weeks of frame-by-frame, hand-drawn animation.

Like the network of drawing layers and effects with which you're now familiar, a particle system is a network of modules connected by cables. At first it may look confusing so it'll help to know what the various modules are and how they affect the particle system. Not all of them will be covered here, but the following will serve as an introduction.

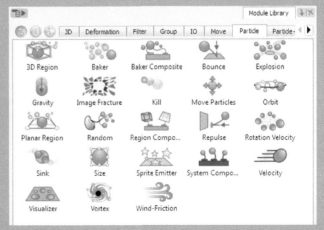

4.129

ANIMATE TO HARMONY

FOUNDATION MODULES

Just like the network of an ordinary animated scene, there are a few 'building blocks' common to all particle systems. As a beginner, it may be some time before you need to build a particle network from scratch, but when the time comes, these are the three you'd start with, and build upon.

PARTICLE-SYSTEM-COMPOSITE

The Particle-System-Composite is just like the main scene Composite, only this one is especially

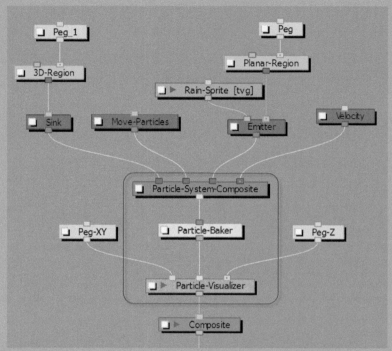

4.130

for compositing particle systems. It simply funnels all the information of the particle system and outputs as a single image.

PARTICLE-BAKER

Taking the composited particles, the Particle-Baker determines how many particles there will be, the quality and randomness of the simulation, the number of Pre-Roll frames (we'll use that in our snowfall exercise), and a few particle behaviours.

348

PARTICLE-VISUALIZER

With all the information read from the Particle-Baker, the system passes into the Particle-Visualizer module, which essentially outputs the final result of the particle network. This module has two Peg inputs at the top: the top left for controlling the x and y position; the top right controls the z position so for example, the particles can appear behind or in front of a character.

ACTION MODULES

Plugged into the Particle-Composite module, there will generally be a number of purple modules. These are the various physics controls and emitters called *action* modules. Most of these tell the particles what to do and how to behave. While there are several action modules, there's one we need to know up front.

THE EMITTER

A fundamental piece of any particle system is the Sprite-Emitter. It defines the point from which the particles are 'born' as well as how they look and behave.

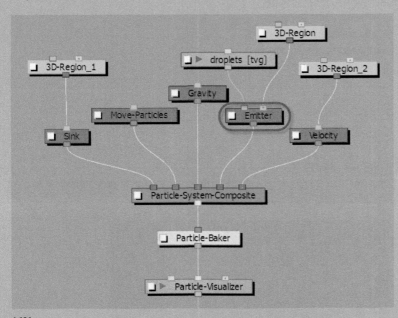

4.131

An Emitter requires two inputs: something to emit (e.g., snowflake art) and something to emit *from* (a region or point). An example of particles being emitted from a point would be from a metal grinder shooting out sparks. An emitter *region* on the other hand is like a sky, or a shower head; it's a broad area from which water is emitted.

The Layer Properties for the Emitter let you control the number of particles emitted every frame, the rate at which they're emitted and when they should 'die', if at all. Don't worry: when particles die, it's very quick, they don't feel a thing. They're simply snuffed out of existence. This is useful where you need particles to be removed once they go outside the scene border. You don't want to waste processing power on particles that you can't see.

4.132

WHAT IS A SPRITE?

Under the hood of a particle system, each particle is a mathematical point; an infinitesimal speck visualised in the software as a tiny placeholder dot.

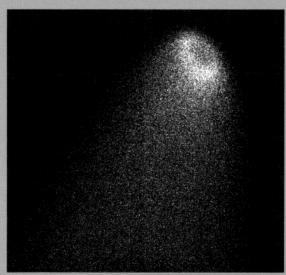

4.133

Only when we replace the dot with images or animation does the particle effect really start to look interesting. A drawing or layer of animation attached to the particle is called a sprite.

A simple example of an animated sprite would be a bee cycle with wing animation. This little bee clip can be attached to the Emitter, so that every dot becomes a bee, forming a swarm.

4.134

The same can be done with static art. You can, for example, apply a static snowflake sprite to a particle system for a wintry snowfall scene, as you'll see in the upcoming exercises.

PARTICLE EXAMPLES

In Harmony you may rarely need to build a complete particle system from scratch. For most standard particle tasks, you can drop one of the pre-built particle systems into the scene and tweak it according to your needs.

Suppose, for example, you need to create gentle snowfall. You could drop in the Rain particle system and alter the art and physics, so each particle falls more gently, like snow. In these next exercises, we'll do just that and learn more about particle systems along the way.

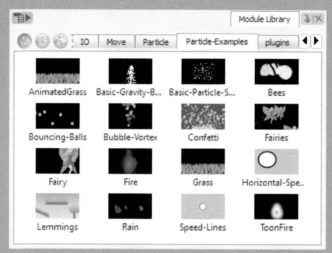

4.135

PARTICLES EXERCISE 1: TURNING RAIN INTO SNOW

Rain is one of the pre-built particle examples and is a fairly 'toony' simulation. Let's add that to a scene and tweak the settings for a snowfall scene.

> 1.   Create a new scene file called 'snow', with half HD resolution (w960 × h540)

> 2.   You won't need the default Drawing layer, so delete it from the Timeline.

> 3.   Open the Module Library and go to the Particle-Examples tab.

> 4.   Drag the Rain example module into your Network and plug it into the main Composite.

> 5.   Using the playback controls, watch the simulation play.

Even though this is a completely different scene to the one we want, we can use some of this simulation's attributes in our snow scene.

> 6.   Stop the playback and look at the Network view.

The particle network is contained inside the Rain group, and there's a Peg attached. Right away this tells us that the entire particle system can be moved around by simply keyframing the Rain Peg.

> 7.　In the Network view, go inside the Rain group and let's see what makes up this system (Figure 4.136).

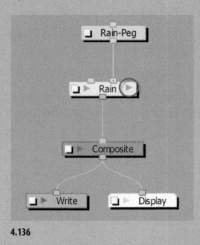

4.136

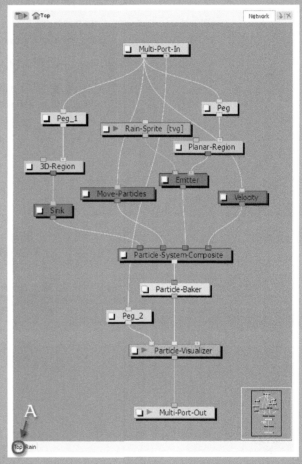

4.137

This network of cables and coloured nodes may be confusing at first, but we can break it down module by module and see that each node controls a specific aspect of the system. Some of the names may be self-explanatory, for example, Velocity, while others with names like Sink and 3D-Region will need some explanation. For now we'll press on with the snowfall scene and things will be explained as we encounter them. Remember, if you want to leave the Group, use the 'Top' link at the bottom left of the Network view (see A in Figure 4.137).

> 8.　In the Network view, inside the Rain group, select the Rain-Sprite module.

> 9.　In the Timeline, press the [O] key a few times until the Rain-Sprite layer is revealed.

This Rain-Sprite module is the drawing layer that contains the raindrop art. In the Timeline you'll see that it consists of three frames, each with a different raindrop.

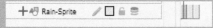

4.138

In a particle system, frames can be used either as different particle states, or as particle animation. For example, you can make six different snowflakes on six frames, so your snowfall has a variety of snowflake shapes. Alternatively you can have six frames for a bee cycle that plays six frames of wing buzzing animation.

In our snowfall scene, we're going to replace the three frames of raindrop art with three snowflakes, though you should feel free to add as many as you like.

> 10. In the Drawing view, zoom in closer to the raindrop. If you can't see it in the Drawing view, turn on the grid with [Ctrl/⌘ '] and you'll find the raindrop at the centre.

> 11. On frame 1, drag a selection around the raindrop art and press your [Delete] key.

> 12. In the raindrop's place, draw your own snowflake design about the same size as the raindrop. Turn on the Onionskin tool if you need the raindrop sizes for reference.

4.139

You'll notice in Figure 4.139 that I've drawn my snowflake in dark blue. Because you're working in the Drawing view with a white background, you'll initially need to draw the snowflake in a dark colour, and then repaint it with white when you're done.

> 13. Repeat steps 11 and 12 to replace the other two raindrops on frames 2 and 3 with snow-flakes.

> 14. If you've used a dark colour to draw your snowflakes, repaint all of them white now.

This is no longer a rain scene, but a snow scene. To avoid any confusion, now is a good time to rename the various parts of this system.

> 15. Wherever you see the word Rain, replace it with Snow, as in Figure 4.140.

4.140

> 16. Finally, if you added more than three snowflakes, you'll need to go to the Emitter properties and enter the new number to Particle Type 1. For example, if you have seven frames of unique snowflakes, add the value 7 to the Particle Type 1 field.

> 17. Save your scene with [Ctrl/⌘ S]

Now that you've replaced the raindrops with snowflakes, go back to the Camera View and use the playback controls to play the simulation.

PARTICLES EXERCISE 2: SNOWFALL SPEED

We've replaced all the raindrops with snowflakes, but it's all falling way too fast. We need to play with some values and find a number that works.

One of the 'actions' (purple) in this system is a Velocity module. This one determines the speed of the particles, controlling how far each one moves every frame.

> 1.   In the Network view, select the Velocity module.

In the Layer Properties, we have X, Y and Z directions. The snow is falling down (Y -1) but it's also falling slightly to the right (X 0. 5). Let's make it fall straight down.

> 2.   In the Velocity module properties, set X to 0 (Figure 4.141).

4.141

> 3.   Just below the Direction fields, in the Speed section, set the maximum to 0.05 (Figure 4.141).

> 4.   Go to frame 1 and play the simulation.

Well, now we have a slight problem. The snow is falling slower, so it takes longer to arrive in the scene. In fact, snow doesn't even enter the scene until about frame 45. We'll fix that in the next exercise.

PARTICLES EXERCISE 3: PARTICLE-BAKER

We don't want the snow to start when the scene starts; we want it to appear as if it's already snowing. For this we'll add some *Pre-Roll frames*. This calculates what the simulation would look like after a specified number of frames and makes that the start position.

> 1. Select the Particle-Baker module and open its Layer Properties.

> 2. Change the number of Pre-Roll frames to a higher number. As shown in Figure 4.142, I've input 1000.

4.142

By adding a high number of Pre-Roll frames, it means that from the very first frame of the scene we'll have a simulation that's well and truly in progress.

TIP
Slow effects like this tend to need more Pre-Roll frames to become established. If the intended effect is fast, however, like heavy rain, your particles will need fewer Pre-Roll frames. If we want the audience to see the beginning of an effect, for example a burst of sparks from a magician's wand, you'll need no Pre-Roll frames at all.

I feel like there are far too many snowflakes in the snowfall simulation. If there are any characters in the scene, I wouldn't want the snow to be distracting. There are a couple of places we can tweak the number of particles, but let's stay in the Particle-Baker for now.

> 3. In the Particle-Baker's properties, reduce the Maximum Number of Particles to 100.

> 4. Play back the simulation.

And we have another problem! The snowflakes are coming down in solid bands, because the simulation generates 100 particles, then stops. We specified that 100 particles should be the maximum, so it waits for some of them to leave the scene before generating more.

> 5.   Change the Maximum Number of Particles to 5000. That's still too many but it should be just enough to fill the entire screen and we'll tweak some other settings.

> 6.   Save the scene ready for use in the next exercise.

PARTICLES EXERCISE 4: EMISSION RATE
We can reduce the emission rate even further via the Emitter module.

> 1.   In the Network view, select the Emitter module.

The Number of Particles is currently set to 20, while the Probability of Generating Any Particles is currently at 100. That means there's a 100% chance that 20 particles will be generated on every frame. Let's reduce them both substantially.

> 2.   In the Emitter's Properties, change the Number of Particles to 12.

> 3.   Change the Probability of Generating Any Particles to 20.

Now there's only a 20% chance that a particle will be generated up to a maximum of 12 per frame. I think these numbers make for a better simulation of gentle snowfall, but you should play around with them and find a rate that you like.

PARTICLES EXERCISE 5: REGIONS
The *Region* modules are invisible 3D areas where particles can be created or destroyed. In the snow network, the Emitter is connected to a Planar-Region module, and there's another module called Sink, connected to a 3D-Region.

While invisible by default, we can make these areas visible in the Camera View, just as we viewed Peg trajectories in the previous chapter.

> 1.   In the Network View, select the Planar-Region module.

> 2.   In the Camera View, press [Shift F11], or go to View → Show → Control.

The Planar-Region is visible in the Camera View. You may need to zoom out using [1] on your keyboard.

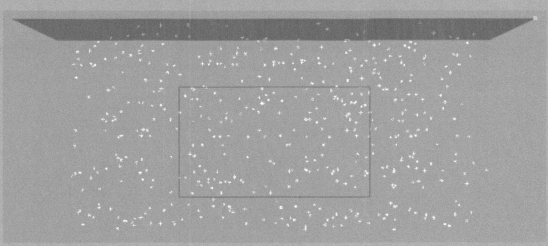

4.143

If you play the scene, you can see how the particles are emitted from the entire plane area. It's quite a bit larger than the scene borders though, so let's resize and reposition it.

> 3. In the Planar-Region's properties, change both **width** and **height** to a value of 25.

> 4. In the Network view, select the Planar-Region's **Peg.**

> 5. Turn off Animate mode and, in the Top view, bring the Planar-Region closer to camera.

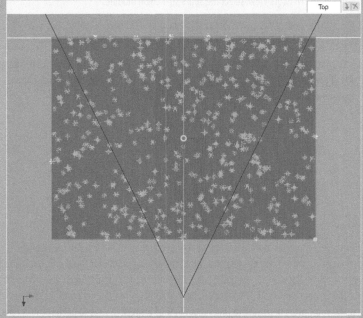

4.144

Play the scene and be amazed! Your snowfall scene should really have some depth now, with some nice distance between the snowflakes being emitted closest to the camera and those at the back of the scene. To give it even more depth, you could increase the height parameter of the Planar-Region. This will put more distance between the furthest and nearest snowflakes.

4.145

The other region in this scene is a 3D-Region, attached to the Sink module. You could think of the Sink as the area in which particles can survive. Once they go outside the Sink, they cease to exist. This is useful for destroying particles that are no longer needed, but could also be used to stop particles going through surfaces; say, an umbrella.

> 6.   In the Network view, select the Sink's 3D-Region module.

> 7.   In the Camera View, press [Shift F11] or go to View → Show → Control.

The 3D region appears in the Camera View now. It's a wireframe cylinder that surrounds the entire particle system. Any particles that go outside this cylinder are removed from the simulation. If you wanted to, you could invert the region via the Sink properties, so that particles only appear outside the region.

4.146

The Layer Properties of the 3D-Region have various shapes that you can use depending on the needs of your scene. We can just stick with the default cylinder for this scene, but take a look at the other shapes if you want and resize them using their properties, or blue vertex handles in the Camera View (you'll need to use the Transform or Translate tool for this). Whatever shape you settle on, be sure to check it out in the Perspective View to get a sense of how it works with your scene.

As always, to hide the regions in the Camera View, simply press [Shift C], or go to View → Hide All Controls.

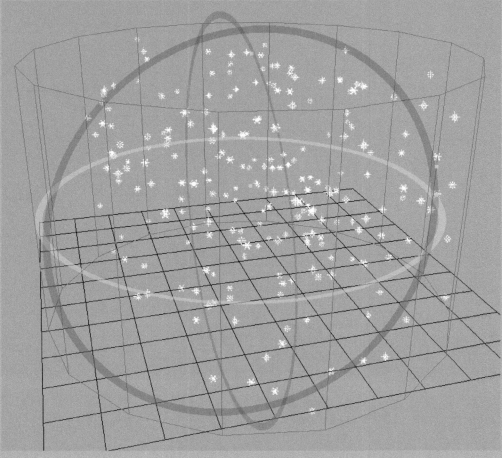

4.147

PARTICLES EXERCISE 6: PARTICLE ROTATION

The only thing that seems to be missing is some rotation on the snowflakes. In this exercise we'll add the Rotation-Velocity module to the system so each flake tumbles gently as it falls.

> 1. From the Module Library's Particle tab, choose Rotation-Velocity and drag it into the Snow network.

> 2. From the Multi-Port-In (where everything else in this system is connected) drag a cable out and plug it into the Rotation-Velocity input.

> 3. Drag a cable from the Rotation-Velocity output into the Particle-System-Composite (Figure 4.149). Plugged in between the Sink and Move-Particles cables will be fine.

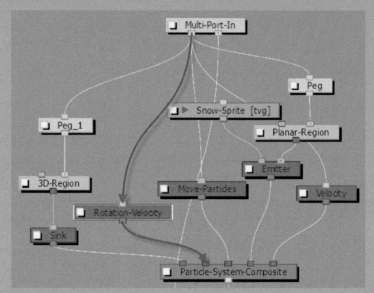

4.149

> 4. With the Rotation-Velocity module selected in the Network, apply the settings via the Layer Properties panel as shown in Figure 4.150.

☑ Enable/Disable		🔒 ⬡
Name:	Rotation-Velocity	

General

Trigger	1	🔄 ▾
Axis Type	Interpolated Axis	▾

Axis

Axis0 X	-1	⬍ 🔄 ▾
Axis0 Y	0	⬍ 🔄 ▾
Axis0 Z	1	⬍ 🔄 ▾
Axis1 X	0	⬍ 🔄 ▾
Axis1 Y	-1	⬍ 🔄 ▾
Axis1 Z	1	⬍ 🔄 ▾

Speed (Degrees/Frame)

Minimum	-5	⬍ 🔄 ▾
Maximum	5	⬍ 🔄 ▾
		Close

4.150

The Axis fields control how each particle rotates. Positive values are a forward rotation; negative values are a backwards rotation; zero is, of course, no rotation. It may help you remember these x, y, z axis rotation values if you think of them as *pitch*, *yaw* and *roll*, or alternatively, *tumble*, *turn* and *spin*, as shown in Figure 4.151.

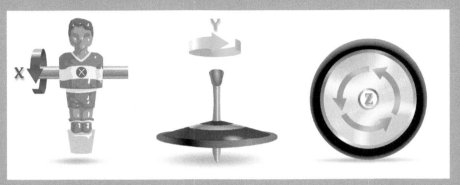

4.151

> 5. Finally, in the Sprite-Emitter properties, go to the Rendering tab and enable 'Use Rotation of Particle'.

4.152

> 6. Play the simulation to see some lovely tumbling, turning, spinning snowflakes.

If you think your snowflakes are too large, you can adjust the Size over Age value, which can be found on the Rendering tab of the Emitter properties.

4.153

This simulation is now ready to drop into any snow scene that comes your way. You can fine-tune the Sprite-Emitter, ParticleBaker, Rotation Velocity and Region settings according to the needs of any given scene. In Appendix A you'll learn how to save modules to your library so they can be shared and imported into any project.

PARTICLE EXAMPLES SUMMARY

The past six exercises have demonstrated that a completely new effect can be built around a pre-configured particle example. This is very much the case with a great number of particle effect needs. You can take something from the Module Library's Particle-Examples tab and reconfigure it to look and behave exactly how you want it.

EFFECTS SUMMARY

This chapter has introduced you to some of the most frequently used effects. For Animate Pro and Harmony, you only need to look at the Module Library to see just how much more there is to explore.

When you use effects and use them well, you breathe life into your characters and atmosphere into your scenes.

CHAPTER 5

Camera

The Camera View is so called because it is the view from a scene camera. If you don't add your own Camera, the scene uses its own static camera which isn't found in the Timeline or Network, nor can it be animated. You do have limited control over this default camera, including the resolution, FOV (field of view angle) and grid settings, all of which you can access in Scene → Scene Settings.

5.1

Generally you would add a Camera only if you want to animate the view, such as panning, zooming, trucking or rotating. If your scene doesn't require any of this camera animation, then there's usually no reason to add one.

5.2

Camera move terminology can differ slightly between animation and live action. In live action film, 'panning' generally means turning left and right on the spot without travelling. In animation, you may hear the same term used for moving left and right, as well as up and down and turning.

☑ Enable/Disable

Name: Camera

Position

(x) Axis   0

(y) Axis   0

(z) Axis   12 F

Angle   0

Pivot

(x) Axis   0

(y) Axis   0

Override Scene Fov ☑

FOV   Camera: FOV: 32

Set Default FOV

5.3

FIELD OF VIEW

When added to the scene, a new Camera inherits the FOV specified in the Scene settings. However, in your Camera's Layer Properties panel, you have options to override the scene Camera settings with your own FOV.

You can animate this value in the Timeline's data view but you can get the same effect by simply animating the *scale* of the Camera Peg, which is much more intuitive.

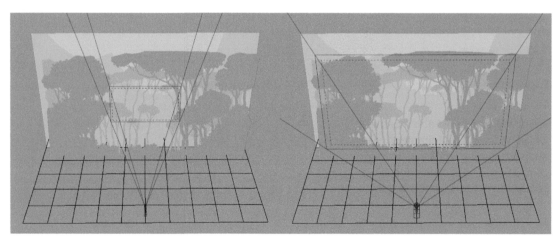

5.4

ADDING A CAMERA

As far as Timeline layers are concerned, a Camera is much like other layers. It can be added via the Timeline ⊕ button. If you're using Animate, this is the only way to add the Camera, but with Animate Pro and Harmony, you have the additional option to add it into the Network from the Module Library. If it's not already on your Favourites tab, you'll find it on the Move tab.

5.5

CAMERA MOVES

In order to animate the Camera transformation, it must first be attached to a Peg. Once this is done, you can simply keyframe the Peg around the scene to create start and end positions, as well as control the easing and trajectories with control points.

> CAMERA EXERCISE 1
  CAMERA PEG AND KEYFRAMES

We'll now create a simple camera movement around a large background. The following exercise steps through a provided scene file, but feel free to create your own scene with a sufficiently large background that the Camera can pan around.

> 1.   Open up the provided scene called camera_basic from this chapter's files.

> 2.   Add a Camera to the scene:

 Animate – use the ⊕ button in the Timeline to add a Camera. The Camera appears at the bottom of the layer stack in the Timeline.

5.6

Animate Pro and Harmony – from the Module Library's Favourites tab, drag a Camera into the Network view and leave it floating off to one side.

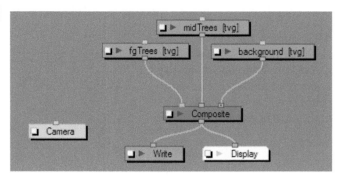

5.7

> 3. In the Timeline, select the Camera layer and add a Peg by clicking the ⊛ button. If you're using Animate Pro or Harmony, you could also simply drag a Peg from the Module Library's Favourites tab into the Network and attach it. However, if you do it in the Timeline, the Peg is automatically named.

> 4. In the Timeline, select the first frame of the Peg layer (Camera-P).

5.8

> 5. Ensure the Animate button is on.

With the Camera Peg selected, the scene border becomes yellow, indicating that keyframes will be set as you move the Peg around the scene. With the Animate button turned off, the scene border is red, so the Camera Peg and all of its keyframes will be moved together without setting any keyframes.

> 6. In the Camera View, using the Translate tool [Alt 2], move the Camera to a starting position.

> 7. In the Timeline, move the playhead to the last frame.

> 8. In the Camera View, move the Camera to its end position with the Translate tool.

5.9

Now if you scrub the playhead in the Timeline, or play back the scene using the playback controls, you'll see the Camera movement in action.

Just like other Peg movements, you can make a function curve for the Velocity parameter and create some easing. Revisit page 204 if you need to a refresher on how to add easing to a function curve.

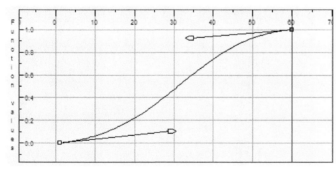

5.10

WHERE IS THE CAMERA?

By now you're well and truly familiar with the Camera View and we've also touched briefly on the Top, Side and Perspective Views back in Chapter 3 in the '3D space' section starting on page 211.

In the Camera View, you can't actually see a Camera because you're looking through it. The only visualisation you have of the Camera itself is the movie border. When selected, this border changes colour (usually red or yellow, depending on whether Animate mode is off, or on).

In the Top and Side Views, however, you can see the Camera, visualised as a V shape, representing the FOV (field of view). When in the Perspective view, you can also show or hide the Camera using the Show/Hide Camera button in the bottom left.

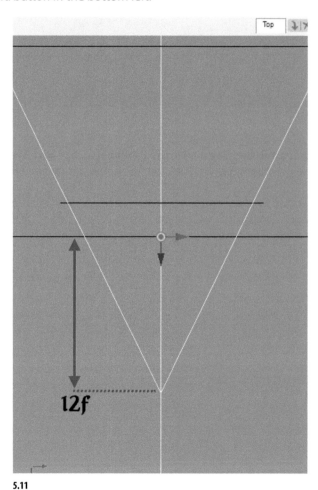

5.11

Enable/Disable

Name: Camera

Position
(x) Axis 0
(y) Axis 0
(z) Axis 12 F

Angle 0

Pivot
(x) Axis 0
(y) Axis 0

Override Scene Fov
FOV 31.4173
Set Default FOV

5.12

As you can see in the Top and Side Views, the Camera is set back from the scene. The exact distance is 12F (12 grid units forward) on the z axis, as shown in the Camera's layer properties.

CAMERA TRANSFORM

Animating the Camera Peg's position, rotation and scale is no different to animating Pegs for other layers. Movement is keyframed, the path manipulated with control points and easing controlled with function curves.

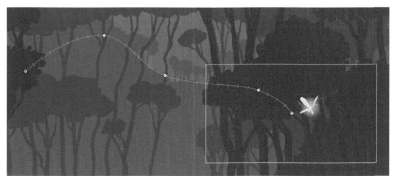

5.13

CONNECTING OTHER LAYERS TO THE CAMERA PEG

Occasionally you'll want scene elements to move with the camera. For example, you may have subtitles or credits over a scene that's panning across a large background. You could attach the titles to a Peg, and then match that Peg movement with that of the Camera.

5.14

However, the better option is to simply attach the titles and Camera to the same Peg. This way, wherever the Camera Peg goes, the titles go.

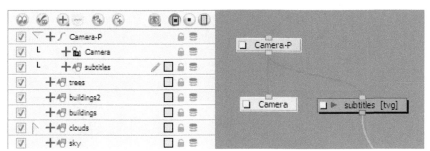

5.15

ANIMATE PRO & HARMONY ONLY

3D CAMERA

As you learned back in Chapter 3, when you enable 3D on Drawing layers and Pegs, you can create entire rooms by rotating walls, floors and ceilings into place. When you add 3D rotation to your scene Camera's Peg, you open up a world of cinematic possibilities.

5.16

In Figure 5.16, an entire set has been built using Drawing layers. In this scene, the Camera sits in the middle of the table and simply rotates to focus on each character as they deliver their lines. Outside the window there are more layers and even a snow particle simulation (Harmony only).

The advantage of this setup is that you can endlessly experiment with the Camera position in the scene. The disadvantage is that unless your camera moves are really carefully planned, characters and other 2D elements can really look flat in the 3D environment, as illustrated in Figure 5.17.

5.17

Z DEPTH AND MULTIPLANE

When your scene layers are separated along the z axis, the scene has *depth*. This z space depth is what turns an ordinary Camera trucking movement into something special.

In the days of traditional animation, this was called a *multiplane* camera move because the camera physically travelled past multiple layers (or the layers were moved past the camera), to give the illusion of real space in the scene.

5.18

Advanced 2D software like Toon Boom allows multiplane camera effects without any additional work. Merely by adding distance between the layers in 3D space, your scenes automatically show that depth whenever the camera moves.

VERTIGO

You can animate characters independent of camera and backgrounds for some special camera effects, like the classic 'vertigo' effect, where a camera moves toward the character while simultaneously zooming out.

5.19

Incidentally, this is called the *vertigo effect* because it was made famous in the 1958 Hitchcock film *Vertigo*. The shot starts with a narrow field of view (zoomed in), then, as the camera moves toward the character, the field of view is widened (zoomed out). As the character's onscreen size is maintained, the world around him appears to widen, or if the effect is reversed, the world closes in.

To achieve this effect, start by attaching the character to your Camera Peg just as you would with subtitles (see Figure 5.15), then animate the scale of your Camera Peg. Your background elements will be affected by scale but the character, attached to the Camera Peg, will not.

MULTIPLE CAMERAS

Your scene can contain multiple Cameras, each with its own FOV, Peg and animation settings. While multiple Cameras are useful for setting up several unique Camera angles in the same scene, there is also the option of using twin Cameras for creating a 3D stereoscopic scene or movie.

5.20

CHOOSING WHICH CAMERA TO VIEW

With multiple Cameras in your scene, you can choose which Camera to view through from the Scene → Camera menu.

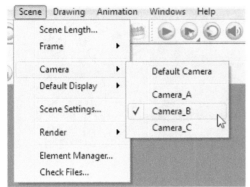

5.21

NOTE
Even with multiple Cameras in the scene, your Timeline may only show the active camera. To see all Cameras in the Timeline go to Scene → Default Display → Display All.

5.22

> CAMERA EXERCISE 2
  MULTIPLE CAMERAS

> 1.   From the chapter files, open camera_multiple.

> 2.   Add a Camera to the scene and rename it 'Camera_A'.

> 3.   Select Camera_A and add a Peg via the Timeline ⊕, so the Peg is automatically named.

> 4. Select the Camera_A Peg and then move it to frame the first character.

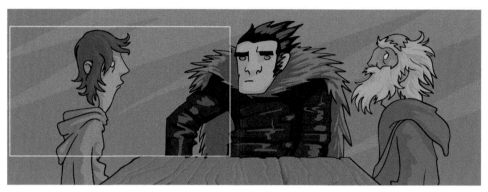

5.23

> 5. Add a second Camera, rename it 'Camera_B'.

> 6. Select Camera_B and once again add a Peg via the Timeline ⚙.

You now have three Cameras in the scene; the two you've just added, plus the original default Camera. Once again, if you can't see the new Cameras in the Timeline, go to Scene → Default Display → Display All.

> 7. Make Camera_B the active Camera by going to Scene → Camera → Camera_B.

> 8. Using the Translate [Alt 2] and Scale [Alt 4] tools, move the Camera_B Peg so that Camera_B frames the second character (Figure 5.24).

5.24

Switching Cameras in this way is useful mainly for workflow purposes, especially when making stereoscopic scenes, but Cameras cannot be switched on the Timeline. That is, you can't have the scene shown through Camera 1 for half of the scene and then switch to Camera 2. For something like that, you'd either keyframe the Camera Peg to jump-cut a single Camera from position 1 to 2, or you would render half the scene from Camera A and the second half from Camera B.

You'll learn all about rendering in Chapter 7 where we'll also touch on multiple Cameras for stereoscopic and 3D output.

SUMMARY

Cameras are the eyes of the director. The audience, therefore, experiences the story through that director's eyes. When you use a Camera, you're directing the audience to look at something the way you want them to see it.

Using your favourite angles, close-ups, wide shots and techniques like camera shakes and vertigo cam, you can develop your own style, creating a unique experience for the audience.

In the next chapter, we'll look at audio: often the final major step in bringing your movie to life.

5.25

CHAPTER 6

Audio

W hat movie would be complete without audio? Even if your script is entirely without dialogue, it's likely that you'll still need to have sound effects, music or both.

A scene that is entertaining in silence will be a hundred times more so with good audio. It's a key ingredient in entertaining animation.

6.1

PREPARING AUDIO

Most audio will require at least some preparation before importing. Only rarely will you be able to buy or record a piece of audio and just plop it raw onto the Timeline. Preparation means converting, editing or trimming the sound so that it works in the scene.

If you plan to do a lot of audio work, it'll help to know your way around a sound editing program, like Adobe Audition, Adobe Sound-booth, Audacity or Apple's Logic Pro. There are some limited tools in Toon Boom's audio interface provided for trimming and volume adjustment. We'll look at that a bit later in the chapter. Generally though, it's advisable to organise and name your audio files well before bringing them in.

sc1_line1_nick.mp3
sc1_line2_jimmy.mp3
sc1_sfx_doorOpen.mp3
sc1_sfx_kettleBoiling.mp3
sc2_line3_nick.mp3
sc2_sfx_footsteps.mp3
sc2_sfx_teacupRattle.mp3
sc2_sfx_waterPouring.mp3
sc3_line4_jimmy.mp3
sc3_sfx_chairCreak.mp3
sc3_sfx_doorSlam.mp3

6.2

WHICH FORMATS CAN BE IMPORTED?

Toon Boom accepts three common audio formats for importing to the Timeline. These are .mp3, .wav and .aiff. If your audio is in a more obscure format, for example .ogg, .3gpp, .m4a or .cda, you'll first need to convert it to one of the three acceptable formats before attempting to import.

NOTE

Converting file formats can be a tricky business and is beyond the scope of this book. Some formats are strictly controlled by their creators; for example, a song in your iTunes library may be protected against conversion and therefore cannot be simply imported into Toon Boom without an evening of online research and messing about with shadowy conversion software.

As well as the potential legal hassles, it's very likely that using some-one else's audio without permission will get your movie taken down from certain video-sharing sites. It's always sensible to obtain the proper permissions before simply converting your favourite song and using it in your project, especially if that project is for public broadcast.

When importing audio, each sound is placed on its own layer; adding three sounds to a scene will result in three additional Timeline layers (Figure 6.3).

6.3

After saving your scene, any imported audio becomes part of the scene structure and you'll find it in the scene's *audio* directory (Figure 6.4).

audio
elements
environments
frames
jobs
palette-library

6.4

THE WAVEFORM

A waveform is a visual representation showing audio levels along a line. Silence is represented by a flat line, while sound makes the line wavy, with peaks and troughs.

Figure 6.5 is a screenshot from Adobe Audition, a sound recording and editing program. When magnified, you can see the string of points that forms the sound wave.

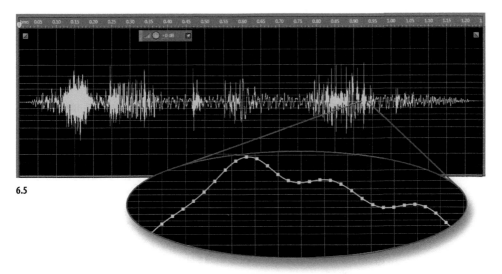

6.5

Audio is imported as a layer into the Toon Boom Timeline, displaying the audio's waveform.

> AUDIO EXERCISE 1
  IMPORTING AUDIO

There are two ways to create a Sound layer; one is to use the ⊕ icon and choose Sound. However, this method only creates a blank sound layer into which audio will eventually need to be imported.

In this exercise we'll import audio directly and then look at the sound layer in the Timeline.

> 1.   From this chapter's files, open audio_newsGuy.

> 2.   Go to File → Import → Sound.

> 3. Browse to this chapter's files and inside the audio folder, choose audio_Line-1.wav.

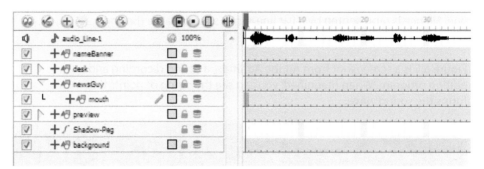

6.6

The newsreader's audio is imported into the Timeline and appears as an audio layer with a waveform.

> 4. Save the scene here because you'll use it in the next exercises.

NOTE

If, for some reason the Timeline doesn't show any audio, it may be that audio layers are hidden from your Timeline. Once again, show sound layers in the panel menu ▤▶ → View → Show → Show Sounds (Figure 6.7). While you're there, make sure Show Sound Waveform is also checked.

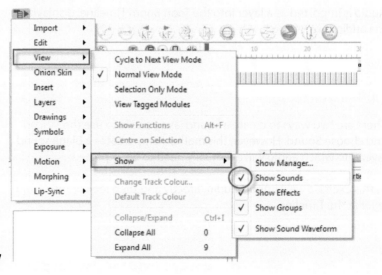

6.7

In the Timeline, an audio layer is identified by a ♪ icon. Where most other layers have a visibility checkbox, the sound layer has a 🔊 speaker icon that can be toggled to mute and un-mute that layer.

6.8

The right-hand side of the sound layer has a ⊕ zoom slider that will increase or decrease the size of the displayed waveform. This is *not* a volume value; merely the height of the waveform displayed in the Timeline. It's useful for when you have low volume audio and need to look closer at the waveform for a visual indicator of where key sounds occur.

> AUDIO EXERCISE 2
SCRUBBING AUDIO

Audio scrubbing is essential in animation. If you are to animate anything in sync with audio, you'll need to hear the sound on the Timeline as you move the playhead back and forth.

> 1. On the playback control, activate audio scrubbing. It's the speaker icon with an S on it (Figure 6.9).

6.9

> 2. Drag the playhead back and forth to hear each frame of the audio: 'Welcome to the evening news.'

I have provided mouth shapes in the library but there's currently no lip-sync in the scene. Later, you'll scrub the audio and insert the appropriate mouth shapes along the Timeline.

THE SOUND EDITOR

There's a couple of ways to open the Sound Editor window. The simplest is to double-click the Sound layer's name in the Timeline. Alternatively, when a sound layer is selected, the Properties panel has a Sound Editor button (Figure 6.10).

The Sound Editor is an advanced Properties panel for your audio. Here you'll be able to scrub, trim, zoom, modify the audio or 'map' it to mouth shapes for Auto Lip Sync.

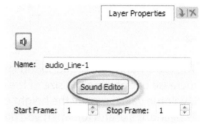

6.10

> AUDIO EXERCISE 3
  EDITING AUDIO

If you play the provided scene file, you'll hear that the audio starts immediately. But it would be better if the news reader paused for around 15 frames before delivering his welcome message. In this exercise we'll adjust the start and end frames of the audio.

> 1. In the newsGuy scene, double-click the audio_Line-1 layer to open the Sound Editor. Alternatively you can click the Sound Editor button in the Layer Properties.

At the top section of the Sound Editor is the Sound Element preview with frame numbers along the top (Figure 6.11).

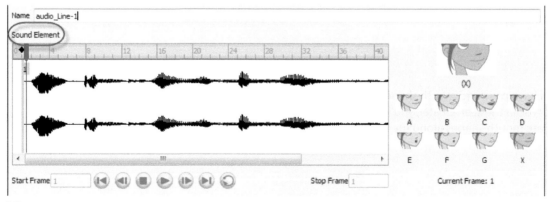

6.11

This preview is the audio *as it will be heard* in the final scene. The news-Guy audio starts at frame 1 and ends at frame 45.

> 2. In the Sound Element (top) section, click the waveform to select it.

> 3. Still in the Sound Element pane, drag the green Start Frame flag along to frame 15 (see Figure 6.12). You can also enter the value in the Start Frame field.

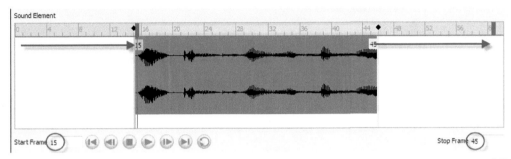

6.12

> 4. Now set the sound's end frame by dragging the yellow End Frame flag to the end of the scene.

> 5. Close the Sound Editor and save your scene.

> 6. In the Playback controls, ensure the audio speaker is turned on (Figure 6.13) and play the scene.

6.13

The audio now starts at frame 15 and finishes just before the end of the scene.

> AUDIO EXERCISE 4
> ADJUSTING VOLUME

We can raise or lower the volume and even fade in/out or silence parts of it. In the lower part of the Sound Editor we have the Current Sound window. Thin, blue, horizontal lines represent the volume level and these can be raised or lowered using the control points.

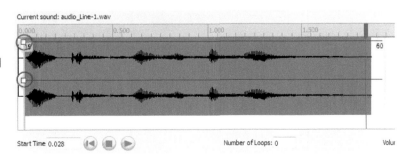

6.14

> 1. Drag the volume control points downward to lower the volume and then play back the audio to hear the effect.

> 2. Click anywhere on the horizontal blue lines to create new control points. Delete any unwanted control points by dragging them off the waveform, just as you would with gradient tacks when mixing colours (Figure 6.15).

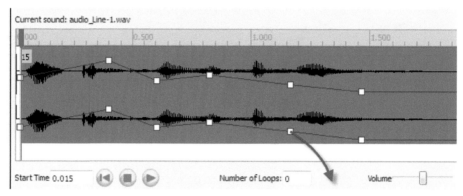

6.15

> 3. Experiment with the volume levels by raising and lowering these controls. Try creating a fade-in or fade-out by manipulating the points.

In the Current Sound section, there are other functions to play with, like zooming, scrubbing, number of loops. There's also the ability to trim the audio using the green and yellow flags.

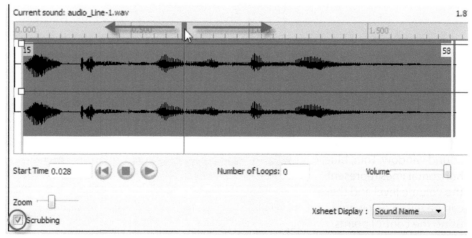

6.16

> 4. Before we move on, delete any experimental control points you added to the volume lines so the audio is at a constant level

> 5. Save the scene for use in the upcoming exercises.

If you're wondering about the mouth shapes images on the upper right, that is for Auto Lip Sync, which is something we'll talk about on page 395.

TIP
It's possible to make a simple echo or reverb on the Timeline, using two instances of the same sound. Simply import the sound onto two separate layers. Open the second layer in the Sound Editor and name it 'echo' in the Name field.

Shift the echo along the timeline by three or four frames and lower the volume considerably. Close the Sound Editor and play the scene to hear the echo.

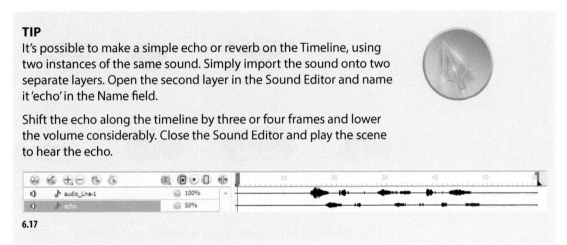

6.17

LIP-SYNC AND PHONEMES

The term 'lip-sync' means that a character's lips are synchronised with the sounds being heard. When the news reader says 'Welcome to the evening news', his mouth will be animated with the individual shapes to appear as if he's actually saying those words.

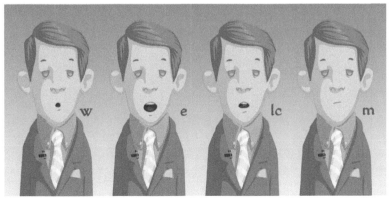

6.18

These individual sounds, called *phonemes*, are what makes up language and are at the heart of lip-sync. Each phoneme will have its own mouth shape, which is something you saw back in Chapter 3's section on Drawing Substitution (see page 280).

Generally speaking, even the most limited animation styles utilise some form of lip-sync. One example is the TV series, *South Park*. It has extremely limited animation, yet the characters have mouth shapes that are synchronised with the dialogue recording.

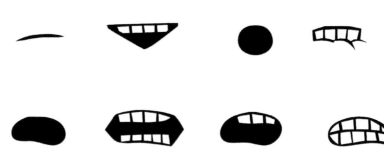

6.19
South Park-style mouth shapes

At the other end of the scale, if you're familiar with Japanese animation, you may have noticed that its lip-sync tends to have very few mouth shapes, so the mouths are not much more animated than that of a sock puppet.

6.20

The number of mouth shapes you use for your lip-sync is up to you, or the style of the project. Naturally, more fluid and realistic lip-sync will require more mouth shapes and take longer to animate.

> AUDIO EXERCISE 5
  LIP-SYNC

In the news reader scene, there is a basic set of mouth shapes in the mouth layer for you to use. This exercise will step you through using Drawing Substitution to place the mouth shapes at the correct spots on the Timeline.

> 1.   Open the news reader scene.

> 2.   Activate audio scrubbing with the button on the playback controls (Figure 6.21).

6.21

> 3.   Drag the playhead along the Timeline until you hear the first sound of the news reader.

As you drag the playhead, the first phoneme heard is the 'w' in the word *welcome*.

> 4.   Position the playhead at the frame where the 'w' sound starts.

> 5.   Select that frame of the *mouth* layer.

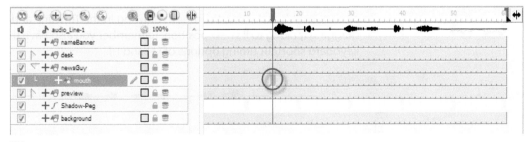

6.22

In the Library panel, you'll see the news reader's mouth preview image.

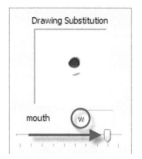

6.23

> 6. In the Library, drag the Drawing Substitution slider along until you arrive at the mouth shape called 'w' (Figure 6.23).

In the Timeline, you'll now see that the 'w' drawing has been inserted. You can scrub the Timeline to hear while you watch the mouth change.

> 7. In the Timeline, position the playhead at the start of the next phoneme: the 'eh' sound.

> 8. Once again, select that frame of the mouth layer.

> 9. Use the substitution slider to find the 'eh' mouth shape.

> 10. Continue along the Timeline, adding the mouth shapes to match the phonemes you hear in the audio.

TIP
One of the first lessons of lip-sync is that it's not necessary to insert a mouth shape for every letter of every word. Watch your own mouth in a mirror while saying the word 'welcome' naturally. This can be animated with just four mouth shapes: *w – eh – l – m*. Perhaps you could even skip the *l* mouth shape if it's spoken quickly enough: *w – eh – m*. Keep this in mind when animating this and future lip-sync scenes; it could save you a lot of work.

When you've finished all of the lip-sync, ensure you have Sound turned on and play the scene using [Shift + Enter] or the playback controls.

If the audio sync is slightly out on any particular mouth shape, you can retime it by selecting the mouth drawing in the Timeline and then dragging it along to its new position. Remember you also have the keyboard shortcut timing options of [+] and [-].

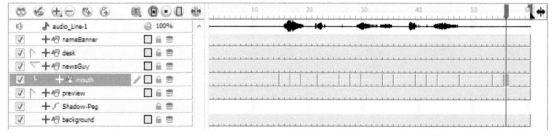

6.24

LIP-SYNC SETUP

The provided newsGuy scene was fully set up with mouth shapes for you in the Library, but in the next exercise you'll see how to do this yourself.

The first step to animating lip-sync is to create a layer of mouth shapes. If your project is in the cut-out style, you should be able to reuse the set of mouth shapes in other scenes.

NOTE
A character's mouth layer may include other parts of the face. Suppose for example that your character has a beard and you'd like the beard and moustache to move and change shape as the mouth does. In this case the mouth shapes may include the facial hair.

6.25

Likewise, if you want the character's jaw and chin to move up and down with certain phonemes, you could draw the chin and jaw on the mouth shapes layer.

> AUDIO EXERCISE 6
  MOUTH SHAPES SETUP

In this exercise you'll draw ten mouth shapes for your own character.

6.26

> 1. In your own scene, draw a character with no mouth. It's not neces-sary to make a finished character design; feel free to use a rough character drawing for this exercise.

> 2. Add a new layer called 'mouth' for the character.

> 3. In the Timeline on the mouth layer, select the first frame and draw a closed mouth shape (see the first mouth in Figure 6.26).

> 4. Still in the mouth layer, move to the second frame and draw the next mouth shape (see the second mouth in Figure 6.26).

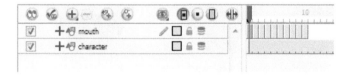

6.27

> 5. Using Figure 6.26 for reference, continue drawing the remaining mouth shapes on new frames of the mouth layer, until finally you have ten frames.

Currently the mouth shapes are named by the frames they were created on. However, in the *newsGuy* file from earlier, you may have noticed the mouth shapes are named A to J. Let's rename the drawings.

> 6. In the Timeline, right-click the first drawing on the mouth layer and choose Rename Drawing. You can alternatively use the keyboard shortcut [Ctrl/⌘ D].

6.28

> 7. Name the first mouth shape whatever you like. Traditionally a closed mouth shape is labelled A, but you could name it 'mbp' (the sounds a closed mouth makes).

> 8. Using the same method, rename each drawing; B, C, D and so on. Or, if you prefer, 'dstz', 'eh', 'uh', 'oh', etc., as explained in the previous step.

TRADITIONAL ANIMATION PHONEMES

In the days of traditional animation, in order to streamline the work-flow for television, lip-sync was standardised with eight essential mouth shapes. These covered most phonemes heard in ordinary speech and allowed very fast lip-sync.

The standard mouth shapes were lettered A, B, C, D, E, F, G. To aid the animator, phonemes were plotted on the X-sheet, to match the sounds heard in the audio (Figure 6.29).

Today, these essential mouth shapes are still used in digital animation, particularly in the cut-out style. This traditional method of lettering mouth shapes is the basis for Toon Boom's Auto Lip Sync tool.

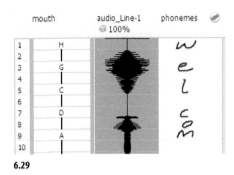

6.29

AUTO LIP SYNC

With Toon Boom's Drawing Substitution method, lip-sync is made easier but it can still be a time-consuming task. Even the simplest lip-sync scenes will require some manual fiddling.

While Auto Lip Sync is an impressive feature of Toon Boom, it's not a magical solution. Much like morphing, it's a robot that attempts to put things in place, but, more often than not, it'll require some fine-tuning. As such, it's a relatively minor tool that merely creates a rough pass for the lip-sync. For this reason, we won't step through any Auto Lip Sync exercises.

Once you know how to animate lip-sync using Drawing Substitution, you may like to learn how to utilise Auto Lip Sync to do some of the heavy lifting. If so, I would recommend reading the Auto Lip Sync section in your [F1] User Guide → Sound Chapter → Lip Sync.

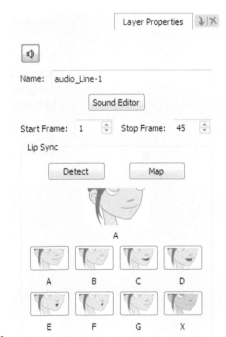

6.30

SOUND EFFECTS

Sound effects are the easiest audio tasks in Toon Boom. Once you know the basics of the Sound Editor, putting a sound effect at the correct place on the Timeline is just about foolproof. If it doesn't quite synchronise with the animation, you can simply shuffle it forward or back in the Sound Editor, as you learned back in exercise 3, starting on page 386.

6.31

6.32

Activate the Sound Scrubbing button for precision when synchronising animation to a sound effect in the Timeline. Also, frequently play back the scene with the Sound on, to test how well the audio synchronises with the animation.

MUSIC AND NARRATION

In Toon Boom, as you know by now, we usually work on individual scene files and then, later, stitch them all together in a video editing program. For sound effects and simple dialogue, that audio can often be contained within each scene, such as the news reader's line.

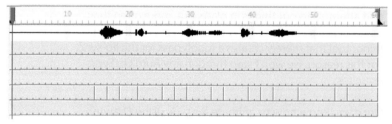

6.33

What about when we have audio that takes place across several scenes; for example, music, voiceover narration or any audio that spans two or more scenes?

6.34

If sync is not important, it may be acceptable to do all the music or narration in your video editing program, later. However, where rock solid sync is important, you have a number of alternative options with cross-scene audio:

Option A: Slicing it up

Using a sound editing program, prepare your audio by slicing it up into parts of individual scene lengths, and then place each part into its respective scene. This may work well for dialogue and narration, but for music it may be quite fiddly, because no matter how hard you try, an audio join can often be audible when the scenes are put together.

Option B: Scratch tracks

Go with option A using temporary placeholder audio, otherwise known as 'scratch tracks'. Later, when the scenes are complete, put it all into your video editing program and replace the scratch tracks with the final, unbroken audio tracks.

Option C: Multiple scenes

Combine several scenes into one scene file. This is rarely advisable, and only then for no more than a few scenes; never for a whole project. If you have say, an explosion sound happening over three scenes, you may consider doing all three scenes in one scene file.

Option D: Toon Boom Storyboard Pro

If you own Toon Boom's Storyboard software, you have a big advantage here. You can storyboard an entire project on the timeline and lay all of the audio down as an unbroken track across all scenes. This is the ideal workflow for music sequences where you want animation to synchronise with a musical rhythm.

Figure 6.35 shows the Toon Boom Storyboard Pro timeline, where an unbroken musical track spans all of the scenes.

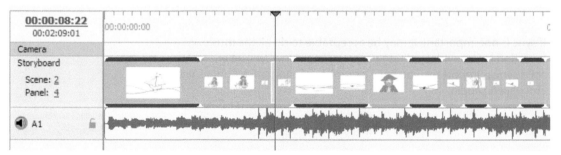

6.35

Once all of the scenes are storyboarded with dialogue, sound effects or music, you go to File → Export → Export to Toon Boom.

From here you can export your entire project as individual scene files, complete in their directory structure. When you open each scene in Animate, Animate Pro or Harmony, the audio is perfectly cut for the specific scene length and synchronising audio with animation is very straightforward.

The big disadvantage to this workflow is that we can't always finalise the audio at the storyboard stage. In most cases, audio is best fine-tuned at, or after, the animation stage.

For most independent animators, one solution is to leave any 'cross-scene' audio, such as music or voiceover narration, until last. After the animation is complete and you've sequenced your scenes together in a video editing program, you can then lay down all your audio tracks, before exporting the complete, final movie.

SUMMARY

In the context of a Toon Boom scene, audio is the final ingredient, appearing as a Timeline layer. With a bit of practice you will grow familiar with the Sound Editor for trimming, moving and volume adjustments.

At this point, you should have a solid understanding of how to create a complete scene in your Toon Boom program, all the way from drawing and animation, to effects, camera and now audio. In the next chapter, we'll look at rendering everything into a format that can be watched, published and shared with the world.

6.36

CHAPTER 7

Rendering

The end game – here we are! Your final working task of any scene is to render all the animation, effects, audio and camera moves, and then output it all as a single video file, which may then be sequenced with the other scenes of the project to create the completed movie. Figure 7.1 is a screenshot of Adobe Premiere Pro CC, where the individual scene QuickTime movies are sequenced on the Timeline. While I personally prefer to use Premiere, the process is very much the same whatever video editing program you use.

7.1

In the same way that rough animation comes before final, you may like to export a series of rough renders for each scene, leaving the final renders until later. Rough renders may be a lower resolution, have rough animation, have effects disabled or have temporary sound and music. These roughs will be quicker to render while giving you a solid idea of how the scenes work together in sequence. Figure 7.2 shows a scene with background and effects complete, while the character is still rough.

7.2

TIP

Without delving too deep into specific video editing software, it's worth mentioning that programs like Premiere don't import your movie files, they merely reference them. In other words, Premiere points to the file's location on your computer, rather than importing the file into the project. What's great about that is you can sequence all of your scenes together on the Premiere timeline long before they are complete, even at storyboard/animatic stage.

Then, back in Toon Boom, you go through your project finishing and rerendering each scene, replacing rough renders with clean ones, they'll automatically appear in Premiere because those file reference links are the same (provided you haven't changed their filenames). This practical method is a fun way to watch your project transform gradually from rough to clean.

PROCESSING POWER

Rendering speed is proportional to the speed of your computer. It'll be much more noticeable on complex scenes with lots of effects and at higher resolutions. This is the case with most video production programs, which demand a certain percentage of your computer's processing power for rendering.

It's not just the final render that can be demanding. The Camera View's OpenGL render, while much less resource-hungry, nevertheless requires a portion of your computer's power. You may therefore experience slowdown with very heavy scenes; for example, a scene with lots of mask/cutters, particles, intricate morphing and so on.

7.3

If your animation workstation is built for such work, or doubles as a gaming beast, then even complex Toon Boom frames should be relatively quick to render. At the other end of the scale, if you are using a slow family laptop that's a few years old and cluttered with files and many other programs, it's more likely to struggle with complex scenes, or even crash from time to time due to CPU overload.

With a 'low-spec' computer (i.e., minimal hardware specifications) that's nevertheless clean and stable, you may find that complex frames are rendered fine, albeit slowly. In this case you could keep your largest scenes aside to render them overnight.

RENDER PREVIEWS

More often than not, before you're ready to render a complete scene you will want to preview how the final frames will look. You can either preview a single frame, or a sequence of multiple frames.

SINGLE-FRAME PREVIEW

The Render View is designed to preview one frame render at a time, rather than an entire scene. This is just to help you see how a single frame will look and is most useful when we're fine-tuning the specific values of an effect.

Previously, especially in the Effects chapter, we've tested our scenes and various values by previewing frames in the Render view. Figure 7.4 is a scene from a music video I created for a song called 'Into the Woods' by Australian musician Cilla Jane.

In the OpenGL Camera view before being rendered, you can see the raw art, including the untreated eye and blush patches. In the final rendered image seen in the render view, the eye and blush patches, the tones, high-lights and background blur have all come together for the final scene.

7.4

MULTI-FRAME PREVIEW

When you'd like to test render a sequence of frames, or an entire scene, you can use the Play preview. Toon Boom Play is an image player built into your Toon Boom software and is opened from the top menu or playback controller (Figure 7.5).

7.5

Before rendering, you can specify the frame range using the Start and Stop frame markers. When you click the Render and Play button, frames are rendered and saved as a sequence of images in the *frames* folder of your scene (Figure 7.6).

7.6

Once rendered, Play loads the frames, at which point you can use the playback controls at the bottom of the window to watch the sequence.

7.7

After you've rendered one preview, any subsequent previews will overwrite the previous image sequence in the frames folder. The overwrite warning appears letting you know that you're about to overwrite the former preview (Figure 7.8).

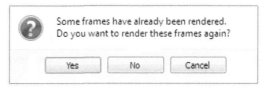

7.8

TIP

If you'd like to archive any earlier previews, you should move them into another folder beforehand so they're not overwritten by the new render. In Figure 7.9, two previous renders are moved to their own folders so they're not overwritten by a new render.

7.9

ANIMATE PRO & HARMONY ONLY

DISPLAY MODULES

Every scene has a default Display that allows us to see what's in the scene. In the Network View, this Display module is plugged into the main scene Composite, which means that everything in the scene will be displayed (Figure 7.10).

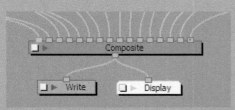

7.10

However, sometimes you want to preview a specific part of the network without necessarily rendering everything in the scene. Connecting your Display module to individual scene elements can lighten the render load, especially in large scenes.

Suppose you have a very complex scene that contains multiple layered characters, effects, particle systems and intricate background art but right now you're just working on the moon glow. You shouldn't need to display the entire scene if you're just working on those glow values. You can simply disconnect the default Display module from the main scene Composite and then plug it into your sky layers.

In Figure 7.11, the Display is connected to a Composite module that has all the sky elements. These will be the only layers shown in the Camera and Render views. Alternatively you can add more Display modules. Simply drag them from the Module Library's IO tab, into the Network and connect them wherever you see fit.

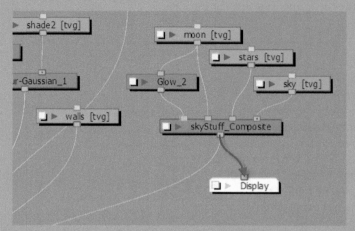

7.11

When you have multiple displays, choose your default from the top menu: Scene → Default Display. You can also use the Display drop-down list as shown in Figure 7.12. If you don't see it on the Toolbar, you'll find it in Windows → Toolbars → Display.

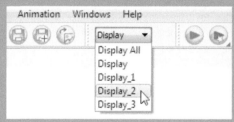

7.12

WRITE MODULE

You could think of the Write module as the 'render settings' module. It is connected to the main scene Composite by default, so that everything in your scene is written to the export. However, just as with the Display module, you can render individual scene elements by connecting the Write module to them.

As shown in Figure 7.13, the Write module's Layer Properties contains options for format, resolution and save destination.

7.13

The options here are mostly for rendering image sequences. When you're rendering a QuickTime movie, there are no format choices, but you can adjust the QuickTime-specific settings using the Customize button.

7.14

Add multiple Write modules to the Network if you want to render several versions of the scene at the same time. For example, you may want to export your scene as an image sequence, but you also want to use one specific frame as a promotional image. For this you can set up two Write modules in the Network as follows:

> **Write_1** exports all frames as a .png image sequence to the 'frames' folder.

> **Write_2** only exports frame 22 in .psd format to folder called 'stills'.

Once the Write modules are set up, simply use File → Export → Render Network [Ctrl/⌘ Shift Y] to render them all at once.

EXPORT FORMATS

Most projects require you to export one specific format or another, whether images or video files. For example, one client may request that your scenes be delivered as an image sequence, while in a separate project, the client may require your export as a video.

IMAGE FORMATS

Exporting individual frames is useful not only for image sequences but also for print. As mentioned earlier in the book, Toon Boom is excellent illustration software. In the following exercise, you'll see how to render a single image, or a sequence of multiple images.

> RENDER EXERCISE 1
  RENDER IMAGES

This exercise contains image export instructions for Animate, Animate Pro and Harmony.

> 1. Open any of the scenes provided with this book's download files, or any scene that you've created.

> 2. Open the Export options from the top menu:

7.15

 Animate –go to File → Export → Images [Ctrl/⌘ Shift Y]. Here you will specify file format and the specific frames to be rendered as images. Once the desired settings are entered, click 'OK' to render the frames (Figure 7.15).

Animate Pro and Harmony – Go to File → Export → Render Network [Ctrl/⌘ Shift Y]. Specify the frame range and click 'OK' to render those frames (Figure 7.16). Note that you should already have specified the file names, destination, file types and frame range in the Write module's Layer properties.

7.16

NOTE
Unless you enter a custom destination in the Path field, all rendered images will be saved in your scene's frames folder.

MOVIE FORMATS

Apple QuickTime (.mov) is a very common video format that works on most computers and is the only video format you can export from Toon Boom.

Should you need your scenes or movie in any other video format, such as .avi or .mpg, you will need to convert your rendered .mov videos using another program. Alternatively, you could export an image sequence, bring it into a video-editing program and export it in your chosen video format.

You'll learn more about exporting a movie on page 414.

TIP

If you already have iTunes installed on your computer, there's a good chance QuickTime is also installed, so you should be able to play .mov files easily. If not, simply head to the Apple website (www.apple.com), download and install the free QuickTime player.

If you don't mind spending some money, QuickTime Pro happens to be a very useful and inexpensive program for quickly sequencing scenes together, simply by copying and pasting scenes together.

SWF EXPORT

There are a few reasons you might export your scene to the Flash .swf format. Here are some possible scenarios:

- You're making a Flash game, but prefer to create the art assets with Toon Boom.

- You're working for a studio that is developing a Flash series and they want your deliveries in .fla or .swf format.

- You want your movie to be a .swf Flash movie that features interactivity, like menus, buttons or playback controls.

- Your client has requested images in a scalable image format.

When it comes to vector graphics Toon Boom does a good job of exporting to the .swf format. However, if your scene contains advanced bitmap effects, such as special blurring, refraction or particle effects, they will not be included in the export. You will probably want to run a few tests to see what works. To test a .swf render, you can use the Test SWF Movie button in the Toolbar (Figure 7.17).

7.17

If you're happy with the test and are ready to go ahead with the .swf render, go to File → Export → SWF. If any particular effects are causing issues, the Export to Flash Movie (Swf) window gives you the option to disable some of them, as shown in Figure 7.18

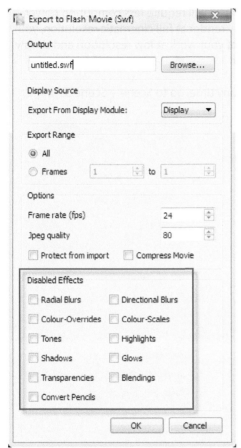

7.18

NOTE
At the time of this writing, Flash CC is the most current version of Adobe Flash, which also happens to be the most stable version yet. Adobe seems to have achieved this (at least in part) by sacrificing a number of Flash features. Bizarrely, one of these features was the ability to import .swf files! Therefore, if you plan on bringing any of your Toon Boom-created .swf files into Flash, you must do it in Flash CS6 or earlier.

RESOLUTION SETTINGS

The resolution of your movie can be changed at any time, higher or lower; it is very useful to work on a low resolution project, and later render it at full resolution. The benefit of working at a low resolution is that even very complex scenes will require less computing power. Even if you plan to eventually render at full cinematic resolution, you may complete the majority of your work at low resolution and simply increase it before you render.

To change the resolution at any time, go to Scene → Scene Settings.

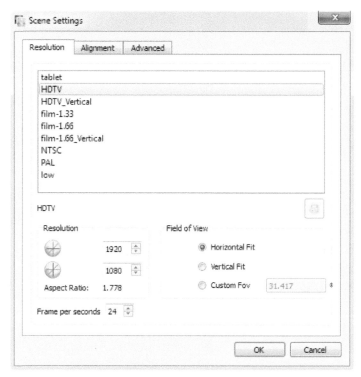

7.19

ASPECT RATIO

Aspect ratio is the proportional relationship between width and height for television and cinema. HDTV for example has an aspect ratio of 16:9 (1.778), while the 'low' and 'film-1.33' resolution presets are 4:3 (1.333). We may be seeing the end of 4:3 (1.333) because it's the ratio of narrow, old-style screens in early television and pre-1953 cinema. Today most screens, including those on mobile devices, accommodate the cinematic 16:9 aspect ratio.

7.20

When you decide to work at a low resolution and switch later to higher for rendering, you should ideally work at the same aspect ratio. For example, if you plan on rendering your scene at 1920 × 1080, you should choose a lower resolution *of the same aspect ratio*. The following resolutions all have an aspect ratio of 16:9 (1.778).

- 1280 × 720

- 960 × 540

- 720 × 405

- 640 × 360

- 480 × 270

Keeping your aspect ratio consistent when switching resolutions ensures your scene will maintain proportions without shrinking or cropping the scene.

MOVIE EXPORT

To export a movie, choose File → Export Movie… This opens a window of settings for the frame range, destination, the Display module and 'Movie Options' (Figure 7.21).

7.21

The Movie Options button allows you to specify additional settings in the QuickTime movie (Figure 7.22).

7.22

COMPRESSION CODEC

By default, the compression codec is set to Animation, which results in large, high-quality files. This codec is a standard in broadcast animation (television and cinema). However, for web video, the Animation codec puts out file sizes that may be unfeasibly large.

WEB COMPRESSION

A very common compression codec for web video is called *H.264*. It's freeware and, at the time of this writing, there's some buzz about the upcoming H.265. If you don't find *H.264* in your codec list, I recommend doing an internet search, downloading it from a reputable site and installing it. When you restart your Toon Boom program, it should appear as an option in your codec list (Figure 7.23).

7.23

If you have a good eye for colour, you will find that a H.264 render appears slightly more 'washed out' than its uncompressed counterpart, but the image quality is still excellent with more web-friendly file sizes.

MPEG-4 (also shown in Figure 7.23) is a sibling of H.264. The two are considered even standards in the digital video industry.

With each codec you will be presented with additional options for quality and frame rate. Experiment with these settings to find something that works for you.

IMAGE SEQUENCE EXPORT

There are many advantages to exporting your scenes as image sequences. Here are just a few:

- Unlike a single large video file, image sequences can be divided up and packaged as smaller manageable chunks for delivery.

- Notice a mistake in your scene after a 40-minute render? It's possible you could rerender and replace only the problem frames, rather than an entire scene.

- If your video editing program doesn't like QuickTime video, it will almost certainly accept an image sequence.

> RENDER EXERCISE 2
   RENDER IMAGE SEQUENCE

To render an image sequence:

 Animate – go to File → Export → Images [Ctrl/⌘ Shift Y]. Choose the image format, frame range and directory, and then click 'OK' to start the render.

7.24

Animate Pro and Harmony –in the Write module's properties, specify the image format and the destination directory. Then, go to File → Export → Render Network [Ctrl/⌘ Shift Y]. When the Render Network window opens, input the frame range if necessary, and then click 'OK' to start the render (Figure 7.25).

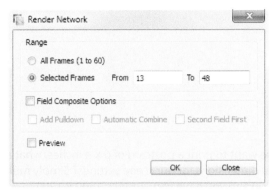

7.25

Once rendered, the images are saved to the specified directory, which by default is the scene's frames folder.

WARNING
When you use Render Network to output an image sequence, there's no overwrite confirmation warning; it simply goes right ahead and overwrites any previous image sequences of the same name. If you want to save a previously rendered image sequence, you should name them differently, or create archive folders (see the Tip Box on page 405) before creating a new image sequence.

EXPORT FOR PRINT

One final consideration for rendering is the capability of Toon Boom to create super high-quality prints. The ease with which you can raise and lower the resolution makes it perfect for working on prints destined for any size.

Print quality is generally expressed in terms of DPI (dots per inch) or PPI (pixels per inch). The accepted minimum resolution for professional print is 300 DPI. This tells us that for every inch of print space, we want

300 pixels, which means at professional print quality, a one-inch × one-inch print must be at least 300 × 300 pixels.

7.26

Therefore, if we want to print a postcard of 6 × 4 inches, what are the minimum pixel dimensions for our scene settings? Simply multiply each inch by 300 and you have your answer: 1800 × 1200.

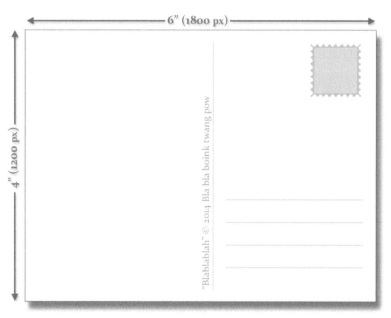

7.27

Using this formula you can work out the minimum resolution for a print of any size. OK, let's get serious: how many pixels for an A2 sized poster? That's 23.4 inches wide and 16.5 inches high.

This comes to 7020 pixels wide and 4950 pixels high; a huge scene resolution! With any level of graphical complexity, it'd likely be very tough even on fast computers. It would make more sense to work at a fraction of that resolution (say 10% = 702 × 495) and when you're ready to render the final, change the resolution to the full A2 size.

The real beauty of this ability to change resolution at any time is that completed scenes may be printed at sizes never considered at the time of doing the work!

TIP
I whipped up my own online print resolution calculator that converts inches to pixels, and vice versa. You'll find the calculator at: bitey.com/px – hope you find it useful!

SUMMARY

With the end of this rendering chapter, you're equipped to take your scenes and entire movie to completion. From here you can start to learn about advanced and more technical aspects of Toon Boom software.

Between now and the end of the book, Appendices A and B will cover some of those in brief detail. There is so much that could not be covered in this book, so when you're ready to take it further – or if you encounter something in your work that demands knowledge not printed here – I suggest delving into the Toon Boom documentation, which is always just a [F1] key press away, or online at docs.toonboom.com.

Advanced Tools

This appendix contains brief information on a handful of advanced tools. Some of these alone could fill up a separate book but hopefully these short introductions can help you get started. You'll find complete documentation on these features in the User Guide [F1] and online at docs.toonboom.com.

ADVANCED COLOUR

Colour in Toon Boom is very powerful, but what you've already learned about creating and mixing colours is just surface functionality. You can link colours to tools, reference external palettes, duplicate, import, tint entire palettes or select strokes by colour. Let's take a quick tour of some of these excellent features.

SELECTING BY COLOUR

Rather than repaint strokes, lines and fills one by one, you can select a colour in the Colour panel, and then press [Ctrl/⌘ Shift A] to select every stroke of that colour in your drawing. This is a great feature of Toon Boom colour, allowing you to quickly delete or repaint multiple areas of a common colour.

As an example, suppose your character is supposed to have a black outline. You've finished the line drawing and are just about done painting all his colours. Then you suddenly notice that you've accidentally drawn all of the character outlines using the dark hair colour instead of the black outline. Don't feel silly – it's an easy mistake to make!

> 1.   In the Colour panel, select the dark brown hair colour.

> 2.   Hit [Ctrl/⌘ Shift A]. Every stroke and spot of that colour in the drawing will be selected.

> 3.   Again in the Colour panel, select the character's outline colour to instantly repaint the selected strokes.

TIP

 You can also use the Select By Colour mode in the Select [Alt S] tool properties. Using this mode just click on any colour and all strokes using that colour will be selected, ready for repainting, deleting or editing.

DUPLICATING PALETTES

A single character palette only goes so far. If your characters visit different locations, in different seasons and at various times of day or night, you'll probably need a few palettes. Once you have created the character's base, or 'day' palette, this is easy to do. The next step is to duplicate that base palette.

In the Colour panel's palette window, right click the palette and choose Duplicate (Figure A1). Rename it according to the palette's intended lighting conditions. For example, I'll duplicate my 'Dashkin_Day' palette and use it as a starting point to create the 'Dashkin_Night' palette.

Don't bother going through and manually changing each colour to a night version though. That's what the Tint panel is for!

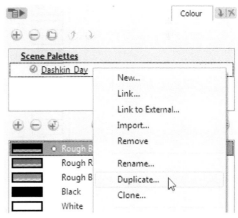

TINT PANEL

A1

Very often, when you're well into a project, you may need to change individual colours. Perhaps you've decided the skin is a bit too green, or brown snowflakes don't really look that great after all. Tweaking individual colours is a simple enough task but what if you want to change a whole bunch of colours – or all of them?

The Tint Panel allows you to adjust multiple colours at once. In the Colour panel, go to the menu ▤▶ → Tint Panel...

If you duplicated your day palette and renamed it night as outlined in the previous section, be sure the night palette is selected in the drop-down list at the top (see Figure A2).

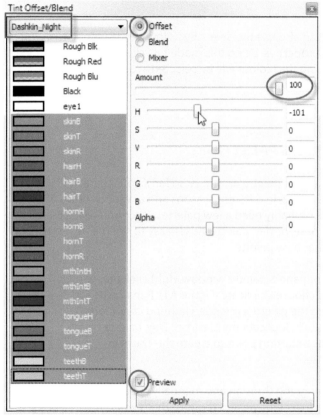

A2

In the left-hand column, as shown above, select individual colours, or [Shift]-select multiple colours that you want to change. Select the Offset option, turn on the Preview checkbox, and start playing with sliders. You'll see the colour swatches updating as you do so and with Preview checked, any art in the scene using those colours will change.

WARNING
Before you click 'Apply' to lock in those changes, be aware that the starting colours will be overwritten. That's a pretty good reason to use duplicate palettes when working on tints.

TEXTURES

When we think of 2D cartoons, we generally think of linework filled with flat colours but in Toon Boom we can paint with texture swatches. Textures can be manipulated with handles in the same way that gradients can be manipulated using the Gradient/Texture manipulator tool [Shift F3].

A3

A texture swatch is created by importing a texture image using the ⊕ button (Figure A4). Any bitmap image in .psd or .tga format may be used as a texture, which you can then use to paint using the Brush tool, or fill with the paint bucket.

A4

IMPORTING PALETTES

Because we work in individual scene files, it's important to be able to use palettes from previous scenes. There are a couple of ways to do this: *link to external* palettes, or *import* them (see below). You will find these options in the 🔻 → Palettes menu, or by right-clicking anywhere in the palette window of the Colour panel.

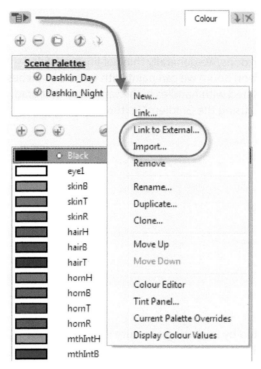

A5

LINK TO EXTERNAL

A6

🔻 → Palettes → Link to External. This creates a reference link in your palette list that points to a palette file elsewhere on your computer. In Figure A6, the Dashkin_Sunset palette is a link to an external palette. Any changes to the colours in this palette will affect the original and will be reflected in any other scene that uses it.

WARNING
Edit linked palettes with care. Linked palettes are incredibly useful for when you want any changes reflected in every scene file (for example, a permanent, project-wide change to the main character's hair colour), but it can be disastrous when you finish an overnight render only to discover a bunch of unwanted colour changes in multiple scenes.

On a studio project, specific palettes may be stored in a centralised location with strict editing permissions. If you're a one-person studio, you may have a folder dedicated to project palettes, or you might just link to the palette in an existing scene folder.

As an example, let's say that in scene 35, snake-rabbit explodes from the bushes with an evil squeak. The last time we saw him was back in scene 3. To bring his colours into scene 35, you can link his palette from the scene 3 → palette-library folder.

> 1.　Go to 📑▶ → Palettes → Link to External.

> 2.　In your project directory, browse to the scene 3 folder → palette-library.

> 3.　Select the snake-rabbit palette and click 'Open'.

IMPORT A PALETTE

📑▶ → Palettes → Import. When you import a palette, you're essentially bringing a duplicate into the scene. You can make changes to it and the original will remain unaffected.

A particularly quick and useful way to import a palette is to simply import a drawing that you created in another Toon Boom scene file. A character model sheet with colours is a good example. When you import it from the library, it brings its palette with it.

ADVANCED DRAWING

We have covered most of the Drawing tools but there are a couple of Advanced Drawing features that you should find useful.

TEXTURES

Textured brushes are different to texture colour swatches. You might use a texture colour swatch as a fill for patterned wallpaper or a coarse fabric effect. A textured brush however is applied as a brush stroke, allowing for, among other things, some natural graphite pencil or crayon effects.

A7

The chalk drawing and concrete texture in Figure A7 was done with the texture brush.

NOTE
Texture brushes were once an advanced feature, available only in Animate Pro and Harmony, but this is no longer the case and they are now a standard feature in Animate 3.

DYNAMIC BRUSH

A dynamic brush is essentially a stamp tool, allowing you to quickly paint complex scenes. For example, you can create a dynamic brush containing several trees and then create an entire forest with just a few strokes. Another dynamic brush may contain a number of different buildings, with which you can paint a cityscape in mere seconds.

To create a dynamic brush, first draw each 'stamp' (for example a tree or bush) as a *single frame* on its own individual layer (see Figure A8). Don't worry, these are temporary layers; once the dynamic brush is created, you can delete them all.

In Edit → Preferences → Camera, make sure *Select tool works on single drawing* is unchecked. This will allow you to select all of your stamp layers at once.

You should now be able to select the whole stack with the Select tool, as shown in Figure A8. Once they're all selected, grab the Brush tool and in the Properties panel, click the 🖌 New Dynamic Brush button. Your new dynamic brush has been created!

You'll find it at the bottom of the brushes list and it's called Dynamic Brush 1. You can rename it using the Ⓐ button or delete it using the 🗑 button.

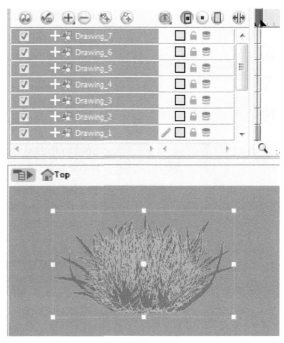

A8

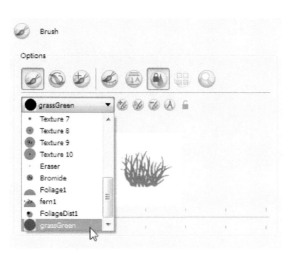

A9

With the brush saved, you may now safely delete the layers on which you created the stamps.

WARNING

Dynamic brushes come with a couple of downsides. Hopefully these will be addressed in future versions of Harmony but in the meantime, here are some things to be aware of:

- **Sub-layers** – dynamic brushes will only work on the sub-layers they were created on. For example, suppose you create grass stamps on the Colour sub-layer; that dynamic brush will never work on the Line, Overlay or Underlay sub-layers. It'll only work on the Colour sub-layer.

- **Stamp colours** – the colours used in your stamps will be saved in your dynamic brush and not in the scene's Colour palette. When you use your dynamic brush in other scene files, you won't find its colours anywhere in the Colour panel. To add the brush colours to the scene palette, save and close the scene; when you reopen it, you'll be prompted to perform Colour Recovery. Doing so will add the colours to your scene palette. Those colour names will appear bold in the list. Just save the scene to add them permanently to the scene palette.

- **Stamp preview** – the slider in the Brush tool properties merely shows you the stamps in the brush. Unfortunately it doesn't let you choose which stamp to place. Your brush stroke will always begin with the first stamp and cycle through them as you draw.

- **Flattening stamps** – dynamic brushes allow you to create hundreds of drawings in seconds. This means an insane amount of curves and vector points which can bring your computer to a crawl. The Auto-Flatten function does not work on dynamic brushes, so as you paint with the dynamic brush, it's a good idea to regularly select and flatten the art from the menu Drawing → Optimize → Flatten [Alt Shift F]. This combines all the stamps into one piece of art, minimising its complexity, as shown in Figure A10.

A10

ADVANCED ANIMATION

Except for Deformers, the Advanced Animation tools covered here are available in all three programs: Animate, Animate Pro and Harmony.

THE X-SHEET

As mentioned earlier in this book, the X-sheet is the father of all Time-lines used by traditional animators. It's likely that you can get by without ever using it, but certain animation tasks can only be performed in the X-sheet view, such as 'marking' drawings.

MARK DRAWINGS

This is another traditional animation tool that allows advanced use of the onion skin, and is particularly useful with pose-to-pose animation. In traditional animation, on a key drawing, the drawing number is circled, indicating that it's a key. All other drawings are numbered without circles.

In Toon Boom, rather than circle the drawing numbers, you can mark drawings with K or B, indicating a Key or Breakdown drawing. These markers are shown in the X-sheet view only.

To mark a key drawing in the X-sheet view, right-click it and choose → Mark Drawing As → Key. You can alternatively select the drawing and press [K] or [B]. Should you ever need to remove a mark from a drawing, just mark it as an inbetween [I].

ADVANCED ONION SKIN

Sometimes you want to see several key drawings without seeing all the inbetweens through the Onion Skin. The best thing about marking drawings is that you can filter what is shown through the Onion Skin. Once you've marked your keys and breakdowns, you can use the advanced Onion Skin toolbar (Windows → Toolbars → Onionskin) to see only keys, or only breakdowns.

A11

NOTE
The Advanced Onion Skin only works in the Drawing View.

A12

SHIFT AND TRACE

Figure A13 illustrates shift and trace in traditional inbetweening. When inbetweening two key drawings that are far apart (A), it's often necessary to lift one key off the pegs and line up the drawings on the lightbox (B), then position the next sheet of paper in order to do the inbetween (C). When the drawings are placed back on the pegs, not only the pose but also the drawing position has been inbetweened (D).

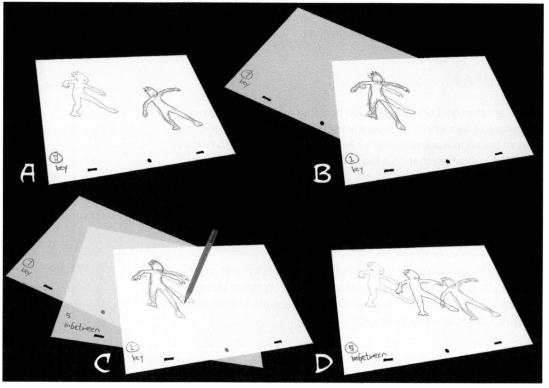

A13

This can also be an issue in digital 2D inbetweening but *Shift and Trace* solves the problem, allowing you to temporarily reposition drawings to make inbetweening easier. It's a process that would take several pages to explain, so check out the [F1] User Guide → Traditional Animation → Advanced Traditional Animation → Shift and Trace to learn how to use it.

HARMONY ONLY

DEFORMERS

Ever since deformers were introduced in Harmony 9.2 it's astounding what some animators have been able to achieve with them.

A deformer allows you bend a drawing using a bone chain, or a curve. Traditionally for example, a swinging vine would require many individual drawings and skilful inbetweening to move smoothly and realistically. Using a deformer however, a single drawing of a vine may be deformed and keyframed so it waves and writhes realistically.

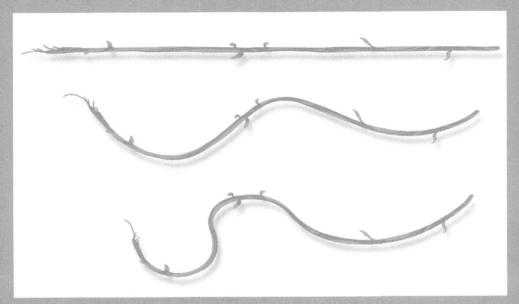

A14

The applications for this are endless; from writhing incense smoke, coiling ropes and chains, to character limbs and even faces!

Deformation and deformation rigging is one of those subjects that could possibly fill a book, so if you'd like to learn how to use it, check out the documentation [F1] → User Guide → Deformation. There's also a Deformers tutorial video on this book's companion website.

IMPORT 3D MODELS

In the early days of traditional animation, backgrounds and solid props, like machinery, were notoriously difficult to animate. In fact, they still are! Even something as simple as a door swinging needs to be carefully planned so it doesn't morph and change shape as it moves. 3D is immune to this problem because a model holds its shape perfectly unless deliberately distorted. So it really was just a matter of time before 3D models could be fully supported in 2D software.

In Harmony, we can easily import 3D models by going to File → Import → 3D models (Figure A15). As of Harmony 10, accepted 3D formats are .fbx, .osb, .3ds and .obj.

As well as models complete with their textures, you can import animated sequences. Bringing in static models is very straightforward, but articulated animation cannot be done within Harmony. This means you'll need to finalise any animation in your 3D program before importing it.

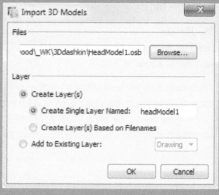

A15

Once you have it in Harmony, the 3D model may be positioned, scaled, rotated or attached to a Peg to move through the scene Remember to enable 3D in the Peg properties to take full advantage of the 3D positioning and rotation. If the model contains any animation, its frames can be sequenced on the Timeline using 🔳▶ → Exposure → Sequence Fill…

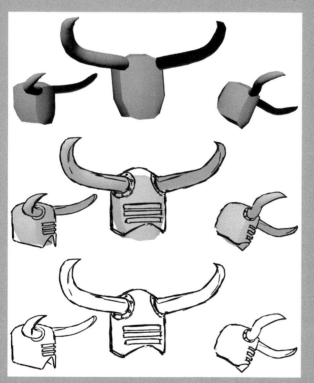

A16

What's truly awesome about 3D import is that you can quickly import free models and use them as construction guides for your 2D animation. Download free 3D models of vehicles and props from the internet (or create your own), import them into Harmony and trace them with the drawing tools. This is a great way to preserve that 2D hand-drawn look, while maintaining the volume of the object as it turns or tumbles in the scene. Perfect for cars, doors, crates, buildings, terrain, even complex rigid character parts, like antlers and horns.

Figure A16 illustrates how even the simplest of 3D models can help with constructing objects and staying on model, whatever the angle.

Thanks to 3D modellers and animators offering their creations for free, there are countless sites from which you can download 3D models. A simple search for 'free 3D models' will turn up pages upon pages of results. Even the official NASA website has a section where you can download more than 100 free 3D models of their creations. If you're interested, go to www.nasa.gov and type '3D models' in the search bar.

TIP
When downloading any pre-built assets for use in your work, *always* be sure to check the licensing info and obtain the proper permissions. Even free models can come with conditions attached, such as non-commercial use or credit to the artist.

TEMPLATES AND THE LIBRARY

You saw the Library earlier in the Drawing Substitution exercises, but it's also where you store assets for use in other scenes. In Toon Boom these assets are called Templates. You can save single or multiple assets – including drawings, pegs, groups, effects, even whole scenes – as Templates, which may then be imported into other scenes.

A colour model sheet for your character is a good starting example. To create a colour model sheet for use in other scenes, start by drawing and colouring the character on a new layer. This can be a single drawing or multiple frames with the various angles.

A17

Later when you import the model sheet into other scenes, it will bring its colour palette into the scene as outlined ahead in Importing Templates (page 435).

SAVING TEMPLATES

First, open the Library with Windows → Library, or via the panel menu. Below the Drawing Substitution slider you'll see a hierarchy of folders on your computer where you can save Templates. The following steps are for saving assets to the Library for use in other scenes.

> 1. Select the layer in the Timeline or the Network and hit [Ctrl/⌘ C] to copy it.

> 2. In the Library, select your Toon Boom library folder. Depending on the program you use, this will be called Animate Library, Animate Pro Library or Stage Library.

> 3. Right click the folder and choose → Right to Modify. Once unlocked, you're cleared to paste your assets.

> 4. With the Library folder selected, hit [Ctrl/⌘ V] to paste. Your drawing appears in the right-hand list. You can rename folders and assets with the right-click menu.

With the right to modify, you can also create new folders in your Library folder for different projects and categories. Do this using the panel menu ▧▶ → Folders → New Folder.

A18

IMPORTING TEMPLATES

Importing templates is as simple as dragging assets from the Library and into your Timeline or Network view. When you import a template, its colour palette will come with it and you'll find it in the palette window of the Colour panel.

NOTE
If you have, say a 'Day' palette in your scene and the imported asset uses the same palette but with some extra (or different) colours, they will be merged into one palette. Bold colour names indicate unsaved colours, so save the scene with [Ctrl/⌘ S] to save the palette.

Slightly Technical Stuff

All over the world, people are operating machinery competently and safely without necessarily knowing exactly how that machinery works. Meanwhile a champion motorbike racer has a much deeper knowledge of his machine and understands exactly what each individual component does.

Similarly, good software must be user-friendly so that anyone can learn to use it without necessarily knowing how it's built. Just like the champion motorbike racer though, once you're comfortable with it – if you aspire to be a power user – this level of understanding can deepen your relationship with the software.

This appendix briefly explains a handful of slightly technical concepts that are useful to know, but not entirely necessary in order to use the software.

WHAT IS VECTOR?

In Toon Boom we create *vector* art. This means that everything we draw and paint is created mathematically, not with pixels but with curves calculated between points. A single brush stroke for example consists of an invisible border filled with colour. This border is made up of points that mathematically define its contour.

As another example, a line drawn with the Shape tool consists of a single line plotted by two points. Everything you draw with the Toon Boom drawing tools is created this way.

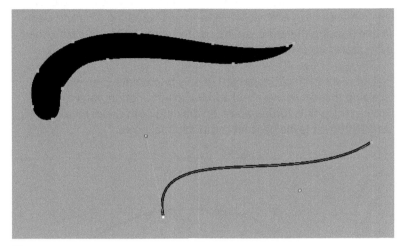

B1

LIMITATIONS OF .SWF

It is possible to export your scenes as vector using File → Export → .swf. Usually this works fine for plain vector art and animation. However if your scene contains effects such as glows, complex blurs, tones and highlights, you'll soon find that very few effects translate to vector format and most of them simply won't appear in the export.

SCANNING, VECTORISING AND IMPORTING

Are you a traditional animator not entirely comfortable using digital drawing tools? You may consider drawing on paper and scanning them with File → Import → From Scanner.

If you plan on scanning line drawings and digitally painting them, they will need to be *vectorised*. In effect this means you're converting bitmap pixel lines to vectors.

B2

WHY EVEN VECTORISE?

The biggest advantage of vector is that it may be scaled up infinitely with no loss of quality. This is how in Toon Boom we're able to change the dimensions of a movie while keeping everything crisp and clean. A line drawing therefore, can be created at say 100 × 100 pixels, then later scaled up to 4000 × 4000 and beyond.

In Figure B3, both circles consist of only four points. Even when you scale up that circle, there's no additional information; you've merely moved the points further apart. So drawing both circles requires exactly the same file size and computational power.

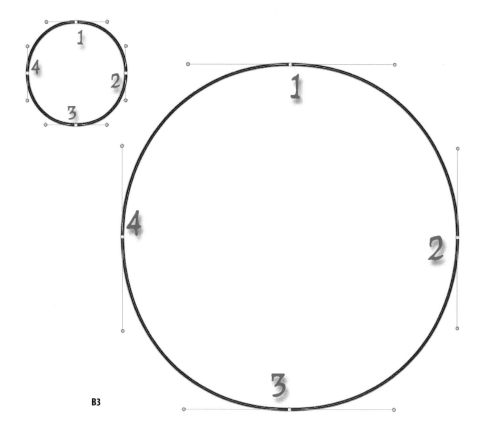

B3

By contrast, when you scale up a bitmap image a few times the mosaic of pixels becomes less and less appealing. To create a large bitmap without jagged pixelation, you need more pixels, which equates to higher file size and more computational crunch.

VECTORISING

When you import bitmap images, whether from a folder or directly from your scanner, you're given the option to *vectorise* shown in Figure B4.

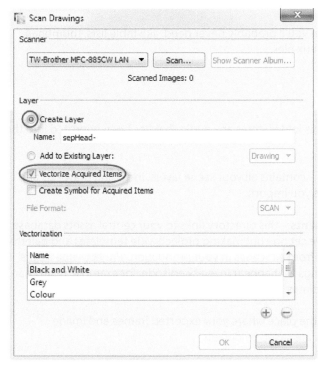

B4

While you can vectorise any bitmap you import, you should ideally use it for line art and avoid trying to vectorise complex, photographic images. These can lock up your computer as it attempts to generate potentially millions of vector points and curves.

TIP
Any linework that you draw on paper should ideally be strong and consistent. Fades or breaks in the linework may result in lots of broken vectorised lines, which makes painting difficult.

audio
elements
environments
frames
jobs
palette-library
newsGuy.aux
newsGuy.aux~
newsGuy.xstage
newsGuy.xstage.thumbnails
newsGuy.xstage~
PALETTE_LIST
scene.elementTable
scene.versionTable

B5

PROGRAM DIRECTORIES AND FILE FORMATS

Your scenes are saved in a folder that contains various files and a number of other folders. These are only created when you save the scene for the first time, while others are created when you do something, for example, import a 3D model or create a new colour palette.

Some of them you'll probably never need, like table lists, thumbnail lists and the .aux files.

FOLDERS

- **Audio** – this folder stores any audio that has been imported into the scene.

- **Elements** – contains all your scene layers, including drawings and 3D models you import.

- **Environments** – this directory links to your central assets database (if you have set one up) making project-wide templates and palettes accessible from all scenes in your production. 'Project-wide assets' means things that appear in every episode, for example, main character templates, key backgrounds/sets and their colour palettes.

- **Frames** – the place where your exported frames and image sequences are saved by default.

- **Jobs** – similar to the *environments* folder, this directory contains links to your asset library or database of *episode-specific* assets and palettes; an example would be assets featured in just one or a few episodes, like a particular monster, a unique prop, or special colours.

- **Palette-library** – your scene palettes are saved here. You can copy the palettes within or link them to other scenes (see Appendix A).

FILES

- **.ple**, **.anim**, **.stage** or **.xstage** – the program file used to open your scene.

- **PALETTE_LIST** – a plain text list of your scene's palettes

- **scene.elementTable** – a list of all the scene elements (layers and drawings).

- **scene.versionTable** – a list of all the scene versions.

- **tilde (~)** – any file suffixed with a tilde character is a backup of your previous save. In the event of corrupted scene files, you may be able to salvage your work by removing the tilde character from the name of these files and opening them.

KEYBOARD SHORTCUTS

Below are two tables of frequently used keyboard shortcuts. For a full list, just hit [Ctrl/⌘ U] or go to Edit → Preferences. On the Shortcuts tab you can see and change every shortcut in the program.

Table B1 Tool shortcuts

FUNCTION	SHORTCUT	OVERRIDE
Select	[Alt S]	[S]
Brush	[Alt B]	[B]
Repaint Brush	[Alt X]	[X]
Resize Brush		[O]
Eraser	[Alt E]	[E]
Eyedropper	[Alt D]	[D]
Pencil	[Alt /]	[/]
Shape (line)	[Alt \]	
Shape (rectangle)	[Alt 7]	
Shape (oval)	[Alt =]	
Paint	[Alt I]	[I]
Repaint	[Alt R]	[R]
Unpaint	[Alt U]	[U]
Paint Unpainted	[Alt Y]	[Y]
Cutter	[Alt T]	[T]
Invisible Stroke	[Alt V]	[V]
Close Gaps	[Alt C]	[C]
Text	[Alt 9]	[9]
Edit Gradient	[Shift F3]	

Table B2 Other shortcuts

CATEGORIES	FUNCTION	SHORTCUT	AVAILABILITY
Animation	Translate	[Alt 2]	All views
	Rotate	[Alt 3]	All views
	Scale	[Alt 4]	All views
	Skew	[Alt 5]	All views
	Transform	[Shift T]	All views
	Morphing	[F3]	All views
	Onion Skin	[Alt O]	All views
Arrange	Flip Horizontal	[4]	Camera, Drawing
	Flip Vertical	[5]	Camera, Drawing
	Bring Selection to Front	[Ctrl/⌘ Shift PageUp]	Camera, Drawing
	Push Selection to Back	[Ctrl/⌘ Shift PageDn]	Camera, Drawing
View	Centre on Selection	[O]	Timeline, Network
	Centre on Mouse	[N]	Timeline, Network
	Zoom in	[1]	All views
	Zoom out	[2]	All views
	Rotate Workspace	[Ctrl/⌘ Alt]	Camera only
	Reset Workspace	[Shift M]	Camera only
	Show/Hide Strokes	[K]	Camera, Drawing
	Line/Colour Sub-Layer	[L]	Camera, Drawing
Timeline	Next Frame	[.]	Timeline, Camera, Drawing
	Previous Frame	[,]	Timeline, Camera, Drawing
	Next Drawing	[G]	Timeline, Camera, Drawing
	Previous Drawing	[F]	Timeline, Camera, Drawing
	Next Keyframe	[']	Timeline, Camera, Drawing
	Previous Keyframe	[;]	Timeline, Camera, Drawing
	Next Layer	[J]	Timeline, Camera, Drawing
	Previous Layer	[H]	Timeline, Camera, Drawing
	First Frame	[Shift ,]	Timeline, Camera, Drawing
	Last Frame	[Shift .]	Timeline, Camera, Drawing
	Play Timeline	[Shift Enter]	Timeline, Camera, Drawing
	Expand all layers	[0]	Timeline only
	Collapse all layers	[9]	Timeline only

THE LICENSE WIZARD

You can open the Toon Boom License Wizard from your computer's Programs directory at any time. However, when you first install a Toon Boom program, the License Wizard should appear before you can start animating. Using the License Wizard to activate and return your license is a straight forward process.

ACTIVATING

After you receive your Toon Boom product code, you can open the program. If your copy of Toon Boom hasn't been activated, you'll receive a popup message and be directed to the License Wizard. If you're connected to the internet, you can use Internet Activation. Just paste your product key into the fields in the License Wizard and click 'Activate'. The License Wizard then contacts Toon Boom's license server, which should then activate your license on that computer.

B6

YOUR LICENCE ON MULTIPLE COMPUTERS

It's common to have a desktop workstation and a laptop for working on the move, or outside the office. Toon Boom can be installed on multiple computers, but the licence can only be activated on one computer at a time. You'll need to transfer your licence to the computer you plan to use.

For example, suppose you have your Toon Boom licence installed on your desktop computer but you're planning a trip away and you'll be using your laptop for your animation. Before you go, transfer the licence from the desktop machine to the laptop in the following way:

> 1. On your desktop computer, open the License Wizard to return the licence. In your list of programs, you'll find it in Toon Boom <program name> → License Tools.

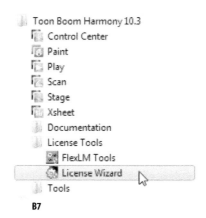

B7

> 2. Choose Manage Licenses → Manage Local Licenses. In the Local License Manager, select your program and click 'Return'.

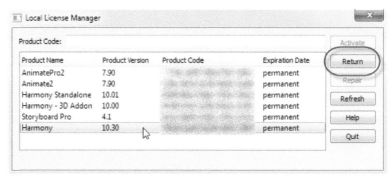

B8

> 3. On the laptop computer, again using the License Wizard, this time choose Activate License.

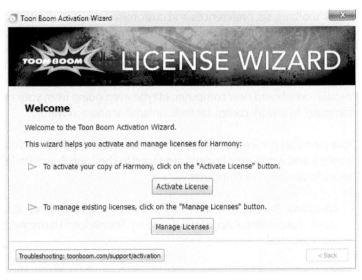

B9

Simple as that! The licence will be transferred from the desktop to the laptop. When you return from your trip, just transfer it back to use your Toon Boom program on your desktop.

NOTE
When you return your licence and then later reactivate it, everything will be just as you left it. Transferring licences does not change anything about the program, your preferences or your scenes, which can be opened on any other computer that has an active licence.

In the event that something terrible happens to your computer, like theft, damage or loss to a poker opponent, and you cannot transfer the licence yourself, you can always contact Toon Boom support and they can return the licence for you. Once you're up and running on another computer, you can then install and reactivate the licence.

YOUR PREFERENCES

Over time, as you work in Toon Boom, you'll readjust your workspace, tweak toolbars, set preferences and customise keyboard shortcuts. As you grow more familiar in the program and make it your own, sooner or later you'll find yourself at a point where you can open your Toon Boom program and immediately feel right at home. That said, the day will come when you need to reinstall Toon Boom fresh on your computer, or install it on a brand new computer. Maybe even going from your home computer to a work computer feels unfamiliar and awkward.

Your personal preferences like keyboard shortcuts, toolbars, dynamic brushes and workspace layouts are saved in the Toon Boom Preferences folder on your computer.

- **Windows:** Back up this directory (Harmony 10.3 example) –C:\ Users\<username>\AppData\Roaming\ToonBoom\Harmony\ full-1030-pref.

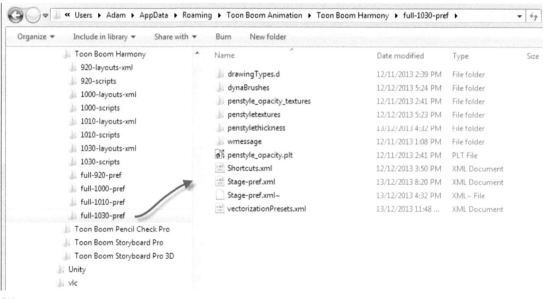

B10

- **OSX:** Back up this file (Harmony example) – Go\MacintoshHD\
  Library\Preferences\com.toonboom.harmony.full.Stage.plist

If the thought of losing your lovingly fine-tuned preferences keeps you awake at night, you can always back them up regularly. Perhaps zip them up and email them to yourself once a month, or just store them on free cloud storage, like Dropbox or Google Drive.

Now you know where they're saved, just take your preferences from one computer and import them to the same location on another. Restart the program and you're home again!

WARNING
When installing your preferences on someone else's computer, it might be considerate to back up their preferences before overwriting them with your own.

Index